# The Complete

# Cookie Jar Book

Mike Schneider

Revised 3rd Edition

Schiffer Publishing Ltd

4880 Lower Valley Road, Atglen, PA 19310 USA

# Dedication

To Betty and Floyd Carson
for their many years of helping writers
inform the public about collectibles

A note from the author about values:

Suggested prices of cookie jars in this book were arrived at through a combination of interviewing collectors and dealers, consulting other price guides, auction and show reports, observations at antique shows, internet sales, and a general feel for the market. They are estimated values only, not rock solid prices.

They are based on what might be paid when a transaction takes place between an informed cookie jar dealer and an informed cookie jar collector. That makes them somewhat higher than what a general antiques dealer could probably charge when looking for a quick turnover. It makes them somewhat lower than what a passionate collector might pay during heated competition at an auction.

Prices will vary according to local area, condition and other factors. The best way to use these estimates is not to base what you pay or charge on them, but to judge one jar's value against another's to arrive at a realistic price.

Two different renditions—and two different glazes—on McCoy's "Happy Face" jar, no. 235. Although the one on the right appears larger, it is only because it is sitting slightly forward in the picture. Each is 11 inches high. They were made from 1972 to 1979. Jar on the left is marked "215/McCoy/LCC/USA" on four lines. Jar on the right is unmarked, while another photographed had the McCoy bull's-eye mark with "USA" below. *Courtesy of Jazz'e Junque Shop, Chicago, Illinois.* $45

**Title page photo:**
This unmarked Hopalong Cassidy cookie jar is 11-1/2 inches high. Courtesy of Jazz'e Junque Shop, Chicago, Illinois. $700.

**Revised price guide: 2001**
Copyright © 1999 & 2001 by Mike Schneider.
Library of Congress Catalog Card Number: 00-111940

Typeset in Souvenir Lt BT

ISBN: 0-7643-1376-2
Printed in China
1 2 3 4

Published by Schiffer Publishing Ltd.
4880 Lower Valley Road
Atglen, PA 19310
Phone: (610) 593-1777; Fax: (610) 593-2002
E-mail: Schifferbk@aol.com
Please visit our web site catalog at
**www.schifferbooks.com**

This book may be purchased from the publisher.
Include $3.95 for shipping. Please try your bookstore first.
We are always looking for people to write books on new and related subjects. If you have an idea for a book please contact us at the above address.
You may write for a free catalog.

In Europe, Schiffer books are distributed by
Bushwood Books
6 Marksbury Avenue
Kew Gardens
Surrey TW9 4JF England
Phone: 44 (0) 20-8392-8585; Fax: 44 (0) 20-8392-9876
E-mail: Bushwd@aol.com
Free postage in the UK. Europe: air mail at cost.

# Acknowledgments

As with the other books I've written on antiques and collectibles, this one was made possible only through the collecting community's unselfish willingness to share collections and information, and the understanding and help of my wife, Cindy.

The more than 600 cookie jars of Michigan residents, Stan and Karen Zera, was the first large collection we photographed, which was no easy chore for Stan as most of the jars were stored in the basement. While I was busy shooting them in the kitchen, Stan shuttled them up and down the steps one and two at a time. His leg muscles must have grown as hard as stoneware from the strenuous exercise. A special thanks also goes to the Zera children, Sean, 8, and Brenda, 7, whose patience and nearly perfect behavior during the three days we commandeered their parents exhibited maturity beyond their years.

The Zeras put us in touch with Mercedes DeRenzo, owner of Jazz'e Junque Shop, the first and only cookie jar shop in Chicago. Two days at Jazz'e Junque resulted in another friendship and many more good photos.

Mercedes introduced us to Jay Blumenfeld and Mark Taylor, both of Chicago, who specialize in collecting head jars and fruit and vegetable jars, and who graciously allowed us to photograph their exquisite collections.

Back home in northern Ohio, Floyd and Betty Carson always invited us to photograph jars not only from their personal collection, but also those they often bought for resale.

Betty and Floyd led us to Richard and Susan Oravitz, enthusiastic collectors who supplied the jars for another several hundred photos.

Central Ohioans Jim and Betsy Coughenour, and John and Carol Bosson, contributed greatly to the Brush chapter. They also helped fill in most of the other chapters. Their collections alone would make a respectable cookie jar book.

McCoy collector Georgina Lilly, and Shawnee collector Robert Smith, of different suburbs in the Cleveland area, provided the jars we so badly needed to complete those chapters.

Maureen Saxby, who with her husband, Clifford, edits the *Crazed over Cookie Jars* newsletter, supplied leads and information. And Maureen, aided by Mercedes DiRenzo, even took some pictures for the book.

Others who provided either jars to photograph or information to use were Cloud's Antique Mall, Dorothy Coates, Country Heirs Antique Shop, Elvin R. and Frances (Jerry) Kulp, Joan Eaton, Elyria Public Library, Mary Jane Giacomini, Carol Gifford, Lisa Diane Golden, Grinder's Switch Antique Shop, Herrick Memorial Library, Mary and Bill Hallier, Keith Herklotz, Mary Huffman, Sharon Isaacson, Charles Kidd, Lorain Public Library, Keith Lytle, Carl and Gari McCallum, Irene Mychul, Allan and Michelle Naylor, Vicki Nitecki, Debbie Preussner, Melanie Rollin, Rosa Sberna, Dan Schneider, Homer and Bev Simpson, Claude and Edna Mae Smith, Fred Strunk and Denise Dakoulis, Connie Swaim, Wellington Antiques, and Rick Wisecarver.

I would be remiss if I didn't mention Lucille Bromberek, of Lemont, Illinois. Although I wasn't able to photograph any of Lucille's jars for the book, it was she who first caught the attention of the national and international media through her cookie jar museum. I, as a writer, owe her a debt of gratitude for long ago planting the seed that made this project necessary. Collector's owe her the same debt for creating the interest that made cookie jar collecting a viable hobby.

I would also like to thank those writers who came before me Pamela Coates, Ermagene Westfall, Harold Nichols, and Fred and Joyce Herndon Roerig for the fine job they did photographing and documenting cookie jars for posterity.

But most of all my thanks goes to you, the reader, for considering the book worthy of inclusion in your library.

Three American bisque animals with hands in pockets. The jars on the outside are 11 inches high, while the one in the center, which has a turnabout bank head, is 10-3/4 inches high. The elephant appears to be a married jar considering the two different colors. In addition to the jars shown, the company also made a cat and a cow, and often finished the jars in solid colors. *Bosson Collection.* $100 each

# Introduction

A Ludowici Celadon lion, 10-3/4 inches high, marked "Belmont/Patent Applied/USA" on three lines. It appears to be repainted. One of the most troubling aspects of these jars is that some of the white jars definitely attributable to Ludowici Celadon appear to be made of the same clay and glaze as white jars definitely attributable to American Bisque and American Pottery. They also have the same crude workmanship on their bottoms. For a detailed explanation of the crossover between these three companies, see Chapter 8. $75

Because the introduction is the most boring part of any book, I promise to keep this one brief. But there are a couple points that should be covered.

The first concerns measurements. Heights of jars are included in most of the captions, but they must be considered nominal because heights of identical jars can vary by as much as 1/4 inch, and even a little more in extreme cases. If you have a collection with many duplicates, you've probably already noticed that your identical jars aren't always the same size. This occurs because pottery shrinks between 5 percent and 15 percent from the time it's removed from the mold to the time it's removed from the kiln. the rate of shrinkage is determined in large part by the clay mixture. When a pottery changes suppliers for one of its clays, or when human error results in a slip recipe not being followed to the letter, finished pieces will end up being slightly different size due to the modified composition.

Even at that, the measurements stated herein will give you a sound idea of what size object to look for when you wish to acquire a particular jar. They are also accurate enough to indicate the average 10 percent shrinkage that occurs when a cookie jar is used as a mold core in order to produce a fake. (See Chapter 5 for further explanation.)

The other thing is identification of cookie jars. Unless there was compelling evidence to the contrary, I accepted previous cookie jar book authors at their word concerning identity. For instance, If Ermagene Westfall (*An Illustrated Value Guide to Cookie Jars*) said an unmarked jar was American Bisque, then I too considered it American Bisque. But where errors clearly existed, such as Harold Nichols's (*McCoy Cookie Jars—From the First to the Latest,*) accidental insertion of a Regal China Quaker Oats jar in place of a McCoy Quaker Oats jar, I labeled the jars as they are supposed to be, and stated the reason.

When style, glaze, color, or unique markings indicated a previously unidentified cookie jar was in all probability made by a certain company, it was included with the rest of that company's jars. An example of this would be the numerous brown, green, and ochre glazed jars typical of Doranne of California. If there was the slightest indication of Doranne origin, such as a raised or indented design, or a mark showing "CJ" plus a number, or "J" plus a number, all of which Doranne is known for, the jar was placed with the rest of the Doranne jars.

In cases where nothing is sure, such as the quagmire in which American Bisque, American Pottery, and Ludowici Celadon are bogged down, I attempted to use the small amount of information available to draw logical conclusions. While most of these are not labeled as theories per se, inclusion of words such as probably or possibly will telegraph to the reader that such information has not been factually proven.

There's really not much else to say except that I hope you enjoy the book, and Happy Collecting!

# Contents

This California Originals mouse is 12-1/2 inches high. It is marked "2630" on the rim of lid, and "2630 USA" on base. *Zera Collection*. $45

# Section I: Cookie Jar Collecting

The thing most people told me they like best about collecting cookie jars is the natural high they experience when they find a long sought jar and acquire it. The low, they said, often comes upon returning home with their new trophy. For some it is discovering that the jar isn't nearly as attractive when sitting on a sideboard that's cluttered with two dozen other jars, as it was when it was sitting by itself in a picture in a book. For others it's removing the new jar from the dishwasher and finding half the decoration has disappeared, or realizing their emotions led them to pay more for the jar than it was worth, or more than they could afford at the time.

The purpose of this section, aside from relating a capsule history of cookie jars, is to inform the potential collector of the pitfalls that might be encountered in the quest for jars, and how to avoid them.

# Chapter 1
# *A Short History*

Decorative cookie jars appeared on the American scene in the early 1930s. It was the glasshouses of Ohio, Pennsylvania, West Virginia, and New York that first recognized that the stock market crash of 1929, and the Great Depression that followed, had eliminated many folks' daily trip to the bakery, forcing them to bake cookies in their home kitchens. Once baked, cookies had to be stored, preferably in a container that not only kept them handy, but also protected them from atmospheric influences that soften crisp cookies and dry out moist ones. A container that enhanced a kitchen's decor, namely an attractive glass or pottery cookie jar, quickly found favor over cardboard oatmeal boxes, coffee tins, and other make-do receptacles available in most of America's homes.

As early as 1931 the McKee Glass Company, of Jeanette, Pennsylvania, added a lid to its 5-1/2 inch, three-footed jardiniere, and advertised it as a cookie jar. In 1932, circulars of the Hocking Glass Company, Lancaster, Ohio, showed a cookie jar with a screw-on metal lid being sold as an accessory to its popular green glass paneled canister set. And it wasn't long before Hocking's catalogs began referring to the covered pretzel jar that came with its 8-piece beer and pretzel set, as a "pretzel or cookie jar." Several other well-known glass manufacturers also produced cookie jars during the early years of the Depression.

Which pottery served up the first ceramic cookie jar is open to debate, but the Brush Pottery Company, of Roseville, Ohio, seems the likeliest candidate. The green canister cookie jar shown below is from the Brush Kolorkraft line, which was introduced in the 1920s. The cookie jar, No. 344, was added late in 1929. Oddly, Brush didn't start making its beautiful figural cookie jars until the mid-1940s, several years after other potteries had begun pouring them out.

Early pottery jars were generally quite simple, usually either in a cylindrical or bean pot shape. Many were made of stoneware. Painted decoration was usually applied to the outside, either over the glaze or directly to the bisque. Leaves and flowers won the public's nod as the most popular theme.

One of the pioneers of these early stoneware jars was the Harper J. Ransburg Company, a decorating and distributing firm in Indianapolis, Indiana. By the mid-1930s, Ransburg's No. 207 jar was selling to the tune of a quarter-million units per year.

This Brush Kolorkraft jar is 10 inches high, marked with an impressed "344." The Kolorkraft line made its debut in the 1920s. The jar was first available in 1929, making it a good candidate for the honor of being the first pottery cookie jar. *Zera Collection.* $35

Around 1940, potteries began test-marketing figural cookie jars—people, animals, fruits, vegetables and other objects—setting the stage for today's collecting hobby.

The greatest output of American pottery cookie jars occurred from the mid-1940s to the mid-1970s, even though many potteries were forced out of business by foreign competition during the 1950s and 1960s. In the 1980s, American production slowed to a trickle as the inflated cost of materials, labor, energy, and transportation that had wracked the previous decade, spelled bankruptcy for the majority of the few American potteries that remained in business.

Today the flow of new cookie jars is increasing. A good number of jars are currently being made by domestic potteries such as

Treasure Craft, and by studio artists such as Carol Gifford and Rick Wisecarver. But most of today's jars are being imported from overseas. While Pacific-Asian countries lead the pack of foreign manufacturers, cookie jars are also made in Europe, South and Central America, and probably most other places, too.

For a long time collectors turned a blind eye toward foreign jars. Unlike their American counterparts, they were light in weight, shoddily executed, and widely available. This was particularly true of Japanese jars that flooded the market in the wake of World War II. But the picture has changed in recent years. Today's Pacific-Asian jars, and those from other areas, while still lighter in weight, generally meet or closely approach the design and manufacturing standards previously adhered to by American potters. As an example, the Vandor radio, shown below, was made in Korea in 1988. It exhibits every bit as much quality although a different style as the Shawnee Mugsey pictured next to it, which was made in America approximately 40 years earlier.

As for the future, it looks good. More non-collectors are beginning to realize that cookie jars have value, which results in the older rarer jars winding up in collections instead of in landfills. Importers are continuing to hold foreign potteries to high standards. Mold companies that cater to the hobby ceramics market appear to be offering more cookie jar molds with greater detail, while companies that specialize in glaze, paints, and decals have greatly broadened the finishing methods available to crafters. Manufacturers of consumer products apparently have recognized the popularity of cookie jars, and are again using jars for premiums and discount offers. Studio artists are turning out many more cookie jars than they were just a few short years ago. And lately some nice reproductions of older jars—marked as reproductions—have appeared on the scene.

Put all these factors together and tomorrow's skies appear bright and sunny for cookie jar collectors.

For a long time after World War II, Japanese cookie jars offered little but low prices to lure the consumer. Perhaps these two are supposed to imitate Wade Irish Porcelain. The jar on the left is 10-1/4 inches high and has a "Japan" inkstamp. The one on the right stands 13 inches and has a "Japan" paper label. *Oravitz Collection.* Left $20; Right $25

Paper label of Vandor radio.

Today's Pacific-Asian jars are well-designed and expertly crafted. This radio, imported from Korea by Vandor, is 5-1/2 inches high. *Courtesy of Jazz'e Junque Shop, Chicago, Illinois.* $65

Shawnee Mugsey, 11-3/4 inches high. Impressed in the bottom is "Patented/Mugsey/USA" on three lines. *Smith Collection.* $350

Here is an early glass cookie jar, dating back to at least 1932. It is 8 inches high and was made by the Hocking Glass Company as an accessory for its green glass paneled canister set. *Zera Collection.* $25

A black glass cookie jar, 8 inches high, made by the L.E. Smith Glass Company, Mt. Pleasant, Pennsylvania. One of three black glass cookie jars illustrated in an early 1930s Smith catalog, it was known as no. 3 and originally included a hand-painted flower decoration. It is unmarked. This jar was also made in clear green glass, as shown in Chapter 35. *Zera Collection.* $90

A real country couple by Roseville, Ohio, studio artist Rick Wisecarver. The jar is 12-1/2 inches high, incised "Wihoa's/Original/Handpainted/Cookie Classic/Roseville/Ohio" on the bottom on six lines, and "Wihoa's/Cookie Classic/By Rick Wisecarver" on the back on three lines. It is hand-signed by the artist. *Oravitz Collection.* $100

Another noteworthy studio artist is Carol Gifford, of Wanette, Oklahoma. This is her pancake mammy, no. 3 in a set of five black jars in a limited edition of 250 sets. Height is 9-1/2 inches. Other Gifford jars and the mark of this jar are shown in Chapter 27. *Courtesy of Jazz'e Junque Shop, Chicago, Illinois.* $200

There wasn't anything fancy about most early pottery cookie jars. This one, by McCoy, is 7-1/2 inches high, made of yellowware. It is no. 7 in the McCoy line, unmarked, and usually referred to as the round ball shape. It was made from 1939 to 1944. Other colors for this jar were blue and green. It also came in a smaller size. *Zera Collection.* $50

This pilfering cat was made by Treasure Craft, formerly an independent company but now a division of Pfaltzgraff Pottery, of York, Pennsylva

Hocking Glass Company originally called this a pretzel jar and sold it as part of its 8-piece beer and pretzel set. When cookie jars began gaining popularity in the early 1930s, the company switched to calling it a pretzel *or* cookie jar. It is 10-3/4 inches high and unmarked. *Zera Collection.* $35

Cookie jars are made in Europe, too. This one, 10-1/2 inches high, is marked "Made in/Western Germany/3802" on three lines. *Blumenfeld Collection.* $125

nia. It is 11-1/2 inches high, with "Treasure Craft/©/USA" impressed on three lines inside the lid. Treasure Craft is one of a handful of American potteries that still makes cookie jars in quantity. *Oravitz Collection.* $60

# Chapter 2
## Types of Ceramic Jars and Decoration

While cookie jars are and have been made in several different media such as metal, glass, wood, and plastic, it is ceramic jars that capture the most attention. The large majority of ceramic jars are made of earthenware, usually the white variety. Redware, which has been used on occasion, most often by the Japanese, is also earthenware. Some forms of what is commonly referred to as yellowware is earthenware, but it hasn't been used much for cookie jars. A very few jars are made of porcelain, a more expensive ceramic material that is denser and more durable than earthenware, and which, if poured thin enough, exhibits translucency. Some jars, like those that were produced by the Western Stoneware Company of Monmouth, Illinois, are made of stoneware, the ceramic medium used for crockery.

But the type of ceramic a cookie jar is made of isn't nearly as important as the type of decoration that's been applied to it. Ceramic cookie jars are decorated by five primary methods—glaze, paint, glaze and paint combination, glaze and transfer combination, and a combination of all three materials.

Glaze is the most durable finish. Simply explained, glaze is minute particles of colored or clear glass, suspended in a liquid carrying agent. Glaze is applied by dipping, brushing, or airbrushing. All glazes are fired after they are applied, giving the clay body of a jar what amounts to a glass coating. Glaze can have a gloss or matte finish.

The main problem encountered with glaze is crazing, the tiny cracks you sometimes see that form an unwanted mosaic pattern over all or part of a jar. Crazing in pottery might be compared to latent genetic defects in life forms. Although it may take decades to appear, if a cookie jar is going to craze, its course is set when the jar is made. Crazing is caused by the glaze contracting more than the body of the jar as it cools after firing. This results in the glaze coming under excessive tension. Years later, when the glaze can no longer sustain the tension, it cracks or crazes. Nothing can be done to prevent it, or to slow its progress once it has started. Fortunately, most cookie jars are manufactured correctly, and do not craze.

Some jars appear to have only minor crazing. This is called primary crazing, long cracks in the glaze that run in generally the same direction. In time, shorter cracks will fill in between the long cracks and form squares, triangles and other shapes. This is secondary crazing, and it is inevitable when primary crazing is present.

While crazing will reduce the price of a cookie jar, it should not deter a collector form purchasing a jar that is a rare one at the right price, or one he has been seeking for a long time. Common jars with crazing should be avoided as better examples are readily available.

Paint decoration, often called cold paint, is not fired. It causes the most problems, whether applied directly to bisque, or on top of glaze. The American Bisque pirate is an example of a painted cookie jar, no glaze having been used on it. The unknown gingerbread boy canister is one on which the highlights were painted after the jar was glazed.

Like the paint on the exterior of a house, paint on cookie jars is subject to deterioration from moisture, humidity, temperature extremes, prolonged exposure to direct sunlight, and contact with

This American Bisque round bottom jar is finished entirely with paint, no glaze having been used. It is 13 inches high, with "USA" impressed on the bottom and "Jolly Pirate" impressed on the collar. *Zera Collection.* $150

foreign objects. Most jars that were painted 40 or 50 years ago suffer to a greater or lesser degree from such deterioration. There's little that can be done to halt its progress.

Never immerse a painted jar in water to clean it. Not cleaning it at all is the best bet. But if cleaning does become necessary, use tepid water and a thoroughly squeezed soft sponge or well-rung cloth. Use very gentle strokes or the paint is apt to disappear before your eyes. Cleaning the glazed portion of a jar that's decorated with both glaze and paint presents no problem if the paint is not touched.

Cookie jars that have transfer designs, an example being the McCoy Yosemite Sam cylinder jar, are decorated with a fired-on decal applied over the glaze. While transfers hold up much better than paint, they are more susceptible to damage from foreign objects than glazes. It will usually be the transfer, not the glaze, that will account for the poor condition of a transfer-decorated jar. Immersing a transfer-decorated jar in tepid water will not cause damage as long as the transfer was correctly applied and fired, and is still in good condition.

McCoy "Yosemite Sam" cylinder jar, transfer decorated, 10-1/2 inches high. No. 224, it was made in 1972. Its inkstamp mark is shown in Chapter 7. *Zera Collection.* $150

This is a stoneware jar, 10-3/4 inches high. That's a real cork in the top. On the bottom is the impressed maple leaf mark of Western Stoneware, shown in Chapter 21. *Courtesy of Jazz'e Junque Shop, Chicago, Illinois.* $20

A 9-1/2 inch high, unmarked jar that has been painted over the glaze. *Zera Collection.* $35

The most common problem encountered with glaze is crazing, most noticeable here to the right of the center flower. This unmarked jar is 9-1/2 inches high and was made by American Bisque. *Zera Collection.* $35

# Chapter 3
## *Prices*

Cookie jar pieces have gone down over the past couple of years. Typically, midrange jars that used to jump off the shelves at $300 now sit and collect dust at $250. Lower priced ones that dealers could always count on selling at $75 go for $50 or less, or sometimes not at all. And some of the declines on high end jars have been even steeper. Speculators hate it but collectors love it as their cookie jars settle down to more affordable prices after years of rising ones.

Prices have declined for three reasons-a glut of reproductions, a glut of new jars, and Ebay. We'll look at them one at a time.

Reproductions are everywhere. Some of them are quite realistic, others are quite nasty. But whether they are good copies or bad copies you see them not only at flea markets but also in the best antique malls and at the best shows. New collectors who do not have enough experience to tell the difference between an original and a reproduction are afraid to lay out much money for fear of getting stung. The problem is compounded when general line antique dealers with established reputations but a lack of specific knowledge about cookie jars occasionally dabble in them and unwittingly display repros as originals. It's happening more and more often as reproductions flourish. As already wary buyers discover they can no longer trust normally trustworthy dealers they choose to trust no one, and good jars go unsold.

Another way reproductions have taken a toll on prices is that in many cases seasoned collectors are opting for suitable repros instead of ultra expensive originals. How many people are going to pay a couple of thousand for an original American Bisque Olive Oyl when you can get a very nice J.D. James reproduction for a couple hundred and save the big money for that special jar that is not being reproduced. Additionally, a collector has no crystal ball to see the future. Does she really want to pay a huge price for a coveted jar when it could be reproduced at anytime, thereby potentially deflating the value overnight.

New jars. They are more prevalent than they have ever been. Since cookie jars came into prominence with the Andy Warhol estate auction in 1988, where $50 jars averaged close to $2000, manufacturers have responded aptly and eagerly. Today the housewares sections of discount and department stores are filled with cookie jars of all types and descriptions. While they are not all terrific they are generally inexpensive, and a good many of them are cleverly designed and very attractive. Most can be had for $20 or $30, and a lot of the new collectors entering the hobby have chosen them in favor of the older, rarer, and more expensive jars. Also, studio artists have popped up all over the country to take advantage of the collecting boom. Their jars are generally not only charming but also affordable, and because in most cases collectors are dealing directly with the artists they do not have to worry as much about getting taken.

This is one of the jars readers of *Newsweek* saw sitting on Andy Warhol's kitchen table when the magazine did a cover story on the auction of the artist's estate. The jar was made by Robinson-Ransbottom, is 9-3/4 inches high, and marked "R.R.P Co./Roseville, Ohio/No-411" on three lines. Some examples of this jar are trimmed in gold (this one is not). *Blumenfeld Collection.* $250

The Brush Purple cow, a jar that sold at the Clum cookie jar auction for $825, a good bit higher than its book value and market value at the time. It is 8-1/2 inches high, and has on its bottom the raised Brush palette mark with a "W10" below it. The jar dates from 1970. *Zera Collection.* $800

An finally, Ebay. Regardless of whether you love computers or hate them, the online auction site has changed the collecting world for the foreseeable future and has taken over as the number one venue for buying and selling what are usually referred to as smalls, or anything small enough to be fairly easily packed and shipped. And that includes cookie jars. They are there en masse. With tens of millions of registered users, jars that appeared somewhat rare before Ebay can now be found not only routinely, but in multiples, 24 hours a day, 7 day per week. While writing this I went to Ebay and did a few searches. Looking for a Shawnee Smiley? Forty-four of them had sold in the previous three weeks, prices averaged $211. Like McCoy cookie jars? One thousand three hundred five (1305) had been offered during that same three week period, 482 were currently for sale. As with anything else the law of supply and demand takes over. With so many jars readily available prices weaken. Toss in the possibility of getting a reproduction, or of a jar not living up to its described condition, which happens a lot, and people are even less willing to pay the higher prices they readily paid just a few years ago.

So where will prices go from here? At this writing they appear to be stabilizing. I suspect they will begin to creep up again as collectors and dealers adjust to the internet and the constant flow of new jars and reproduced ones. But really it's anyone's guess, and you still build a great collection today the same way you did years ago, usually one at a time by looking for the best jar at the lowest price.

# Chapter 4
## *Condition*

A collector of fine china dinnerware would probably turn up his nose at the two McCoy clown heads pictured below. He would consider one to be in bad condition, the other worse. And no wonder. The typical piece of fine china dinnerware is finished totally with fired-on decoration, spends most of its life behind glass in a protective cabinet, is used only on holidays and special occasions, and normally isn't subject to handling by children.

Cookie jars are not so privileged.

Many cookie jars are decorated with unfired paint applied on top of the glaze or directly to the bisque. Cookie jars are usually forced to endure the hazards of everyday life on a kitchen counter. And they are often used by youngsters who aren't overly careful when handling them.

The clown on the left is in excellent condition considering it was decorated with paint over the glaze 50-odd years ago, sometimes between 1945 and 1947. It's about the best you'll find short of one that's been restored. And the example on the right is pretty good, too, far better than most that are seen today. Consequently,

knowledgeable collectors use a sliding scale when evaluating the condition of painted cookie jars. They often accept jars in worse shape than they would accept them had the jars been decorated entirely with glaze.

Chips on pottery cookie jars reduce value. So do cracks. Knock off 40 percent or more for a chip that shows, 25 percent for one that doesn't show. Jars with tight cracks should be reduced at least 50 percent, open cracks 75 percent. Pay about 35 percent, or less, of the going price for bottoms without lids, or lids without bottoms.

Sometimes jars exhibit factory flaws. Thin spots in the glaze, or small shards that adhered to the bisque and were then covered with glaze, are two examples. When you see these types of flaws on jars that are for sale, throw up a caution flag. Don't give any more credence to an antique dealer who tells you there's nothing wrong with a flawed jar because it came from the factory that way, than you would give to an automobile dealer who feeds you the same line about a brand new car with a dented fender. You

McCoy clown bust, no. 19, 10-1/2 inches high. It was made between 1945 and 1947, and is in excellent condition for a jar painted over the glaze that long ago. Mark is shown in Chapter 7. *Oravitz Collection.* $75

Same clown bust, but decorated differently. It is in better shape than most. *Lilly Collection.* $70

can bet the manufacturer of the flawed cookie jar originally peddled it through a factory outlet store at a reduced price. Full value shouldn't be paid on the secondary market, either, considering that jars in better condition are available at the same price.

Sometimes you'll notice several little holes in the glaze on the underside of a cookie jar. These don't decrease the value because they're not defects. They're caused by stilts, small nail-like objects that pottery sits on during the glaze firing. If they weren't used the glaze would contact the kiln, and the jar and the kiln would become permanently bonded.

One thing that's inevitable is finding tiny spots of wall or ceiling paint on cookie jars. Apparently many people who dutifully cover furniture and appliances when painting their kitchens, are lackadaisical when it comes to protecting cookie jars from the spray of the roller. Paint spots on glazed jars, for example the Holiday Designs pumpkin shown below, seldom cause much problem. If you're not very particular, they may be left as they are. Most people to whom you show your collection won't notice them. If you are the particular type, paint spots can sometimes be removed from glazed jars with household solvents. Be sure to test the solvent first in small area that doesn't show to make sure it won't damage the glaze. Spots of paint may also be scraped from a glazed jar with either a fingernail or a razor blade. If working with a razor blade, use a light touch to avoid scratching the glaze.

Spots on painted jars are best left alone because the razor, fingernail, and solvent will likely take off the spots and the decoration beneath them at the same time.

Restoration of cookie jars is a hotly debated issue. Some collectors prefer to have jars in poor condition restored, others vehemently oppose it.

Restoration most often comes into play in the case of painted jars. Paint is subject to chipping, peeling, and washing off. Restoring painted jars is fairly easy to accomplish when compared to restoring glazed jars, or transfer-decorated jars. But there's more to true restoration than simply brushing on more paint.

The American Bisque fire chief shown below is a sad example of what can happen when a butcher gets hold of a brush. The jar looks nothing like it did when it was new. The colors are wrong, and the paint has been applied to the entire jar. As originally decorated, the fire chief would have been largely unpainted bisque. The jar lacks authenticity, and the repainting has probably reduced its value a significant amount.

But the Donald Duck-Joe Carioca turnabouts are a completely different matter. They show how a competent restorer can benefit a jar that the years have not treated kindly. The

Originally, the body of this American Bisque fireman was largely unpainted. The jar might still be saved by firing off the paint and starting from scratch. The mark is "USA" impressed in the bottom. *Courtesy of Jazz'e Junque Shop, Chicago, Illinois.* $90

This pumpkin looks pretty nice from a distance, but, as the close-up reveals, it is loaded with paint spots from a previous owner's do-it-yourself project. The jar is 8 inches high, has a "6951" inkstamp on the bottom of the base, and a "6483" inkstamp inside the lid. Often called a McCoy jar, it was actually made by Holiday Designs, which, like Nelson McCoy Ceramics, is a subsidiary of Designer Accents. *Zera Collection.* $30

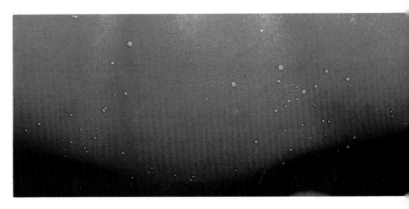

Paint spots on the pumpkin. They are a part of the hobby from which there seems to be no escape.

original colors have been placed where they belong, and the work is a monument to neatness. Regardless, you'll seldom find anyone willing to pay full price for a restored jar, no matter how well it has been done.

As collectors continue to debate the pros and cons of restoring jars, it might be noted that restoration is not looked down on in the art world. Museums routinely pay large sums to restore the works of great masters. It could be that until restoration is no longer looked down on in the cookie jar world, the cookie jar will continue to linger as just another of many collectibles, instead of rising to its deserved place of honor among American art forms.

Here is the result when someone who knows what he's doing restores a cookie jar. This turnabout of Donald Duck and Jose Carioca, from the movie "The Three Caballeros," was sold by the Leeds China Company, a Chicago distributor that worked closely with Ludwici Celadon, American Bisque, and other potteries. (A turnabout is a jar that can be turned about to present a different front. The picture shows different sides of the same jar.) The height is 14 inches, and it is marked "Donald Duck and Joe Carioca from The Three Caballeros Walt Disney USA," although it is unreadable on this particular example. Ludwici Celadon is known to have used this mark when filling contracts for Leeds, but possibly other potteries did, too, and to say which one made this turnabout would be guessing at best. *Bosson Collection.* $200 each

# Chapter 5
## Counterfeits, Reproductions and Fakes

Back in 1989 and 1990 when I was writing the first edition of this book, reproductions were on everyone's mind, almost to the point of being paranoid about them. This jar is being reproduced, people would say, and that jar is being reproduced. The problem was that no one could show me any of the reproduced jars. Not in collections, not at flea markets, not at antique malls. Not anywhere. Matter of fact, the best I could do on photographs was the four Oscar jars, all of which are probably original. Reproductions just weren't there—yet. But six months after the book was published it was like someone opened a floodgate. Reproductions abounded. Everywhere you looked you saw them. Unfortunately, you still see them, and in ever increasing numbers.

Here's two facts to remember about reproductions. Number one, they are here to stay. Number two, you can deal with them. Let's discuss these facts one at a time.

No matter how much anyone complains about reproductions, or how badly they wish they would go away, they will be with us as long as people continue to collect. Some manufacturers are going to mark them as reproductions, some aren't. Some dealers are going to unwittingly sell them as originals. Other dealers are going to sell them as originals, knowing full well they are not. And even the most knowledgeable collectors will be taken in once in a while. It's what I like to call one of the three inevitables of cookie jar collecting. The other two are discovering damage after the purchase, and occasional breakage. Trying to avoid them and getting upset when they happen is fine. Letting them spoil your enjoyment of the hobby is not, as all three go with the territory.

Now, on to fact number two, you can deal with reproductions.

The big thing here, the only thing here, is for you to know your product, know your collectible. And I can't stress this to you enough. Not me. Not the Roerigs or the Huxfords or the Kovels. You. You are the one laying down the money. You are the one who has to know what you are buying.

That old saw about knowing your dealer and only purchasing from reputable dealers? Worst advice ever written. Forget it. What you really need to know is what you are buying, not whom you are buying it from. Even reputable dealers make mistakes. So do knowledgeable ones.

I know a very knowledgeable dealer who several years ago made a special trip to a huge flea market that I attend regularly. While there his wife happened onto a vendor who was putting out a McCoy Chairman of the Board at a very low price. She bought it from him and a week later, after one thousand dollars had changed hands, the jar was sitting proudly in a collection in another part of the country. And another Chairman of the Board was sitting on that vendor's table, by my conservative estimate it was about the 10th one he had for sale that summer.

Another case. A dealer and collector for whom I have the greatest respect bought a rare Brush Purple Cow at a low price at a long established antiques show in Ohio, only after inspecting it with the utmost care, and being assured by the dealer that it was an original. My friend resold the jar and made a tidy profit. Felt really good about it, too, until he did a show in Michigan the next month and the same dealer told him he had another Purple Cow for sale for the same price. "My stomach knotted up when he told me about the second jar," he said.

Both of these people were knowledgeable and, perhaps more importantly, honest and trustworthy. Both got swindled. Both unwittingly swindled others. So forget about trusting other folks, including those who could normally be trusted, and trust only yourself. You do that by learning as much as possible. View, feel

The Cookie Monster on the right, made by California Originals, is marked "© Muppets Inc. 1970" along the base. The jar on the left is believed to be a counterfeit. It is 11 inches high and unmarked. *Zera Collection.* Left $30; Right $50

This is the reproduction of the Brayton Laguna mammy, commonly called the "Married Mammy" because of her 24 kt gold wedding ring. The jar was sold by Mary Jane Giacomini, of MJ's Collectibles in Sonoma, California, who said she intended to make about 100 of them before destroying the mold. The color of this one is periwinkle blue. *Courtesy of Mary Jane Giacomini.* $150

George Williams' limited edition commemorative of McCoy's Pontiac Indian. The jar is 10-3/4 inches high. Its mark is shown. In 1990 Williams made 300 of these jars and sold them for $79 apiece. *Bosson Collection.* $200

Brayton Laguna mammy reproduction in yellow. These jars are 12-1/4 inches high. Originals are 12-5/8 inches high. Inside the lid of each of the "Married Mammies" is an incised "90" or "91," which is not present on the originals. Neither are the decals on the apron. Other colors for this jar are dusty rose and light green. *Courtesy of Mary Jane Giacomini.* $150

Mark of the Williams Pontiac Indian, showing the jar to be no. 94 of 300.

and pick up every cookie jar you can at malls, shows, shops, and flea markets. Also those in other collections. Read everything you can find on the subject. Talk about cookie jars with other collectors and dealers. Eventually you will become the most knowledgeable person you know and will be able to buy just about any cookie jar with confidence, knowing you are getting an original, not a repro.

To be sure, not all reproductions are bad. Those of J.D.James of Buckeye Lake, Ohio, for example, have filled a niche in that they offer collectors a means of having normally very expensive jars at reasonable prices. A few examples are shown on pages 295 and 299. As you can see, James not only does a very nice job, he also clearly marks his jars as reproductions under the glaze. That's important as it would make it incredibly tough for any shyster to pass one off as an original at 10 or 20 times the price.

Jars of American Bisque's line reproduced by James include Casper, Fred Flintstone, Rubble House, Sitting Horse, Popeye, Olive Oyl, and Swee' Pea. From the Brush Pottery he has done Formal Pig, Hillbilly Frog, Little Angel in both white and black, Little Boy Blue, and Peter Pan. McCoy's Davy Crockett, Leprechaun and Hillbilly Bear, Gonder's Sheriff and Pirate, the Lane Indian, DeForest Halo Boy, and the Regal China Peek-A-Boo are also among James' offerings. Additionally, he has done a Nancy head and Nancy full-bodied jar, Sluggo, Little Lulu, Gleep, Weller dog, and many others.

Roger Jensen, of Rockwood, Tennessee, made reproductions and marked them all McCoy for awhile, according to an article by Stan and Karen Zera in *Antique Week* December 14, 1992. While his McCoy mammy might snag a few unsuspecting collectors, it wouldn't take a long time in the hobby to realize something was awry with Jensen's Mosaic Tile Mammy, Luzianne Mammy, and Hull's Little Red Riding Hood—all with McCoy marks on their bottoms!

Many other companies and individuals have jumped onto the repro bandwagon. Look for the trend to continue as long as prices of rare originals remain high.

A related problem is that of counterfeits. A counterfeit jar is a copy of one that is currently being manufactured, or a copy of a jar that's protected by copyright, trademark, patent or other legal means. The Cookie Monster on page 17 is believed to be a counterfeit as there is no copyright notice on it.

Oscar is 10 inches high, and was made by Robinson-Ransbottom. There seems little doubt this jar is an original. *Zera Collection.* $150

Oscar still looks old, but is in better shape than the one with the blue hat. In all liklihood this is also an original. *Zera Collection.* $150

Two more Oscars, the one on the left looks like it came off the shelf yesterday. Did it? Probably not, but it pays to be careful. *Blumenfeld Collection.* $150 each.

Mark of the single Oscar with the red hat. Somewhat hard to read, it says "USA/ 202/OSCAR" on three lines.

Jars that are often confused with reproductions and fakes are those made from molds produced for the hobby ceramics market. The mammy and granny below are an example. While it appears one might have been copied from the other, both were made from the same mold, sold by Alberta's Molds, Inc., of Atascadero, California. Making and selling jars from these types of molds is a legal and very common practice.

Mark of the Carol Gifford mammy.

Studio artist Carol Gifford, who made the mammy on the left, is sometimes criticized for copying the design from the older jar on the right, thereby producing a fake. Nothing could be further from the truth. Both jars were rendered from identical Alberta's molds, a fact Gifford doesn't attempt to hide. These jars, 9-3/4 inches high, have been made and sold at craft shows by hundreds of home ceramists across the country. The jar on the right is unmarked, and the mark of the Carol Gifford jar is shown. *Courtesy of Jazz'e Junque Shop, Chicago, Illinois.* Left $150; Right $50

# Chapter 6
## *Problems of Collecting*

Until a few years ago cookie jar collectors faced three major problems in pursuing their hobby—a lack of information about jars and their makers, financial resources to purchase jars, and the large amount of space jars require for display and storage.

Problem number one, a lack of information, has been eased considerably by the publication of several excellent books. In addition to this book, all cookie jar collectors should consider familiarizing themselves with the following volumes:

1. *An Illustrated Value Guide to Cookie Jars, books 1 and 2,* by Ermagene Westfall.
2. *McCoy Cookie Jars—From the First to the Latest,* by Harold Nichols.
3. *The Collectors Encyclopedia of Cookie Jars, books 1, 2 and 3,* by Fred and Joyce Herndon Roerig.
4. *Dictionary Guide to United States Pottery and Porcelain (19th and 20th Century),* by Jenny B. Derwich and Dr. Mary Latos.
5. *Lehner's Encyclopedia of U.S. Marks on Pottery, Porcelain & Clay,* by Lois Lehner.

The information contained in the above books, along with the information in this book, will not tell you everything there is to know about cookie jars, but it will enable you to enjoy the hobby to a much greater degree. At the same time it will drastically reduce your chances of being taken advantage of by unscrupulous or misinformed dealers.

Sources of the above publications are listed in Appendix 1.

Problem number two, financial resources to purchase jars, relates directly to the amount of disposable income at hand, the amount of time available to search for jars and, let's face it, a collector's skill at what might be called creative budgeting. There are few true collectors, myself included, who haven't used part of the house payment, the vacation savings, or money designated for some other specific purpose, to take advantage of an unexpected good deal.

The cookie jar collector's money crunch has become more severe the past few years as jar prices have shot up at a rate many times that of the average growth in personal income. But good buys still exist for those willing to ferret them out.

Flea markets are the best hunting grounds for the person limited on both time and cash. Get there early before everything has been picked over.

If you have more time than money on your hands, a common syndrome among parents of college-aged children, garage sales are a good route. Many families have a cookie jar or two, a lot don't realize what they're worth. At garage sales where no cookie jars are displayed, ask the people if they have any. The results might surprise you.

Don't overlook antique shops and shows, either. While shooting cookie jar pictures at antique malls, I spotted a tan Brush squirrel on log jar for less than one-third of its average book value, a McCoy asparagus jar for $10, a Shawnee Smiley pig for $16, and many other good buys. Make the round of shops often because good deals don't remain on the shelves very long.

At antique shows you'll have the greatest success by arriving two to three hours before the show opens, while the dealers are still setting up. Some shows charge a premium for early admission, others don't.

Auctions can be good, too. At auctions where many jars have been advertised, the bidding is nearly always very competitive. You might find the jars you want, but be prepared to pay book price or more for them. At estate auctions you'll find less quantity but usually better prices, especially when the jars haven't been advertised.

By displaying cookie jars on modular aluminum shelving units, you focus attention on the jars themselves, not the piece that is holding them. (Note American Bisque Olive Oyl on middle shelf, not shown elsewhere in the book.)

Close-up of aluminum shelving.

Bookcases and similar storage units can easily be used for displaying cookie jars.

You don't need anything fancy to exhibit your cookie jar collection. Here, construction grade pine lumber, stained but not varnished, has been used to create basement shelving.

Bookcases can serve double duty by holding books and displaying cookie jars at the same time.

The third problem cookie jar collectors face is an eternal one: space. There's no way around it, cookie jars take up a lot of room. Start a collection and before long your house will be taken over by it. But houses can be taken over by many things, such as pets, so its no big deal, providing you love your jars.

Space problems are greater in the early stages of collecting when a person has gone beyond the point of being able to pass up a great jar, but has not yet committed to a long term, if not a lifetime, endeavor. Once that commitment is made, most people devise attractive display units and adequate storage facilities.

The built-in and modular displays shown here will give the neophyte some ideas to copy or enhance. While work by skilled tradesmen can be quite expensive, the cost of a professionally built display unit will pale when set against the value of the jars it holds. The competent do-it-yourselfer can get by for much less.

Storage of undisplayed jars can be easily accomplished by building rough shelves of inexpensive grade lumber in a basement or garage, or even a dry unheated shed if you live in the proper climate. Doors made of 1 x 3 furring strips with clear plastic stretched across them will protect your cookie jars from dust, smoke and other undesirable elements while they're being stored.

# Section II: The Cookie Jar Giants

Numerous American potteries in business between the 1930s and the present have made cookie jars, but two—McCoy and American Bisque—stand above the others as giants of the industry, both in the number of different jars they produced and in the standard of quality they maintained. It's probable other potteries noted the success of these two companies and decided to grab their own share of the market, thereby making McCoy and American Bisque the driving force that gave today's cookie jar collectors their hobby.

They've been placed at the beginning as a tribute to their contribution.

# Chapter 7
# *McCoy*

No other pottery has made more different cookie jars—well over 300—than McCoy. While an entire book could be written on the history of this company, suffice to say its roots go back to 1848 when W. Nelson McCoy went into the pottery business in Putnam, Ohio, to produce stoneware crocks and other utilitarian pieces for local consumers. W. Nelson McCoy's uncle, W.F. McCoy, assisted in the venture. Putnam, incidentally, no longer exists as it was later annexed to Zanesville. As time went on the quality of the pottery's wares improved to the point they were eventually transported by flatboat down the Ohio and Mississippi rivers to eager wholesale buyers as far away as New Orleans.

W. Nelson McCoy taught the business to his son, J.W. McCoy, who founded the J.W. McCoy Pottery in Roseville, Ohio, on September 5, 1899. Like its predecessor, the new company dealt mainly in domestic use stoneware, but also dabbled in glazed spittoons, jardinieres, pedestals, and other large pieces popular at the time. These met with considerable success, encouraging the firm to experiment with artware of the type produced by trend setters such as Weller and Rookwood.

J.W. McCoy continued the family tradition of handing down the craft, and in 1910 formed a separate corporation with his son, Nelson McCoy. It was called the Nelson McCoy Sanitary Stoneware Company. This is the company that eventually made McCoy cookie jars. Meanwhile, the J. W. McCoy Pottery became the Brush-McCoy Pottery Company in 1911 when General Manager George Brush bought into it. The affiliation lasted until 1925 when the McCoys sold their interest and redirected the capital to the Nelson McCoy Sanitary Stoneware Company, which at some point along the way changed its name to the Nelson McCoy Pottery Company.

In 1967 Chase Enterprises bought the firm, sold it in 1974 to Lancaster Colony Corporation. In 1991 it was owned by Designer Accents, of Sebring, Ohio, and goes by the name Nelson McCoy Ceramics. It is now out of business.

The first McCoy cookie jars are believed to have been made in the late 1930s, but the exact date is unknown. These were very plain bean pot type jars. The first figural jar to come from McCoy was the mammy with cauliflowers, which emerged from the kiln in 1939, and is highly prized by collectors today.

The McCoy Indian head, made from 1954 to 1956, is marked "McCoy/USA" on two lines. No. 50, it is 11-1/2 inches high. Long said to be finished in both a light and dark glaze, the glazes are actually one in the same. The shade depended upon how thickly the glaze was applied. The proof is inside each jar. Compare the inside of a light Indian head jar to the inside of a dark Indian head jar and you will find they are both the same color. To paraphrase our forefathers, all McCoy Indian head jars were created equal, but only on the inside, not on the outside. The insides of the cookie jars are finished by pouring glaze in, then dumping it out, giving each interior an even coating. Exteriors are finished by brushing or airbrushing, both of which result in varying thicknesses of glaze. As a further test, lightly rub your finger over the part in the Indian's hair. On a darker jar, (which has a thicker glaze) you will notice less of a depression than on a lighter jar (which has a thinner glaze). *Blumenfeld Collection.* $300

While the 1950s are often thought of as the golden age of McCoy cookie jars, the company actually hit its stride in jar manufacturing during the 1960s, and peaked in the 1970s, both in terms of the number of different jars offered during any particular year, and number of new designs offered. Peaks and lulls of McCoy cookie jar production are shown in the two graphs in Appendix III.

Most McCoy cookie jars exhibit very detailed mold features, yet rather plain decoration, a combination that obviously pleased consumers. Airbrushing was used sparingly, hand-painting of de-

tails on top of the glaze was used extensively. So were decals. McCoy made more fruit and vegetable cookie jars than any other company. More canisters, too.

McCoy marked most of its jars. The many different marks it used are shown at the end of the chapter. Jars that aren't marked can often be identified by the three bars they have across the bottom, which are shown along with the marks. The names and numbers in the accompanying captions are those used by Nichols.

This 9-1/2 inch high sad clown is McCoy no. 255, made in 1970 and 1971. It has the McCoy bull's-eye mark. *Zera Collection*. $130

McCoy's W.C. Fields jar has become very popular with collectors in recent years. No. 153 in the McCoy line, it is 11 inches high, and was made from 1972 to 1974. Its mark is shown below. *Zera Collection*. $210

It seems all Davy Crockett cookie jars command a premium, and McCoy's jar is no exception. The jar, no. 140, is 10 inches high, and was made in 1957. It is marked "USA." *Zera Collection*. $550

A much earlier clown bust, 1945 to 1947, 10-1/2 inches high. It is no. 19, and marked "McCoy." *Zera Collection*. $70

This hand-decorated chef (bust) is 11 inches high, marked "McCoy/USA" on two lines on the hat band, which is an unusual place for a McCoy mark. Made from 1962 to 1964, it is McCoy no. 206. *Blumenfeld Collection.* $130

The unmarked McCoy leprechaun is an exceptionally rare jar. Besides green, it was made in brown, red, and multi-color. Seeing very limited production, the 12-1/2 inch high jar never appeared in McCoy catalogs. Nichols assigned it no. 169. Exact date of the jar has not been ascertained. While a debate rages among collectors as to how many were made, most estimates range from a few hundred to a few thousand. Now the jar has been heavily reproduced and most collectors are afraid to buy it. *Bosson Collection.* $1500

This late addition to the McCoy line stands 11 inches high, and has "McCoy Limited" impressed in the bottom on one line. *Blumenfeld Collection.* $200

The McCoy Christmas tree is 11-1/2 inches high. It is no. 174, made in 1959, and marked "McCoy/USA" on two lines. *Bosson Collection.* $900

Here is McCoy's giant economy size Santa. Standing 21-1/2 inches high, it is really a lawn ornament but is often called a cookie jar because it was made in two pieces, split at the belt. It is unmarked. A close-up of the accompanying Keebler jar appears elsewhere. *Bosson Collection.* Value not determined.

"Cookie Boy," no. 16, manufactured in 1944 and 1945. This 11-1/4 inch high jar was also finished in aqua. The incised mark of the yellow jar is shown below. *Zera Collection.* $125 white; $150 yellow.

The "Boy on Football" was made in 1983, and stands 11-/12 inches high. The jar is McCoy no. 222, according to Nichols, but it is marked "127/McCoy/ LCC/USA" on four lines. *Lilly Collection*. $250

Not surprisingly, "Betsy Baker" is no. 184. Apparently not as popular as Bobby, it was made in 1974 only. The jar is 10-3/4 inches high. The example shown is unmarked, while others are marked "184/McCoy/USA/LCC" on four lines, and still others have a similar mark without the LCC logo. Finding different marks on identical McCoy jars is not unusual. Several different hats, or lids, were made for this jar. *Zera Collection*. $275

In addition to the three colors shown, the "Clown (in barrel)" was also finished in blue. *Bosson Collection*. $100 each

"Boy on Baseball" is 13-1/2 inches high. Offered in 1978, it is no. 221, and marked "221/McCoy/LCC/USA" on four lines. *Bosson Collection*. $275

"Bobby the Baker" is the name the McCoy Company gave to no. 183, the 10-3/4 inch chef, manufactured between 1974 and 1979, and again beginning in 1983. Impressed into the bottom of this particular jar is "183/ McCoy" on two lines, while other examples are marked "USA." *Oravitz Collection*. $45

This is called "Animal Crackers," made in 1960. Some examples have raised dots on them; this one does not. It is no. 175, and is marked "McCoy"/U.S.A." on two lines. *Oravitz Collection*. $110

The "Clown (in barrel)" was sold from 1953 to 1955. Standing 11-1/2 inches high, it is McCoy no. 40., and is marked "McCoy/U.S.A." impressed on two lines. *Coughenour Collection*. $100

This clown is 8-1/2 inches high. It is no. 27, made in 1945. Like most older jars that were painted over the glaze, it is difficult, if not impossible, to find it in perfect condition. The mark, shown below, is "McCoy" in raised letters. *Courtesy of Jazz'e Junque Shop, Chicago, Illinois*. $110

The mammy on the left has been repainted, the mammy on the right has not. This 11 inch high jar, no. 17, has a bit of intrigue connected to it. According to Nichols, it originated in 1944 with the words "Dem cookies shor am good" on it; it was made like this until 1946 when the degrading phrase was dropped in favor of "Cookies." However, no collectors who were interviewed, including many aficionados of black collectibles, reported ever seeing the jar, and most indicated they believe it was never made. Either way, production on this model ended in 1957. Both of these examples are marked "McCoy." *Zera Collection*. $125 each

Not all McCoy mammies wore white dresses. Size and mark are the same as above. *Bosson Collection.* $600

The example on the left was made in 1972 and 1973, while the one on the right was made the following two years. Both are "Granny," no. 159, and are 11 inches high. The mark is "159/USA" on two lines, though it is often unreadable. The plainer version is generally considered to be more desirable, which is reflected in the price guide. *Oravitz Collection.* Left $130; Right $150

"Mammy with Cauliflowers," no. 8 (assigned by Nichols), is 11-3/4 inches high. Made in 1939, this is one of the most sought after—and expensive—McCoy jars, even in this condition, which is typical for old jars that were painted over the glaze. This jar is said to be McCoy's first figural cookie jar. *Zera Collection.* $900

"Rag Doll" (Raggedy Ann) is 11 inches high. Its mark, "U.S.A./ 741" on two lines, includes its model number. The jar was made from 1972 to 1975. *Courtesy of Jazz'e Junque Shop, Chicago, Illinois.* $100

Monk in solid color, 12-1/2 inches high, and unmarked. *Lilly Collection.* $50

One of the things to be aware of when collecting cookie jars is the potential of running into repainted jars. This "Mammy with Cauliflowers" has indeed been repainted, but so long ago it now looks like the original. As far as is known, however, all scarfs were originally painted yellow by the company. *Coughenour Collection.* $900

The unmarked McCoy monk is 12-1/2 inches high. It is no. 846, made from 1968 to 1973. Many others companies made monk jars. *Zera Collection.* $50

One of two kangaroos the company made, this model was first produced in 1965. Standing 11-1/2 inches high, it is no. 234, marked "McCoy/USA" on two lines. *Coughenour Collection.* $500

McCoy's second kangaroo, 13 inches high, no. 234, identified by its three-bar bottom, an example of which is shown below. While it is known that the other model was taken out of production in favor of this one, the exact dates of manufacture for each have not been determined. *Lilly Collection.* $400

"Teddy Bear and Friend," no. 154, is 11-1/2 inches high, mar "154/USA." Made in 1986 and 1987, it also came in dark brown. *Lilly Collection.* $70

Occasionally you find a cookie jar that has been customized to suit a previous owner's specific purpose. While this generally devalues a jar (perhaps if it said something like, To Lady Bird from Lyndon, it might increase the value), it certainly makes it a more interesting piece of Americana. *Zera Collection.* $300

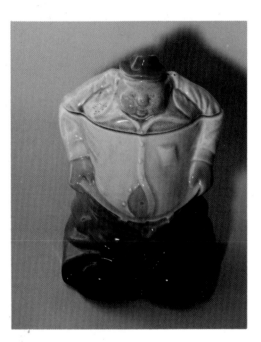

McCoy's "Chairman of the Board," a jar whose price has skyrocketed since 1985, the only year it was made. It is 10-1/2 inches high, no. 162, and marked "162/USA" on two lines. Very good reproductions exist. *Coughenour Collection.* $600

"Hamm's Bear," McCoy no. 148, made in 1972. It is 13 inches high, marked "148/USA." *Lilly Collection.* $300

Bottom of customized "Hamm's Bear." Note faint mark to the right of "Love," an impressed "148," but no USA as on above jar.

"Chairman of the Board" with brown pants instead of burgundy as above. The difference is much more apparent than conveyed in the pictures. The size and mark are the same as above. Because the tops of both these jars are tinted differently than the bottoms, the first impulse is to consider them to be married. They're probably not, as the example Nichols shows is the same way. Slight color variations between tops and bottoms is a common occurrence with McCoy cookie jars, far more prevalent than with any other company. *Bosson Collection.* $600

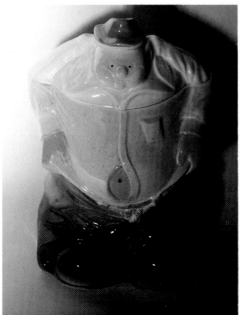

This jar, "Bear (cookies in vest)," no. 22, is seen in two different styles. The original, shown here, was made in 1945, and does not have "Cookies" in raised letters between the feet, as the next example does. The jar is 10-3/4 inches high, with "McCoy" impressed in the bottom. *Zera Collection.* $75

"Honey Bear" is 9 inches high, and was made from 1953 to 1955. McCoy no. 37, it has a "McCoy/USA" mark on two lines. *Zera Collection.* $110

Brother to the jar in the previous picture, this model was manufactured in 1953, and has the lettering between the feet. The mold appears to have been altered a bit, too, specifically in the area below the bow tie. This version is the rarer of the two. *Zera Collection.* $125

Panda, 11 inches high, no. 141. Made in 1978, its mark is "141/USA." *Bosson Collection.* $250

"Honey Bear" with a different color lid, plus one other difference. This one is marked "McCoy" in raised letters. *Zera Collection.* $110

The koala bear is 11-1/4 inches high, no. 216. The jar was made in 1983. Its mark is shown below. *Oravitz Collection.* $100

This is "Brown Bear," also no. 22, but according to Nichols, not shown in any McCoy catalog. The height is 10-3/4 inches, and the mark is "McCoy" impressed. *Coughenour Collection.* $900

Everything the same as the previous bear, except for the bright yellow clothes. *Bosson Collection.* $900

What's happening here is hard to grasp. Apparently the bear is supposed to be wrapped around the beehive, but it looks very unnatural. No. 143, the jar stands 9 inches high, and is marked "143/U.S.A." impressed on two lines. It has been made since 1983, and could still be bought at discount stores in 1990. *Oravitz Collection.* $50

Labeled "Snow Bear" by the company, this 1965 jar, no. 235, is 11 inches high. It is marked with an impressed "USA," but examples are also seen marked "McCoy/U.S.A." in raised letters on two lines. *Lilly Collection.* $80

"Upside Down Bear" is 11-1/2 inches high, marked "McCoy/U.S.A." on two lines with LCC logo impressed quite far below. McCoy no. 210, it was made in 1978 and 1979. *Lilly Collection.* $60

Now it is 1953 and the elephant emerges with a new designation, no. 41, and a trunk that is no longer split between top and bottom. This version is occasionally seen in red. Height is 11 inches. The jar is unmarked. *Zera Collection.* $150

The "Rocking Chair (Dalmatians)" cookie jar is highly prized by collectors. It is 10 inches high, and marked "McCoy/U.S.A." in raised letters on two lines. No. 189, it was made in 1961. *Courtesy of Betty and Floyd Carson.* $350

"Upside Down Bear" with clear glaze. *Courtesy of Jazz'e Junque Shop, Chicago, Illinois.* $60

"Dog House," no. 206, 13 inches high, made in 1983. The one on the left is the eyes-closed version, the one on the right the eyes-open version. The left jar is marked "206/McCoy/LCC/USA" on four lines. The right jar is unmarked. *Coughenour Collection.* $350 each

These two jars are McCoy's "Elephant with Split Trunk," manufactured prior to the "Elephant without a Split Trunk," shown below. Note that one has round eyes, the other pointed eyes. It is believed the round-eye version was manufactured around 1940, and the pointed-eye version, in 1945. McCoy no. 20, some of these jars are impressed "McCoy." They are 11 inches high. Both of these have been restored. *Bosson Collection.* Left $200; Right $275

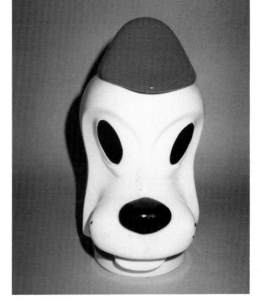

Some dogs are deep thinkers, others are deep sleepers. "Snoopy," no. 247, is 11-1/4 inches high, and was made in 1970. Its mark is "USA" impressed, plus gold stamp, "© 1970 United/Feature Syndicate, Inc./World Right Reserved/Made in USA" on four lines. This is a fairly expensive McCoy jar, which is strange because, according to Nichols, it was made for Sears meaning they must have made kennels full of them. *Courtesy of Jazz'e Junque Shop, Chicago, Illinois.* $250

This is "Mac Dog," no. 208, 11-1/2 inches high. It was made in 1967 and 1968, and is marked "208/USA" on two lines. *Zera Collection.* $100

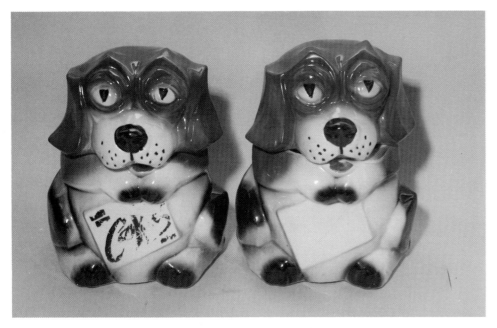

"Clyde (dog)," McCoy's no. 182. It is 12 inches high. The mark is "McCoy/182" on two lines, and the year of production was 1974. *Saxby Collection.* $400

"Puppy with Sign," no. 185, is a 1961-1962 offering, 10 inches high. It is marked "McCoy/USA" on two lines. Although the paint on the sign wears off rather easily, the jar is believed to have been made with the sign both painted and unpainted. While the jar on the right appears taller than the one on the left, look closely and you will see the lid is not seated properly. *Oravitz Collection.* $80 each

"Coalby Cat," no. 207, 11-1/4 inches high. Manufactured in 1967 and 1968, it is marked "USA/207" on two lines. *Bosson Collection.* $450

"Thinking Puppy," 11 inches high, is McCoy's no. 272. It was offered between 1977 and 1979. The mark, shown below, includes the Lancaster Colony Corporation logo. *Courtesy of Mary and Bill Hallier.* $15

Another rendition of no. 272, this jar's mark, also shown below, is different than the mark on the darker model. *Zera Collection.* $15

31

"The Kittens on Ball of Yarn," 9 inches high, dating from 1954 and 1955. The jar is no. 24, and marked "McCoy/USA" on two lines. *Zera Collection*. $100 each

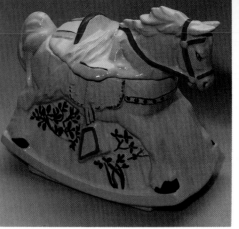

While the "Rocking Horse" was made in these basic colors is a repainted jar. As they came from the factory, the flowers were not painted. Size and mark as above. *Coughenour Collection*. $190

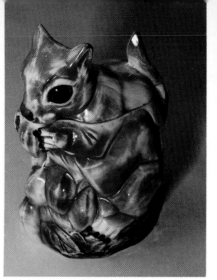

The "Chipmunk" was made in 1960 and 1961. It stands 10-3/4 inches high, and is marked "McCoy/USA" on two lines. Its McCoy number is 172. *Zera Collection*. $150

The same jar in green, with size and mark identical to above jars. *Oravitz Collection*. $100

"Circus Horse," no. 193, is from 1961. It stands 9-1/2 inches high, and is marked "McCoy/USA" on two lines in raised letters. *Zera Collection*. $225

Besides the colors shown, this jar was also made in blue and possibly other colors. Called "Hocus Rabbit," it is quite tall measuring 14 inches. The number is included in the mark, "211/McCoy/LCC/U.S.A." on four lines. "Hocus Rabbit" was made in 1978 and 1979. *Zera Collection*. $50

"The Kitten on Coal Bucket" jar, no. 218, was made in 1983. It is 10 inches high, marked "218/McCoy/LCC/USA" on four lines. *Bosson Collection*. $300 each

No. 36, "Rocking Horse," is 10-1/4 inches high and was sold between 1948 and 1953. The mark is "McCoy" in raised letters. *Zera Collection*. $190

Two more colors of "Hocus Rabbit." Size and marks are the same as above. *Oravitz Collection*. $50 each

"Yellow Mouse," no. 208, 11-1/2 inches high. The mark is "208/McCoy/LCC/USA" on four lines. This jar is also seen without painted eyes. *Lilly Collection*. $50

From wren on house to hen on nest, sounds like Dr. Seuss no less. Made in 1958 and 1959, this jar is 10-1/2 inches high, marked "USA." No. 139, it also comes with a yellow bottom. *Zera Collection*. $100

"White Rooster," 1970 to 1974. It is no. 258, stands 13-1/4 inches high, and carries the McCoy bull's-eye mark. *Lilly Collection*. $50

The McCoy "Wren House," no. 153. Check out the two different lids. Jar on the left is 9-1/2 inches high, jar on the right is 10 inches high. Both are marked "McCoy/USA" on two lines in raised letters. The standard version, on the left, was made from 1958 through 1960. The one on the right, believed to be extremely rare, undoubtedly dates from the same era. *Coughenour Collection*. Left $200; Right Value Undetermined

"The Rooster," no. 55, was made between 1956 and 1958. It is 10-3/4 inches high, marked "McCoy/U.S.A." on two lines. *Oravitz Collection*. $110

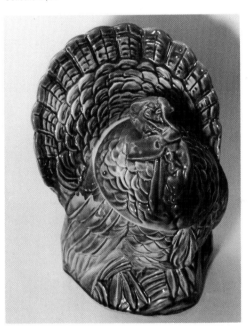

McCoy made two turkey cookie jars, one in 1945, another in 1960. This one, finished in brown and green, is the 1945 model. No. 23, it is 11-1/2 inches high. The mark is "McCoy" impressed. *Coughenour Collection*. $250

Another turkey, vintage 1945, in a different color scheme. *Zera Collection*. $250

Variation of "Wren House," 9-1/2 inches high, with the same mark as above. *Zera Collection*. $200

Gray version of above, but made only in 1957 and 1958. Same size but different mark, "McCoy" impressed. *Bosson Collection*. $125

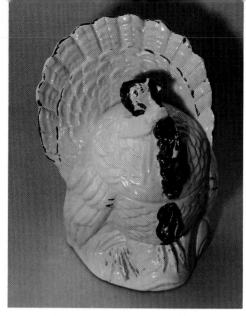

The 1945 turkey was also made in white. *Coughenour Collection.* $250

"Woodsy Owl," no. 201, 12 1/2 inches high. The jar is marked "USA." It was made in 1973 and 1974. *Zera Collection.* $325

"Mother Goose," made between 1948 and 1952, and shown in two different glazes. It is 10-3/4 inches high, no. 34, and has a "McCoy/USA" mark on two lines in raised letters. *Bosson Collection.* $150 each

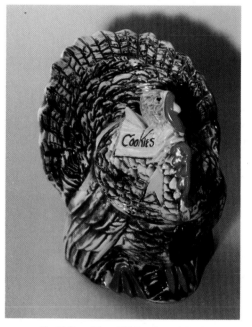

The 1960 model, no. 176. Standing only 9-1/2 inches high, it is considerably shorter than its predecessor. Note that the feet are different, and, although it doesn't show in the pictures, the tail feathers flare more on this one. The mark is different, too, "McCoy/USA" on two lines. *Coughenour Collection.* $250

"Mr. and Mrs. Owl," 1952 to 1955, no. 38. Written on the back of this 10 3/4 inch high jar is, "When shadows fall." It is marked "McCoy/USA" on two lines. *Oravitz Collection.* $110

While McCoy cookie jars are notorious for poor lid fits, this might well be a married jar because it appears the leaf edges and veins won't line up no matter how the lid is adjusted. It is called "The Duck," and was made in 1964. Unmarked, the 11-1/2 inch high jar has the McCoy three-bar bottom. *Zera Collection.* $85

While this jar is simply called "Owl," the owners of this trio like to refer to them as "patriotic owls" because they envision the birds standing to say the pledge of allegiance. The owls were made in 1978 and 1979. They are all McCoy no. 204, but aren't marked the same. The left and right owls sport "204/McCoy/LCC/U.S.A.," impressed on four lines, while the one in the middle has "204/U.S.A." impressed on two lines. *Oravitz Collection.* $40 each

Modern chick, offered in 1976 and 1977. It is 9-1/2 inches high marked "McCoy/LCC/U.S.A." on three lines. *Oravitz Collection.* $300

"Goodie Goose," 12-1/2 inches high. McCoy's no. 166, this jar is unmarked. Production began in 1986. Goodie has also been made with pink and yellow ribbons. *Lilly Collection*. $20

This penguin is "Chilly Willy," no. 155, which began production in 1986. It is 12 inches high. The mark is "155/U.S.A." impressed on two lines. *Oravitz Collection*. $75

The glaze on this "Stump with Frog Finial" could almost be mistaken for a Frankoma glaze (Chapter 21) if seen from a distance. The jar, no. 216, is 12 inches high, and was made in 1971. It has a McCoy bull's-eye mark. *Zera Collection*. $50

"The Love Birds (kissing penguins)," 8-3/4 inches high, no. 29, was also finished in a black glaze which is much more valuable. This jar, made in 1946, is marked "McCoy." *Zera Collection*. $85

"Timmy Tortoise," no. 271, sold from 1977 to 1980. Timmy is 10-1/2 inches high, and marked "271/McCoy/LCC/U.S.A." impressed on four lines. *Oravitz Collection*. $45

A close cousin to the "Stump with Frog Finial" is the "Cookie Log with Squirrel Finial." The 11-1/4 inch high jar was made from 1965 to 1969, and has the McCoy three-bar bottom. The designation is no. 240. *Oravitz Collection*. $35

McCoy labeled this big-billed bird a penguin. Westfall coined it a "pelguin," which seems more appropriate. It is McCoy's no. 18, stands 11-1/4 inches high, and was made from 1940 to 1943. In addition to solid yellow, it was also glazed in solid white and solid green. On the painted versions the head is sometimes black. *Oravitz Collection*. $140

Another relative, the "Monkey on Stump," no. 253, is 11-1/2 inches high, and marked "253/(bull's-eye) ©/USA" on three lines. It was made in 1970. *Lilly Collection.* $45

"Winking Pig," no. 150, 13-1/2 inches high. The mark is "150/USA" on two lines. The jar was made in 1972. *Coughenour Collection.* $500

Nichols doesn't show animals on cylinder jars, but the Roerigs show two, a pair of puppies and a kitten. Said by some to be a McCoy impostor, this "Lamb on cylinder" is 11-1/2 inches high, and is stamped "McCoy" on the bottom. *Courtesy of Jazz'e Junque Shop, Chicago, Illinois.* $150

The "Pig," no. 201, is 8 inches high. It was made in 1978 and 1979, is marked "McCoy/USA/201" on three lines. The lid of this jar has an L-shaped catch that prevents it from sliding off. On this example, the catch is on the same side as the tail. On others, it is placed opposite the tail, which puts the tail too high up on the back of the pig. *Zera Collection.* $50

This McCoy jar is 8 inches high, and marked "8166/USA" on two lines. *Lilly Collection.* $80

Look closely at the head of this pig and you'll see a slot that allows it to serve double duty as a bank. It is 10-1/2 inches high, and was made in 1985. McCoy number is included in the mark "224/U.S.A." impressed on two lines. *Oravitz Collection.* $200

McCoy made several different tops for its basketweave bottom. They're referred to as "Lamb on Basketweave," "Dog on Basketweave," etc. Their average height is 10-1/4 inches. No. 127 is on the left, no. 128 on the right. Both of these were made in 1956 and 1957. The marks are "McCoy/USA" in raised letters on two lines. *Zera Collection.* $65 each

The "Duck on Basketweave" has two heads, one in the front, one in the rear. It was made in 1956. McCoy's no. 129, its mark is "McCoy/USA" in raised letters on two lines. *Oravitz Collection.* $80

The McCoy "Pear" is 10 inches high, marked "McCoy USA" in a circle in raised letters. It is no. 18, made from 1952 to 1957. *Coughenour Collection.* $85

Yet another color. *Zera Collection.* $50

"Pinecones on Basketweave," no. 133, 1957, and "Kitten on Basketweave," no. 126, 1956 to 1959. Both are marked "McCoy/USA" in raised letters on two lines. *Zera Collection.* Left $50; Right $80

"Pears on Basketweave," no. 135, made in 1957. A similar top, made the same year, has apples on it. The mark is "McCoy/USA" in raised letters on two lines. *Zera Collection.* $60

One of several colors for the McCoy "Apple," no. 20. It's 7-1/2 inches high, and is marked "McCoy USA" in a small circle around the blossom end. Long popular, this apple was made from 1950 to 1964. *Zera Collection.* $35

Basically the same apple, but it has a "M" impressed in the lid. *Zera Collection.* $50

The model number and years of production are not known for this 7-1/2 inch McCoy apple, but it is obviously older than those above. Note the saw-tooth edge on the leaf. *Zera Collection.* $85

Here is another style of apple, no. 261, 9-1/2 inches high, made from 1972 to 1979. McCoy mark on bottom. *Zera Collection.* $60

This is called the "New Strawberry," no. 263, as opposed to the "Old Strawberry," no. 54. This one was made from 1972 to 1979, is 9-1/2 inches high. It was glazed in these two colors plus white, shown below. The mark is "263/USA" on two lines. *Taylor Collection.* $40 each

This orange isn't exceptionally tall, 12 inches to the top of the stem, but its girth makes it a really large cookie jar. No. 257, it carries the McCoy bull's-eye mark, and was made during 1970 and 1971. *Zera Collection.* $50

Same as above but marked differently, "263/McCoy/LCC/U.S.A." on four lines. The McCoy bull's-eye mark, with the number "263," was also used on this jar. *Taylor Collection.* $50

Same strawberry but minus the white drip glaze. It has a different mark, too, "McCoy" in raised letters. *Lilly Collection.* $75

A 7-1/2 inch high tomato, made in 1964. No. 210, it is marked "McCoy/USA" in raised letters on two lines. *Zera Collection.* $40

Strawberry with white drip glaze, made from 1955 to 1957. Note the different top than in above examples. Mark is "McCoy/U.S.A." in raised letters on two lines. This jar is McCoy's no. 54, measuring 9 inches high. *Taylor Collection.* $95

The lemon is 9 inches high, was made in 1972, and of has McCoy bull's-eye mark. It is no. 262. As seen here, McCoy used the same lid for several different fruit jars. *Zera Collection.* $80

This pineapple with gold tint, no. 52, goes for more money than the pineapple in natural colors shown below. It is 10-1/2 inches high, was made from 1955 to 1957, and is marked "McCoy/USA" on two lines. *Zera Collection.* $130

Natural color version of above pineapple. Same size and mark. *Zera Collection*. $90

"The Bananas," no. 33, was made from 1948 through 1952. The jar is 11 inches high, and marked "McCoy" in raised letters. Most examples have tops that vary slightly in color from their bottoms. While such a mismatch often indicates a married jar, in this case it is probably the result of being glazed by different people at the factory, or perhaps the tops being done at different times than the bottoms. *Courtesy of Jazz'e Junque Shop, Chicago, Illinois*. $130

McCoy crock jar, no. 3, from 1939 to 1944. It is 9-3/4 inches high. *Oravitz Collection*. $30

Same jar as above in tan. *Courtesy of Jazz'e Junque Shop, Chicago, Illinois*. $30

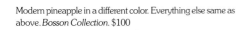

This is McCoy's "Modern Pineapple," no. 823, 13-1/4 inches high, "USA" impressed. *Lilly Collection*. $100

Modern pineapple in a different color. Everything else same as above. *Bosson Collection*. $100

Just like at the supermarket, cookie jar bananas come in different stages of ripeness. *Taylor Collection*. $130

The McCoy "Asparagus" cookie jar was a 1977 to 1979 offering. It is 10-1/2 inches high, no. 267. It is unmarked but has the familiar McCoy three-bar bottom, an example of which is shown below. *Zera Collection*. $60

Nearly white bananas. *Lilly Collection*. $130

The "Coffee grinder," 1961 to 1968. Standing 10 inches high, it is marked "McCoy/USA" on two lines. The jar is no. 179. *Courtesy of Vicki Nitecki and Irene Mychul.* $40

McCoy "Kettle," no. 188, 9-1/2 inches high. Marked "McCoy/USA" on two lines, this jar was made from 1961 to 1967. Nichols shows one with flowers on it. *Lilly Collection.* $30

"Kookie Kettle," no. 171. This was made from 1960 to 1977. It stands 12-1/2 inches to the top of the handle and the mark is "McCoy/USA" on two lines. It has also been seen in white. *Courtesy of Claude and Edna Mae Smith.* $30

According to Nichols, McCoy called this jar "Aladdin." It is 9-3/4 inches high, no. 244, and was made in 1965. The mark is "McCoy/U.S.A." *Zera Collection.* $50

The "Cookie Pot" is 12 inches high, no. 220 in the McCoy line. It is also seen in light blue and with various decals. The jar was made from 1964 to 1974. The mark is "McCoy/U.S.A." in raised letters on two lines. *Courtesy of Jazz'e Junque Shop, Chicago, Illinois.* $50

The "Tea Kettle" is 7 inches high. No. 185, it was made in 1974, and is marked "McCoy/USA" on two lines. *Zera Collection.* $40

The company titled this cookie jar "Chuck Wagon," apparently because it is the type of coffee pot found on chuck wagons. The height of the pottery is 10-3/4 inches. McCoy's no. 206, these jars were not marked. They were made in 1974 and 1975. *Bosson Collection.* $110 each

The "Coffee Mug" is 9-1/4 inches high with a three-bar bottom. It is McCoy's no. 232, made from 1963 to 1966. *Lilly Collection.* $40

This is the "Cookie Kettle," no. 243. Made from 1965 to 1968, it is unmarked but has the McCoy three-bar bottom. Most of the gold lettering has worn off on this one. *Lilly Collection.* $50

Called the "Nibble Kettle," and often shown with title in gold lettering on the front, this jar is marked "McCoy/USA" on two lines. It is 8 inches high not including the handle. Nichols assigned it no. 167, date is unknown. *Zera Collection.* $35

"Gay Time Pitcher," made in 1974. McCoy no. 184, it is 9-1/2 inches high. The mark is "McCoy/USA" on two lines. *Bosson Collection.* $45 each

The "Jewel Box (cookie box)," no. 215, is 9-1/4 inches high, marked "USA," and was made in 1963. *Zera Collection.* $110

McCoy's "Little Red Bean Pot" is 8 inches high, not including the wire handle. No. 259, the jar is marked "McCoy/USA" impressed on two lines. It was made in 1971. This example is incomplete, it should have a coil grip. *Lilly Collection.* $35

Here is McCoy's "Gypsy Pot," which was also finished in white. The jar is 7 inches high not including the handle, and dates from 1975. Although not marked, it is McCoy's no. 7056. *Zera Collection.* $35

The "Early American Chest (chiffonier)" was made from 1965 to 1968. The mark is shown below. No. 245, the jar is 11-1/2 inches high. *Zera Collection.* $90

McCoy "Grandfather Clock," 12-1/4 inches high, no. 203. It was made between 1962 and 1964. In addition to having a McCoy three-bar bottom, "U.S.A." is impressed on the back. *Courtesy of Jazz'e Junque Shop, Chicago, Illinois.* $95

Similar to "Time for Cookies," but antiqued, and numerals in gold, much of this has worn off. *Zera Collection.* $30

On the left is the "Coke Can," no. 1003, on the right the "Coke Jug," no. 1004. Can is 10-3/4 inches high, jug 9-3/4 inches high. Both have "McCoy" impressed in their bottoms. Year of production was 1986. *Oravitz Collection.* Left $90; Right $90

This is called "Time for Cookies" because "Time for" is written directly above the word cookies, although you probably can't make it out on either of these two examples. It is easy to read on other models that have gold lettering, gold hands, and gold numerals. No. 848, it is 13-1/2 inches high, and was made from 1968 to 1973. It has no mark but it does have the McCoy three-bar bottom. *Oravitz Collection.* $30

"Pirate's Chest," no. 252, 1970. This jar is 9 inches high, has the McCoy bull's-eye mark with "252" above, "USA" below. *Zera Collection.* $175

"Keebler Cookie Jar," no. 350, made by McCoy in 1986, 1987, and possibly later. It stands 9-1/2 inches high. Also made by Haeger Potteries. Although the sizes are different, the best way to tell the difference is that the Haeger jar displays a molded, hand-painted elf, while McCoy's elf is a decal applied to a flat surface. There is a side-by-side comparison in Chapter 21. *Lilly Collection.* $30

"Cookie Jug," no. 144, made from 1958 through 1970. The first of several McCoy cookie jar jugs, it is unmarked but has the three-bar bottom. That is an actual cork in the top. This example is 9-1/2 inches high, was also made in another size. Sometimes these jars have brown lettering. *Lilly Collection.* $30

Here's a jar that creates a certain amount of confusion due to Regal China having also made a Quaker Oats jar. This one, measuring 10 inches high, is McCoy's no. 208. It was made in 1970, and is marked "USA." (For a side-by-side comparison of this jar and its Regal counterpart, see Chapter 16). *Bosson Collection.* $800

This "Cookie Jug" made its debut in 1971, and lasted through 1978. It is no. 145, and stands 11-1/4 inches high. It has a McCoy three-bar bottom, and was also made in brown and white. *Zera Collection.* $20

"Cookie Jug" with two handles and rope bottom. The McCoy number is 240. It was made from 1965 to 1968, is 9-3/4 inches high, marked "McCoy/USA" on two lines in raised letters. *Lilly Collection.* $45

The "Pitcher (blue willow)" was available from 1973 to 1975. The jar has a McCoy bull's-eye mark, and is 9-1/8 inches high. It is no. 202. *Zera Collection.* $60

Same pitcher, different look. Different mark, too: "202/McCoy/LCC/USA" on four lines. *Lilly Collection.* $20

McCoy "Tilt Pitcher," an unmarked offering from 1939. No. 6, it is 8-1/4 inches high. This jar was finished in an assortment of colors such as yellow, green, black, and the blue shown below. *Oravitz Collection.* $35

No. 213, 10-3/4 inches high, sold in 1978 and 1979. Marked "213/McCoy/LCC/USA" on four lines, the jar was also made in brown and in a blue and gray combination. *Lilly Collection.* $40

"Tilt Pitcher" in blue. *Oravitz Collection.* $35

This is "The Drum," no. 170, vintage 1960. It is 9-1/2 inches high, has "McCoy/USA" in raised letters. *Zera Collection.* $90

Called "Burlap Bag," this cookie jar was made from 1973 to 1977. In 1972, it was produced with a bird finial. This one is 11-1/2 inches high, and the top with a bird finial is slightly higher. The number is part of mark, "158/U.S.A." impressed on two lines. *Courtesy of Jazz'e Junque Shop, Chicago, Illinois.* $45

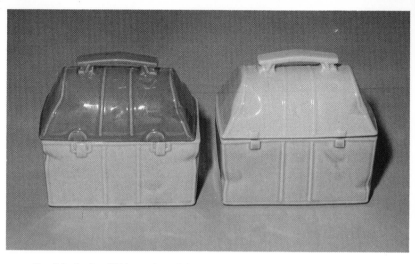

The "Barrel" cookie jar on the left is 10 inches high, the one on the right 8-3/4 inches high. Both have three-bar bottoms. No. 147, it was produced from 1958 to 1968. *Lilly Collection.* $30 each

"Lunch Bucket," no. 357, first made in 1978, continued into 1980s. It is 7 inches high. The jar on the left is unmarked, and the jar on the right is marked "357/U.S.A." on two lines. *Lilly Collection.* $60 each

This "Barrel" replaced the one pictured above in 1969, was made through 1972. No. 146, it stands 12 inches high. It is marked with the McCoy bull's-eye mark with "©" next to it, "146" above, and "USA" below. *Lilly Collection.* $35

"Liberty Bell," from 1975. The height is 7-3/4 inches, and the mark is "McCoy/LCC/USA" on three lines. Nichols assigned it no. 264. *Lilly Collection.* $65

"Fortune Cookie (Chinese lantern)" is 9-1/2 inches high, and was made from 1965 to 1968. McCoy no. 242, it is marked "McCoy/USA" in raised letters on two lines. It also came in other colors. *Zera Collection.* $65

"Cookie Bell," 9-1/2 inches high, McCoy three-bar bottom. No. 231, its years of manufacture were 1963 through 1966. *Courtesy of Jazz'e Junque Shop, Chicago, Illinois.* $35

The "Garbage Can" came out in 1978, and sold until 1987. It is no. 356, 9 inches high, marked "USA/356" on two lines. *Zera Collection.* $45

This plain Jane is McCoy's no. 1, called the "Ball Shape," and made sometime prior to 1940. The unmarked jar is 7-3/4 inches high, was glazed in different colors including a darker brown, light blue, maroon, and green. *Courtesy of Charles Kidd.* $45

The "Hobnail Pattern" jar, no. 15, is 8 inches high. Circa 1940, this model was also made in several different colors. Many examples sport an angled finial instead of the rectangular finial that this one has. The jar is not marked. *Zera Collection.* $35

Made from 1969 to 1979, the "Round Canister" is no. 7024, 8-1/2 inches high. The mark is "U.S.A." impressed. Besides the brown drip glaze, it was made with a yellow glaze, and also with a cream bottom and very dark top. *Zera Collection.* $20

Marked "1420L/McCoy/LCC/U.S.A." on four lines, this jar is 8 inches high. It was probably made around 1979. *Courtesy of Jazz'e Junque Shop, Chicago, Illinois.* $25

"Round Ball Shape," no. 7. Both jars are 7-1/2 inches high. These jars, with the angled finials, date from 1939 to 1944. The "Round Ball Shape" was offered again in 1948, 1950, and 1952 in similar colors but with rectangular finials. *Bosson Collection.* $50 each

Called simply "Canister," this jar is McCoy's no. 131, 9 inches high. The example on the left is marked "USA," while the example on the right shows "McCoy/LCC/USA" on three lines. Both jars have rubber gaskets similar to canning jar seals in their lids. This same basic shape was finished with a wide variety of decals. On some lids the company replaced the knob finial with a disc about 3 inches wide by 1-1/2 inches high. *Lilly Collection.* $15 each

"Round Ball Shape" in green. *Oravitz Collection.* $50

"Canister Jar" with brown drip glaze. The height is 10 inches, and the mark is "133/USA" on two lines. Nichols shows it as no. 7083, marked "7083/LCC USA/McCoy" on three lines enclosed in a circle. It was made in 1976 and 1977. *Lilly Collection.* $15

Actually a bean pot but collected as a cookie jar, this piece is 6-1/2 inches high. It is marked by an impressed "McCoy." The length of time the jar was made is unknown, but it was offered in McCoy's 1947 catalog. *Lilly Collection.* $45

This old crock jar (1939 to 1944) doesn't have a name. It is made of yellowware, is 9-3/4 inches high, and is unmarked. It is McCoy's no. 3. Chances are good this one was repainted. It comes in several colors. *Zera Collection.* $35

Here is a bit of nostalgia put out by McCoy. The height is 8-1/2 inches, the year is unknown, and the mark is shown. *Courtesy of Betty Carson.* $30

Same jar and mark, but with attractive pheasant decal. *Coughenour Collection.* $30

Old milk can shape in green, 9-3/4 inches high. *Oravitz Collection.* $35

Mark of tan glazed reproduction crock.

More of the same, everything as above. *Bosson Collection.* $30

Same jar as above in gray. *Courtesy of Jazz'e Junque Shop, Chicago, Illinois.* $35

On the left is "Dutch Girl (round shape)," 7-1/2 inches high, on the right is "Dutch Boy," 9-1/2 inches high. The boy, no. 24, was made in 1946. The girl, no. 25, was made one year later. Both are marked "McCoy" in raised letters. *Zera Collection.* Left $50; Right $50

McCoy made cylinder jars like these from 1946 to 1954, and again beginning in 1961. The one on the left is 9-1/2 inches high, and is marked "McCoy/USA" impressed on two lines. The jar on the right is slightly more than 1/4 of an inch taller, and obviously bigger around. It is marked "McCoy" in raised letters. *Oravitz Collection.* $30 each

Two more cylinders, 9-1/2 inches high, both marked "McCoy/USA." *Zera Collection.* $30 each

This jar is 9-3/4 inches high, marked "McCoy" in raised letters. *Zera Collection.* $35

Cylinder with peach cobbler recipe decal, made 1983 or later. The jar is 9-1/2 inches high, and marked "McCoy/USA." *Lilly Collection.* $35

Yellow glaze with flower decal, 9-1/2 inches high, marked "McCoy/USA" on two lines in raised letters. *Lilly Collection.* $30

"Cylinder with Poinsettia," 9-3/4 inches high, marked "McCoy" in raised letters on bottom. *Courtesy of Allan and Michelle Naylor.* $25

Close-up of peach cobbler cylinder jar showing 1983 date at bottom.

This jar is 9-1/2 inches high. Its impressed mark is "USA" with the curved tail at the right bottom of the "U," typical of many McCoy "USA" marks. It also has the McCoy cylinder lid. *Zera Collection.* $35

"Gingerbread Boy" is 10-1/4 inches high, marked "USA" in raised letters. The jar, no. 158, was made in 1961. *Zera Collection*. $60

The "Bugs Bunny" cylinder jar is one of three jars made in the early 1970s with cartoon character transfers. This one was offered in 1971 and 1972. It is 10-1/2 inches high, no. 223. In addition to the McCoy three-bar bottom, all the jars are marked with a "McCoy/USA" inkstamp shown below. *Zera Collection*. $150

A cylinder shape referred to as "Modern," this jar was made in different color glazes. No. 254, it sold from 1970 through 1974. The height is 11 inches. Its mark, the McCoy bull's-eye, is shown below. The design is contact paper, which often falls off. *Bosson Collection*. $45

"Mary, Mary Quite Contrary" is the theme of this nursery characters cylinder jar, no. 225, 8-3/4 inches high. The finial is metal. It has no mark but it does have the McCoy three-bar bottom. *Lilly Collection*. $75

"Popeye," no. 222, 1971 and 1972. The third jar, "Yosemite Sam," appears in Chapter 2. *Zera Collection*. $150

"Modern" cylinder with darker glaze. This is how they are usually seen—minus the contact paper. The size and mark are the same as above. *Zera Collection*. $45

Three more as above: "Humpty Dumpty," "Baa Baa Black Sheep," and "Little Miss Muffet." Also in the set but not shown are "Little Boy Blue" and "Little Bo Peep." *Oravitz Collection*. $75 each

McCoy "Milk Can (Antique Dutchland)" is 9-3/4 inches high, marked "USA." Dating from 1974, it is no. 190. *Zera Collection*. $40

"Milk Can with Brown Drip Glaze," no. 7019, was made from 1972 to 1977. It is 10 inches high, has '76 emblem on its reverse as shown below. Its mark, shown at the end of the chapter, includes the Lancaster Colony Corporation logo. Note the thinner lid and narrower handle than in the following example, the "Early American Milk Can," no. 154. *Zera Collection.* $40

"Spirit of '76 Milk Can," no. 333. It is 9-3/4 inches high, and was sold from 1973 to 1975. The mark is "9/U.S.A." impressed on two lines, plus printed information about the eagle, which is shown below. In 1973, Avon bought a large quantity of these jars, along with bean pots and pitchers of the same design, packed them in Avon boxes and gave them as prizes during sales campaigns. *Zera Collection.* $50

The same style as above but smaller, only 10-1/4 inches high. This one was made in 1975 and 1976. Mark is "253/USA." Both these jars have rubber seals in their lids. *Lilly Collection.* $40

Reverse of milk can with brown drip glaze. The riveted seam is a nice detail.

"Early American Milk Can," no. 154, made from 1972 to 1974, is marked "USA/154" on two lines. It is 10-5/8 inches high. It was also made with the can silver, the Liberty bell gold, and the flags red, white, and blue. *Zera Collection.* $45

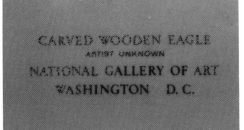

CARVED WOODEN EAGLE
ARTIST UNKNOWN
NATIONAL GALLERY OF ART
WASHINGTON   D. C.

Inkstamp on bottom of "Early American Milk Can."

Another style of milk can, this one without handles, was made in 1978, and again from 1980 through 1985. It is McCoy's no. 253, and is 12 inches high. Mark is "254/McCoy/LCC/USA" on four lines. *Lilly Collection.* $40

Another descriptive name, "Square Jar." No. 30, it was made in 1947, stands 8 inches high, and is not marked. *Zera Collection.* $50

This hexagon jar was made from 1947 to 1949. It is 9 inches high, and is marked "McCoy." The company referred to it as both no. 31 and no. 32. *Oravitz Collection.* $40

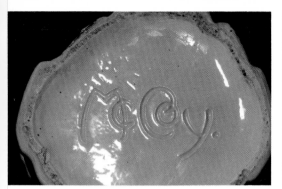

Mark of "Clown (bust)." Note period.

Mark of "W.C. Fields Head" jar.

Bull's-eye mark variation on "Happy Face (Have a Happy Day)."

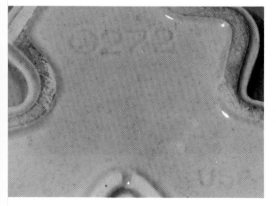

Raised mark of "Decorated Clown (Little Clown)."

Mark of McCoy "Old Apple." Note detail of dead blossom.

Mark of "Bicentennial Milk Can." Note squared letters in LCC logo.

Mark of "Koala Bear."

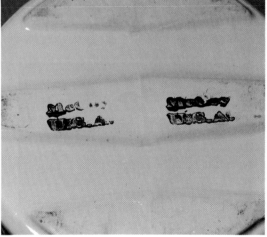

Mark of "Early American Chest (chiffonier)."

Three-bar bottom of "Spaceship (Friendship 7)," the telltale clue that often identifies unmarked McCoy cookie jars.

Mark of "Brown Thinking Puppy," showing Lancaster Colony Corporation logo.

Inkstamp mark of "Yosemite Sam Cylinder" jar, showing three-bar bottom.

Mark of "Gingham Patchwork Cylinder."

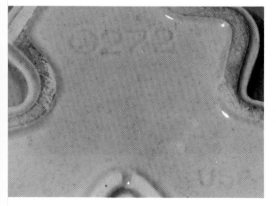

Mark of "Rattan Thinking Puppy," with LCC logo absent.

McCoy bull's-eye mark on "Brown Cylinder (Modern)" jar.

Mark of "Nabisco" jar.

# Chapter 8
## *American Bisque*

American Bisque appears to be second only to McCoy in the number of different cookie jars it produced, although it could actually be ahead because the total number is not known. As a general rule, American Bisque jars are more detailed than those of McCoy, both in the amount of relief design and in the way they were decorated. American Bisque made very few solid color jars. It also shied away from fruit and vegetable motifs. With few exceptions, American Bisque glazed its jars by airbrushing.

Located in Williamstown, West Virginia, the company got its start in 1919 as a maker of Kewpie Doll heads, World War I having cut the European supply line. B.E. Allen purchased the company in 1922. It remained in the Allen family until being sold in 1982. The plant closed in 1983.

When the Ohio River overflowed its banks in 1937, depositing more than 10 feet of water in the pottery, all stock, molds, and materials were lost. This may have been when American Bisque began making cookie jars, the total loss providing a perfect opportunity to abandon some of the old line and experiment with some new ones. The plant was struck by fire eight years after the flood, and had to be entirely rebuilt.

Identifying American Bisque cookie jars can be a frustrating experience. In most cases the company did not mark its jars with anything other than a simple "U.S.A.," and sometimes a number. Most of the paper labels it used have long since disappeared.

One of the easiest ways to recognize American Bisque cookie jars is by the pattern on their bottoms, as shown below. Heavy lugs, often called wedges, were generally incorporated into the bottoms of its jars. The unglazed wedges gave the jars a firm footing when being fired, and later when resting on a homemaker's kitchen counter. The same feature is also prevalent on jars American Bisque made for the Cardinal China Company, a New Jersey distributor.

Several of American Bisque's incised marks show the abbreviation, "A.B. Co." Note that several of the jars in this chapter previously credited to American Bisque were actually made by Ungemach Pottery, which operated in Roseville, Ohio from 1937 to 1984. These are "Pinky Lee," square cat jar with tail handle, fawn jar, and the puppet jars. Captions reflect the changes.

### American Pottery Company
### Ludowici Celadon, and Terrace Ceramics

It is impossible to adequately cover American Bisque without discussing American Pottery, Ludowici Celadon, and Terrace Ceramics at the same time. Because of interaction between the four companies, it often can't be determined which company made which jars.

The American Pottery Company stemmed from the Stoin-Lee Pottery company, of Byesville, Ohio. Byesville is a small town 70 miles east of Columbus, just south of Cambridge. Stoin-Lee incorporated in 1942. Two years later it came under the control of J. B. Lenhart, who changed the name to American Pottery Company. Lenhart then moved at least part of the operation to Marietta, Ohio, directly across the Ohio River from Williamstown, West Vir-

ginia, home of American Bisque. That's not surprising because at the same time he was running American Pottery, Lenhart was sales manager of American Bisque. To complicate matters further, Lenhart sold half his interest in American Pottery to American Bisque owner, A.N. Allen. Consequently, there is a crossover between the two companies' products. Jars normally attributed to American Bisque sometimes bear the mark of American Pottery, and vice-versa.

The jars and marks shown below seem to indicate American Pottery functioned, to a certain extent, as an arm of American Bisque. In all likelihood, American Pottery and American Bisque caught each other's overflow, one filling the orders of the other when it proved expedient. Barring cookie jars learning to talk, there will probably always be questions as to which company made which jars. (Text continued on page 75).

For a more thorough explanation you may want to consult *American Bisque-Collector's Guide With Prices*, by Mary Jane Giocomini (Schiffer 1994).

American Bisque's people cookie jars reflect some of the company's best work. This granny is 12-3/4 inches high. The jar has the letters "USA" impressed in the back. *Zera Collection.* $125

The same granny but with gold trim, a feature that generally increases the value of a jar. *Coughenour Collection.* $150

A Pennsylvania Dutch girl 11-1/4 inches high with an American Bisque bottom. The jar was also made with a yellow hat, and possibly other colors. Additionally, American Bisque made a Pennsylvania Dutch boy with a broad brim hat. *Bosson Collection.* $300

To avoid confusion, compare this American Bisque churn boy to Regal China's version in Chapter 16, which currently sells for nearly twice the price. Height is 11-3/4 inches. *Bosson Collection.* $275

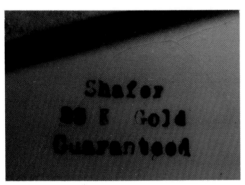

Mark from the bottom of the gold trimmed granny. It's from the G.C. Shafer Pottery Company, of Zanesville, Ohio. Between 1939 and 1980, Shafer provided a gold decorating service for many potteries, American Bisque, McCoy, and Hull to name three.

Dutch boy, 13 inches high, sometimes seen in white. *Zera Collection.* $350; White $150

The umbrella kids stand 11-1/2 inches high with "USA-834" impressed in bottom. *Zera Collection.* $325

One of several clowns American Bisque produced, this jar is 11 inches high. "USA" is impressed in back at base. *Zera Collection.* $100

Same as above but with colors reversed. Probable repaint on hat, nose, and mouth. *Bosson Collection.* $100

This chef stands 11-1/4 inches high, and looks like he enjoys his work. The jar is unmarked. *Oravitz Collection.* $115

Another funny fellow, 12 inches high, unmarked. Some references say this jar is not American Bisque; however, its American Bisque bottom strongly suggests that it is. $200

A third American Bisque clown, also 12 inches high. *Bosson Collection.* $90

Compare this Davy Crockett with the one in the previous picture, and you'll know why it's best to never use generic price guides to evaluate cookie jars. In this case, a non-specific listing such as "American Bisque Davy Crockett cookie jar" could lead to a mistake costing hundreds of dollars. The jar is 11 inches high. It is not marked. *Zera Collection.* $600

Sometimes you can date cookie jars by the characters they portray—like this 12-1/4 inch unmarked Davy Crockett,. Walt Disney and Fess Parker unveiled Davy Crockett to the American public in 1955, creating a marketing phenomenon of a caliber that hadn't been seen since the days of Shirley Temple movies. Potteries, including American Bisque, were quick to get in on the action. *Zera Collection.* $450

Obviously the same jar as above, but with one subtle difference—it was poured in a much newer mold. Look closely and you'll see much more detail on this example: the ribbing going up the left side of the hat, the indentations on the bottom of the hat, and many more. Even the ruffle is crisper. While both jars have basically the same value, this one is more desirable. *Bosson Collection.* $260

American Bisque accessories for its Davy Crockett cookie jars. All have raised areas similar to wedges on their bottoms. *Coughenour Collection.* $65 each

The yarn dolls are 12 inches high. Neither is marked. *Zera Collection.* $130 each

This girl with sandwich board is marked with an inkstamped "Patent Pending U.S.A." and also has "USA" at base on the reverse side. The first mark is shown. American Bisque also made a boy companion. *Courtesy of Jazz'e Junque Shop, Chicago, Illinois.* $300

Same doll in green. *Courtesy of Jazz'e Junque Shop, Chicago, Illinois.* $130

Blackboard hobo, reminiscent of the sandwich board days of the Depression but made much later. It's 14 inches high and has "U.S.A." in raised letters at base on reverse side. The blackboard the hobo is carrying can be used as a chalkboard for leaving message or reminders. *Zera Collection.* $250

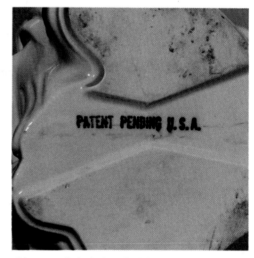

Inkstamp mark of girl with sandwich board. Note the telltale wedges.

Blue yarn doll with gold trim. *Bossom Collection.* $150

Reverse of hobo with sandwich board showing white surface and mark at bottom.

The blackboard clown is 13-3/4 inches high, marked with "Patent Pending U.S.A." ink-stamp. *Oravitz Collection.* $250

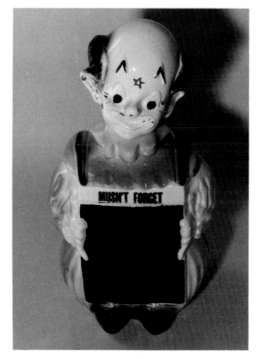

American Bisque paper label from the blackboard clown. It was designed to represent a child's toy block. Paper labels aren't seen very often on American Bisque cookie jars.

"The Cheerleaders" is distinguished for two reasons. It is one of American Bisque's flasher face jars, and also a corner jar, triangular in shape. The corner jar idea seems like a good one, but it apparently never caught on with the public as there wasn't a lot of them made. The flasher faces themselves are made of plastic and glued in place. They show the eyes open or closed depending upon the angle from which the jar is viewed. Marked "802-USA," "The Cheerleaders" is 11 inches high. *Blumenfeld Collection.* $350

"The Cow Jumped Over the Moon" flasher stands 11 inches high, is marked "806 USA" on back at base. *Blumenfeld Collection.* $750

This somewhat rare jar is commonly called Pinky Lee. In case you're not old enough to remember the former vaudevillian's one-half hour comedy series, which ran on NBC from 1950 to 1955, imagine Pee Wee Herman in black-and-white with a checkered sports coat and derby hat, and you'll pretty much have the picture. This jar was made by Ungemach Pottery, of Roseville, Ohio. *Bosson Collection.* $650

Reverse of "The Cheerleaders" corner jar. These must have appealed to the company as only one surface had to be decorated.

This flasher, 9-3/4 inches high, is not marked. Most, however, are marked "801/USA." *Blumenfeld Collection.* $300

The American Bisque majorette is a popular jar, and like the chum boy above, very similar to the one made by Regal China (Chapter 16). This jar is 11-1/4 inches high. It is not marked but has the American Bisque bottom. *Blumenfeld Collection.* $300

Another corner flasher face, this one is 10 inches high, "804/USA" impressed on two lines. In addition to the corner jars shown here, there was also one made with oak leaves on the front and a lid in the shape of an acorn cap, a corner chiffonier, and possibly others. *Oravitz Collection.* $450

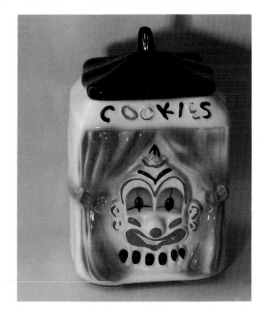

"The clown on Stage" flasher face is 10-1/4 inches high. Impressed at the base of the reverse side is a mark that appears to read "905 USA" on one line. Considering that the other flashers carry 800 series marks, in all probability that's what the mark actually is, the 8 not printed fully due to a problem with the mold. *Blumenfeld Collection.* $300

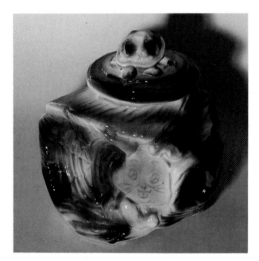

"Tortoise and the Hare" flasher face but with the face missing, which decreases the value a considerable amount. It's 9-3/4 inches high. *Bosson Collection.* $700 w/ flasher; 200 w/o

Yogi Bear with a dark sign. This variation is similar to the Brush Davy Crockett jars in Chapter 10 that have light and dark gun stocks, but it doesn't draw the same interest. *Zera Collection.* $300

With character jars such as this "Yogi Bear," it is often difficult to identify the pottery that made them because the only mark they generally carry is the name of the copyright holder, in this case, "© Hanna Barbera-1961 Productions USA" incised on one line. But identification is a snap here because of the jar's American Bisque bottom. *Courtesy of Betty and Floyd Carson.* $300

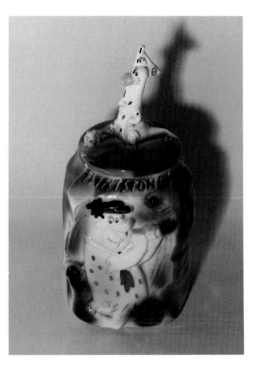

"Fred Flintstone" is 12-1/2 inches high and unmarked except for its American Bisque bottom. *Oravitz Collection.* $800

Dino carrying Fred's golf clubs. The jar is 13-1/2 inches high, has American Bisque bottom. Other jars in the company's Flintstone series are Barney and Betty Rubble's house and Wilma sitting in a chair while talking on the telephone. All American Bisque Flintstones jars are expensive and highly prized. *Courtesy of Betty and Floyd Carson.* $900

Popeye, 10-1/2 inches high, unmarked. The pipe is not original. *Blumenfeld Collection.* $700

Popeye's little buddy, Swee'Pea. The jar is 9-1/2 inches high. American Bisque also made a head jar of Olive Oyl, shown at a distance in Chapter 6. *Bosson Collection.* $2000

Casper, 13-1/2 inches high, unmarked. $700

A different rooster, this one is 12-1/2 inches high. It isn't marked. *Courtesy of Jazz'e Junque Shop, Chicago, Illinois.* $50

Collegiate owl, 11-1/2 inches high, with "USA" in raised letters at base. *Oravitz Collection.* $90

The "Kitten on Beehive" is 11-3/4 inches high, unmarked. It was shown in American Bisque's 1959 catalog. *Zera Collection.* $55

This American Bisque rooster was made in several different colors, including multi-color. Yellow is somewhat rare for the 11-1/4 inch high jar. It is unmarked except for its American Bisque bottom. *Zera Collection.* $80

Hen with chick, 9-1/4 inches high. American Bisque bottom and "USA" impressed. *Bosson Collection.* $50

Mystery time. This rooster lacks wedges but is taller, 12 inches. Impressed in the bottom is "Marston of California" on one line. Although shot facing the opposite direction of the yellow rooster, if you compare to Westfall's and the Roerigs' pictures, you'll see this is the same jar. Marston may have been a distributor or a retailer for which American Bisque made pottery in the same manner that it did for Cardinal. Or it may have been a company that bought an American Bisque cookie jar patent, waited for a patent to expire to make the jar, or just plain ripped it off. *Courtesy of Betty and Floyd Carson.* $100

This cat jar was produced by Ungemach Pottery. The piece is 10-1/2 inches high and unmarked. *Oravitz Collection.* $180

Same Ungemach cat jar. This one is marked "U.S.A." on the base. *Zera Collection.* $180

This kitty is 12 inches high. *Bosson Collection.* $90

What an appropriate place to keep snacks for the family dog. The poodle jar is 10-1/2 inches high with a "USA" mark. *Zera Collection.* $100

The "Kittens with the Ball of Yarn" jar in two sizes. The one on the left is 9-1/2 inches high, and the other is 10-1/2 inches high. While both have American Bisque bottoms, only the one on the left carries a mark, "USA" in raised letters on the back. *Oravitz Collection.* $90 each

Blue poodle. It is the same size as the previous poodle with no mark. *Courtesy of Jazz'e Junque Shop, Chicago, Illinois.* $100

The larger jar in blackish green. *Bosson Collection.* $150

A puppy and a kitten on quilted bases, perhaps pillows. Each jar is 13 inches high. *Bosson Collection.* $150 each.

Another color scheme. *Courtesy of Jazz'e Junque Shop, Chicago, Illinois.* $100

This "Bear with Cookie" was made in at least two different versions: with the shirt pocket (*above*) and with the bib (*below*). It is 11-1/4 inches high and marked "USA." *Zera Collection.* $100

Bibbed version of the "Bear with Cookie." Same size as above, but unmarked. *Courtesy of Betty and Floyd Carson.* $100

This 9-inch high jar was made by Ungemach. As with Pinky Lee above, and a few other Ungemach jars, it has the U-shaped dry foot shown below. *Zera Collection.* $90

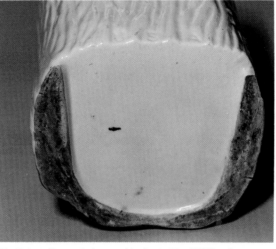

The U-shaped foot on the bottom of the deer jar. Note "USA" mark near top of picture.

The lamb with paws in pockets is just one of several similar jars. It is 11 inches high, unmarked. *Zera Collection.* $120

The horse is 11-1/2 inches high. Like most American Bisque cookie jars, it has the wedges on the bottom. *Coughenour Collection.* $1000

Some of the "paws in pockets" jars were made with turnabout heads, such as this pig. It's a boy on this side, a girl on the other. Note that the head is also a bank. The jar is 10-1/2 inches high, marked "USA" on the base. *Zera Collection.* $120

Reverse of the turnabout pig.

Not only does this jar have a brown ruffle, as opposed to the green ruffle above, it is also much shorter, only 8-3/4 inches. *Zera Collection.* $120

American Bisque's boy pig, 11-1/2 inches high, is a splendid example of how airbrushing can be combined with hand painting to make attractive, yet reasonably priced ceramic art. *Zera Collection.* $110

Here's a lady pig. She is 11-1/2 inches high. *Oravitz Collection.* $150

The lamb is 13 inches high with an American Bisque bottom. *Coughenour Collection.* $110

Another boy pig, but 12 inches high instead of 11-1/2 inches. Like the previous example, it has the American Bisque bottom. The difference in size is probably due to the jar being redesigned. Among the slight changes, note that there are no coverall straps on this version. *Oravitz Collection.* $110

This jar is referred to as "Pig-in-Poke" in American Bisque's 1959 advertising. It is 12-1/2 inches high, has "USA" in raised letters at rear of base. *Oravitz Collection.* $100

Rabbit, 11-3/4 inches high, with an American Bisque bottom. *Courtesy of Betty and Floyd Carson.* $200

The rabbit in hat, or "Magic Bunny" as the company called it, is 12-1/4 inches high, unmarked. *Courtesy of Jazz'e Junque Shop, Chicago, Illinois.* $100

Meet farmer pig, 13-1/2 inches high. The foreign copy that's sometimes seen lacks the American Bisque bottom and "USA" marking that this one has. *Bosson Collection.* $130

Lid to the "Magic Bunny" jar. The pieces of cork will help prevent accidental damage.

Nothing like a baseball player with a built-in bat. The elephant is marked with a "USA" impressed in its base. *Coughenour Collection.* $130

Canister-shaped cookie jars didn't hold a very high priority with American Bisque, ranking just above fruits and vegetables on the company's design ladder. This animal cookies jar is in pretty good shape for being painted over the glaze. The jar is 8-1/2 inches high. In addition to the paper label, it is marked "USA" on the back. *Zera Collection.* $30

Brown rabbits in hats. Hats also show up in blue. *Oravitz Collection.* $100 each

The "Puppy in Pot" jar, showing both front and back of bottom. Puppy on the left has a star on his head. Each jar is 11-1/2 inches high. These bottoms were also made in blue and possibly other colors. *Oravitz Collection.* $85 each

Animal cookies jar with a flat lid. The height is 8-3/4 inches, and it has "USA" impressed at the base. *Oravitz Collection.* $30

Baby elephant in two different sizes. *Left:* 11-1/2 with American Bisque, bottom. *Right:* 13-1/4 inches with a flat bottom and marked "Cookies/USA/Jar" on three lines. These jars are sometimes found with gold trim. *Bosson Collection.* $200 each

Ring cookie jar, 8-1/2 inches high. *Oravitz Collection.* $30

This is the apple jar. It is 9 inches high. *Zera Collection.* $25

Close-up of recipe jar panel.

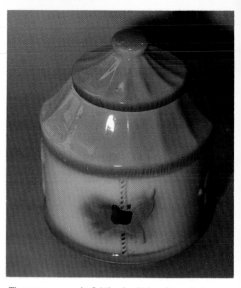

The merry-go-round is 9-1/4 inches high and is marked "USA" on its side. *Courtesy of Jazz'e Junque Shop, Chicago, Illinois.* $100

This attractive jar with its gold "Cookies" is 9-1/4 inches high. It is unmarked, but has an American Bisque bottom. A very similar jar, but with sides tapered toward the bottom, was made by Abingdon. *Oravitz Collection.* $75

Cookie barrel, 9-1/2 inches high, marked "USA." *Courtesy of Jazz'e Junque Shop, Chicago, Illinois.* $40

Jack-in-the-box, 12 inches high, with "USA" impressed in back. *Oravitz Collection.* $150

American Bisque hexagonal recipe jar. It stands 9-1/2 inches high and is marked "USA." *Zera Collection.* $70

Like characters, animals, and people, objects were also a favorite at American Bisque. The train jar is 7-1/4 x 11-3/4 inches and has "USA 200" impressed. This is one of the few American Bisque jars that was completely hand decorated on top of a clear glaze. It also has gold trim. *Zera Collection.* $130

This is the plain version of American Bisque's "Toy Soldier" jar. It is 11 inches high, is marked "USA 743" at rear. *Courtesy of Betty and Floyd Carson.* $120

The "Treasure Chest," 8-3/4 inches high. *Oravitz Collection.* $200

Fancy version of "Toy Soldier" jar. The Roerigs show another version stamped "Walt Disney Productions, copyright 1961." *Blumenfeld Collection.* $120

"Sad Iron," 11-1/2 inches high, no mark. *Courtesy of Grinder's Switch, Avon, Ohio.* $100

Bottom of the "Treasure Chest" showing diagonal variation of American Bisque wedges.

These are Ungemach Puppet jars. *Bosson Collection.* $250 each.

This jar is called a "Sea Bag." It is 10-1/4 inches high and has "USA" in raised letters on base. *Oravitz Collection.* $150

The "Thread Spool" is 10-3/4 inches high. *Bosson Collection.* $150

This coffee pot is 9-1/2 inches high measuring the jar only, not the handle. It's marked "USA." *Zera Collection.* $50

71

A second coffee pot, also 9-1/2 inches high. Note that the lids are of identical design. *Bosson Collection.* $50

A water bucket, 9-3/4 inches high, with the American Bisque bottom and "USA" impressed in back. *Lilly Collection.* $150

"Pot Belly Stove," 11-1/4 inches high, no mark. *Zera Collection.* $40

Hot chocolate mug, 9 inches high, American Bisque bottom. *Bosson Collection.* $50

Same design as above (check knot and other details) but larger, 11 inches high, and with a finish not on a par with American Bisque. Possibly not American Bisque. *Bosson Collection.* $100

This lantern is 13 inches high, not marked. *Courtesy of Grinder's Switch, Avon, Ohio.* $150

The churn on the left is 10-1/2 inches high and unmarked. The one on the right is 10-3/4 inches high and is marked with an impressed "USA." Both jars have American Bisque bottoms. *Oravitz Collection.* $40 each

The clock is not marked. It stands 9 inches high. This is another American Bisque cookie jar that was completely hand decorated aside from the initial clear glaze. Sometimes seen with gold trim, including hands. *Zera Collection.* $90

The "Milk Wagon" is 9 inches high, unmarked. *Zera Collection.* $175

Yellow version of the "Milk wagon," pulled by a palomino. *Bosson Collection.* $175

Another four-wheeled vehicle, the "Cookie Truck" in two different sizes. *Left:* 13-1/4 inches high, marked "USA/744" on two lines on the opposite side above the running board. *Right:* 11-1/2 inches high. *Bosson Collection.* $100 each

Close-up of "Cookie Truck" mark.

Not only is the locomotive similar in shape to the cookie truck, it also has the same top. The jar is 12 inches high. *Bosson Collection.* $125

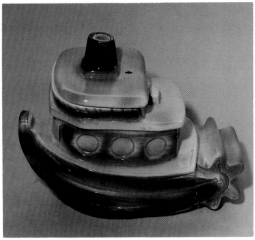

"Stern-wheeler," 8-3/4 inches high, has a "USA" mark. This jar's lid contains a bell. *Bosson Collection.* $200

"Spaceship," 12-1/4 inches high, no mark. *Blumenfeld Collection.* $350

Here is an example of how American Bisque made jars for Cardinal. The one on the *left*, 10 inches high is impressed "USA, Cardinal" on two lines. The one on the *right*, 8 inches high, is not marked. Note that the bases of the jars are the same size. Both have American Bisque bottoms. *Oravitz Collection.* $50 each

"Cookie Bag" with different bottom colors, and showing reverse view of lid. Like the one above, it is 10 inches high but is unmarked. *Courtesy of Betty and Floyd Carson.* $50

A "Cookie Basket," 11-1/4 inches high, marked "USA." The Roerigs show it with a chartreuse bottom and blue top, probably made complete in both those colors and possibly others. *Bosson Collection.* $90

The cookie feed sack is 9-1/2 inches high. *Bosson Collection.* $150

The "After School Cookies" jar was made with a bell on the lid, too. It is 10-1/2 inches high, unmarked. It is also seen with gray sides and brown roof. *Zera Collection.* $100

This saddle not only displays reversed lid colors, but also does not have a blackboard on either side. It is 12 inches high. *Coughenour Collection.* $250

Although hard to see in black, the top says "COOKIE TRAY" in raised letters. The jar is 6-3/4 inches high, marked "USA-602," and has the American Bisque bottom. *Bosson Collection.* $75

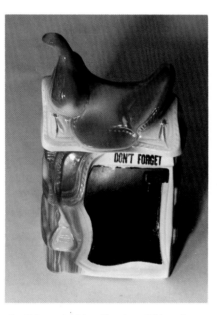

As with the sandwich board jars above, this is another message center waiting to be used. This "Saddle Blackboard" is marked "USA" on one line and "Pat Pend/USA" on two lines. The jar is 12-1/4 inches high. *Zera Collection.* $200

There is no mark on this cowboy boots jar. The height is 12-1/2 inches. *Zera Collection.* $150

This bell has some unreadable letters impressed in its lid. The lid also contains a real bell, just the thing to foil the plans of a potential cookie thief. The jar is 10 inches high, marked "USA" on back. *Zera Collection.* $50

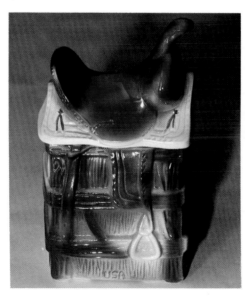

Reverse of "Saddle Blackboard." Note "USA" at bottom.

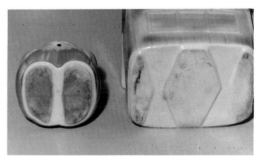

On the left are the modified wedges of a "Paws in Pockets" animal jar, on the right are those of the after school cookies jar.

The "Lamb with Red Suspenders," 11-1/2 inches high. Mark is "Design/Pat. Pen. 117120/ABCO" on three lines. *Zera Collection.* $70

The only good news in this incestuous maze of free enterprise is that the American Pottery Company went out of business in 1965. The plant has since been torn down, never to befuddle cookie jar collectors again.

But there is more. some time after World War II, the Ludowici Celadon Company, of New Lexington, Ohio, peddled some, or perhaps all, of its cookie jar molds to American Bisque. This means there are certain jars that might have been made by any one of the four companies, American Bisque, American Pottery, Terrace Ceramics, or Ludowici Celadon. In case you've ever wondered why the Belmont lion smacks of American Bisque and American Pottery, it's because "Belmont" was a mark used by Ludowici Celadon. So was "Fluffy," as on the cat jar referred to above.

Ludowici Celadon began in 1902 when Celadon Terra Cotta purchased the former Imperial Brick Company, to convert it to a roofing tile operation. Four years later it was bought by a person or a company named Ludowici, and the name changed to Ludowici Celadon. (Celadon is a gray-green stoneware of Chinese origin.) When World War II shut down the construction industry the demand for roofing tile plummeted. Ludowici Celadon then explored other avenues, including cookie jars, to survive the conflict. It made Walt Disney jars including turnabouts, and other jars. The end of the war in 1945, and the construction boom that followed, allowed Ludowici Celadon to get out of the cookie jar business and back into the roofing tile business.

Looking over the jars below, it appears that after American Bisque bought Ludowici Celadon's cookie jar patents, it restyled the jars to its own liking, then produced them with a greater degree of sophistication than the original maker had.

Now let's bring Ludowici Celadon into this crossover mess. This 13-1/4 inch high jar has "Fluffy" incised in script on the bottom, a mark known to have been used by Ludowici Celadon. *Courtesy of Jazz'e Junque Shop, Chicago, Illinois.* $35

Scale "Fluffy" down to 12 inches and it turns into a cat with indented spots, a jar commonly credited to American Bisque and American Pottery. Some, in fact, are known to carry the American Pottery mark. This jar, probably a repaint, is marked "USA/131A" on two lines. *Bosson Collection.* $75

The "Animals with Red Suspenders" series is an example of the crossover between the American Bisque and American Pottery Company. This "Pig with Red Suspenders" is 11-1/4 inches high. Its mark, shown below, clearly indicates it was made by American Bisque. *Zera Collection.* $70

Here is a series mate, the "Cow" (or bull if you prefer) "with Red Suspenders." Standing 11-1/4 inches high, its mark shows it was made by American Pottery Company. Included in the series but not shown is the "Lamb with Red Suspenders." *Zera Collection.* $70

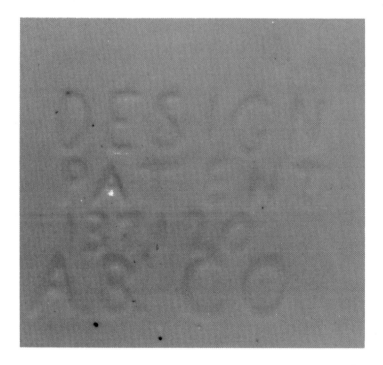

Mark of "Pig with Red Suspenders." A bit dark, it reads "Design/Patent/132170/ABCO" on four lines.

Mark of the "Cow with Red Suspenders." It reads "Design/Patent/Applied/APCO" on four lines.

The bear with eyes closed on the left is American Bisque all the way—style fits and the jar has wedges. The one on the right has indented spots, no wedges, and is marked similar to the cat with indented spots, "USA/130" on two lines. The left jar is 10-3/4 inches high, and the right jar is 12 inches high, probably repainted. Considering that "Fluffy" was scaled down to make the cat with indented spots, it is possible that this could be a mold American Bisque bought from Ludowici Celadon, immediately made some jars with it, then trimmed it to a smaller size and finished it in much the same manner as most of American Bisque's other jars. *Bosson Collection.* $Left, 75 ; right, $95

Here is the "Bear with Eyes Open." It is unmarked, 11-3/4 inches high, and appears to have the same bottom as the two jars above. *Oravitz Collection.* $60

Teddy bear with indented spots, 12-1/4 inches high. The mark is "USA/123A" on two lines. *Bosson Collection.* $95

Pig with indented clover, 11-1/2 inches high and unmarked. Matching salt and pepper shakers are 4-1/4 inches high. While this is basically the same jar as the pig with indented spots, the airbrushing is characteristic of American Bisque. *Bosson Collection.* Cookie jar $125; Salt & Pepper Shakers $35

"Bear with Eyes Open," glazed but not painted. The same size, with no mark. *Zera Collection.* $75

Pigs with indented spots, each 11-1/2 inches high, no marks. Matching bank is 5 inches high. All three have probably been repainted. American Bisque or American Pottery? *Bosson Collection.* Cookie jars $95 each; Bank $65

Another pig with indented clover, and a jar with a similar top but having a different bottom. Pig with indented clover is 11-1/2 inches high. Neither of these jars is marked. *Oravitz Collection.* Left $100; right $100

Here is an interesting trio, all 12-1/4 inches high. The chicks on the right and left both have wedges, but come from different molds as revealed by close inspection of their jackets and berets. The Roerigs show the one on the left on a 1959 American Bisque catalog sheet. The chick in the center with indented spots has a flat bottom and is marked "USA/129A" impressed on two lines. *Oravitz Collection.* $75 each

The bottom of pig on the right in above photo. The bottom of pig on the left matches it.

Canister with indented spots. It is 9 inches high, marked "Pat Applied For/USA" impressed on two lines. $50

This clown is 8-1/2 inches high, marked "Design/ Patent/Applied/APCO" impressed on four lines. *Zera Collection.* $50

The angle of the picture belies the difference in size between these two jars. The one on the left is 11-1/2 inches high, the one on the right 13 inches high. The brown jar looks like it might have been finished by an amateur. Both jars have wedges, as shown. This is another design that American Bisque apparently reduced in size, which makes it likely that there may be some white jars floating around in the larger size. *Oravitz Collection.* $65 each.

There is no doubt about this 8-3/4 inch high bear. Its mark, shown below, identifies it as a product of American Pottery Company. *Zera Collection.* $75

The glazed wedges on the brown jar support the theory that it was finished by an amateur. There is no advantage to glazing them. It seems unlikely a profit-minded company would do so considering the added time and material it would have required.

APCO mark of above bear.

"Horseshoes" and "Spots." The bases are the same, but the lids are different. The clown with indented spots appears earlier in the chapter with a ruffle added and American Bisque airbrushing. *Left*: 11-1/4 inches high with an unreadable mark. *Right*: 11-1/2 inches high, "USA" impressed. *Oravitz Collection.* $80 each

Mickey-Minnie turnabout with original paint. It is 13-1/2 inches high, marked "Patented/Turnabout/4 in 1/Mickey and Minnie/Walt Disney" on five lines. Both Ludowici Celadon and American Pottery use marks that include the word "turnabout." *Zera Collection.* $180

Same turnabout but repainted. *Zera Collection.* $180

This is basically the same bottom as the clowns above. It is 12 inches high, unmarked. *Zera Collection.* $45

Reverse of Mickey-Minnie turnabout.

Reverse of repainted turnabout.

This repainted Dumbo turnabout jar is 14 inches high. Here again, it might have been made by Ludowici Celadon or American Bisque since Ludowici Celadon sold its turnabout molds to American Bisque. Or it might have been made by American Pottery Company because of its ties to American Bisque. In any event, it was probably marketed through the Leeds China Company, a Chicago-based distributor. *Oravitz Collection.* $150

Both sides of a turnabout bear. Parts appear to be repainted. It is 12-1/2 inches high, marked "Turnabout/the four in one" on two lines. An identical jar that was photographed had a mark that read "Patent Applied/Turnabout/The 4 in 1/USA" on four lines. Ludowici Celadon, American Pottery, or American Bisque? *Zera Collection.* $65 each

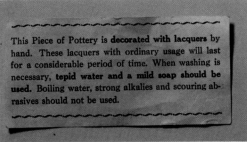

This Piece of Pottery is **decorated with lacquers** by hand. These lacquers with ordinary usage will last for a considerable period of time. When washing is necessary, **tepid water and a mild soap should be used.** Boiling water, strong alkalies and scouring abrasives should not be used.

Original instructions packed in Mickey-Minnie turnabout jars.

Reverse of the turnabout Dumbo. The jar is 14 inches high.

This 13-inch high Dutch girl is marked "Pat Des/138597/ USA" on three lines. *Zera Collection.* $60

The mate to the Dutch girl, 13-1/4 inches high. *Courtesy of Jazz'e Junque Shop, Chicago, Illinois.* $60

On the right is the same Dumbo as above with what's left of the original paint. It is marked "Patented/Turnabout 4 in 1/Dumbo/©Walt Disney" on four lines. On the left is a Dumbo-Pluto turnabout, 13-1/2 inches high. It is marked "Dumbo Pluto/ USA/5231/©Walt Disney" on four lines. It is the same story as above—American Bisque, American Pottery, or Ludowici Celadon? *Courtesy of Jazz'e Junque Shop, Chicago, Illinois.* $150 each

The same Dutch girl in different colors. *Courtesy of Jazz'e Junque Shop, Chicago, Illinois.* $60

The jar on the left is 12 inches high. "Royal Ware" is impressed in the bottom. The jar on the right is 10-1/2 inches high with no mark. Both appear to be repainted. This is the same bear shown with American Bisque airbrushing earlier in the chapter. At some point the design was changed to eliminate the bib and add a shirt pocket, which is how it appears in the company's 1959 catalog. *Oravitz Collection.* $50 each

Reverse of the above turnabout jars.

This one is 11-1/4 inches high, also appears to be repainted, and has a gold cookie. The mark is "Royal Ware." *Zera Collection.* $50

Charcoal Royal Ware bear with cookie, 12-1/2 inches high. *Bosson Collection.* $50

This unmarked basket jar is 11-3/4 inches high. *Oravitz Collection.* $60

According to the Roerigs, these unmarked basket jars have been identified as early American Bisque. They are undoubtedly early something, as they are very heavy and much more crudely made than the photos show. They are, in fact, about what you would expect from a roofing tile company that decided to take a stab at making cookie jars. The puppy is 13 inches high, the kitty 12 inches. Both are marked "Pat./Pen." on two lines. *Oravitz Collection.* $60

## The American Bisque-Robinson Ransbottom Controversy

Probably the greatest revelation for cookie jar collectors since cookie jar collecting began came in 1990 with the publication of *The Collector's Encyclopedia of Cookie Jars,* by Fred and Joyce Herndon Roerig. In it, the authors presented a compelling argument that the round bottom jars shown below were made by American Bisque. Previously, the nearly universal belief had been that the jars were products of Robinson-Ransbottom, mainly because they resembled Robinson-Ransbottom's Oscar cookie jar. But according to Fred Roerig, a letter from former American Bisque owner A.N. Allen, now deceased, states that American Bisque did indeed manufacture the jars. Also according to the Roerigs, a confirmation from J.C. Woodward, who was president of Robinson-Ransbottom in 1982, states that Robinson-Ransbottom did not make them.

Opponents of American Bisque attribution, a group not small in number, point out that Robinson-Ransbottom has always been known for its yellowware—more accurately stoneware of yellow color—while American Bisque specialized in whiteware. They also question how reliable people's memories are in recalling rather insignificant events that took place 50 or more years ago.

Since the best evidence to date indicates these jars were made by American Bisque, they've been included in this chapter. Also included are a few similar jars previously attributed to Robinson-Ransbottom.

No doubt this debate will continue until a catalog or sales sheet verifying the origin of the jars surfaces.

Mark on the collar of the brownie.

This is the "Captain," 12-1/2 inches high. "Captain" is inscribed on the collar. *Zera Collection.* $150

All of the controversial round bottom jars have basically the same bottoms, but different tops. Each jar's collar is marked with the name of the jar, as shown. On the left is the "Brownie," 12-1/2 inches high, on the right the "Preacher," 12-3/4 inches high. *Zera Collection* $150 each.

This repainted jar, 13 inches high, is marked "Jolly Pirate" on its collar. It was obviously worked on by someone who either didn't know how it was originally decorated, or who simply wanted to change it. A "Jolly Pirate" with original paint appears in Chapter 2. *Oravitz Collection.* $150

This jar and the two that follow are similar to the above jars except that only their hats, instead of the entire heads, form the lids. They might or might not have been made by American Bisque, but according to Joyce Roerig, officials at Robinson-Ransbottom deny ever having offered them. Some collectors call this jar a "pilgrim," others call it an "Amish man," while still others refer to it as a "waiter." It is 9-3/4 inches high and unmarked. *Courtesy of Jazz'e Junque Shop, Chicago, Illinois.* $150

The "Cop" is the largest jar in the series, 13-3/4 inches high. "Cop" is marked on the collar. *Zera Collection.* $150

The same jar but with an orange hat and red pants, commonly called a "waiter." No mark. *Oravitz Collection.* $150

"Fire Chief," 12-3/4 inches high. "Fire Chief" is marked on the collar. *Zera Collection.* $150

American Bisque? Robinson-Ransbottom? Teddy Roosevelt? Someone else? Correct lid? All that is known for sure about this jar is that it is 8-1/4 inches high, unmarked. *Bosson Collection.* $175

Here is the "World War I Soldier." Note the "U.S." on the helmet. Unmarked, the jar is 8-1/2 inches high. *Zera Collection.* $175

# Section III: Major American Producers

The firms included in this section weren't determined by company inventory lists, annual reports, or other supposedly reliable data historians often get balled up in . They were chosen by collectors themselves, through their appreciation of the companies' cookie jars, a much more accurate indicator when evaluating the size of any organization's contribution to a collecting hobby.

The criterion was simple. After photographing the more than 1800 cookie jars that appear in the book, manufacturers that were represented by at least 15 different jars, including variations, were admitted to this section, No doubt this method of selection belies actual production figures. On the other hand, it is likely the firms that made the most cookie jars deemed worthy of saving by today's collectors, are the same ones whose quality wares commanded the most respect on the primary market, too.

# Chapter 9
# *Abingdon*

Unlike some companies that allowed cuteness to win the race against usefulness, the Abingdon Potteries, Inc., of Abingdon, Illinois, made cookie jars that were generally designed with utility in mind. There are few Abingdon jars that you can't get your whole hand into when your sweet tooth suddenly demands attention.

Abingdon started out about as far from cookie jars as a pottery can get. From its 1908 inception as the Abingdon Sanitary Manufacturing Company, until 1934, it specialized in commodes and other toilet fixtures. Many of them were built specifically for the penal system, Abingdon at one time being the country's leading manufacturer of prison lavatories. By 1934, the Depression had shut down the building trades and forced the pottery to turn to artware. It kept the name, Abingdon Sanitary Manufacturing Company until 1945 when it switched to Abingdon Potteries, Inc., which was used until the firm was sold in 1951.

An Abingdon cookie jar is somewhat of a lesson in geography as the company used clays from several different places to make its slip. Slip is clay that has been thoroughly mixed with water to make a homogenized, pourable liquid. Abingdon's slip formula consisted of ball clays from Tennessee and England, China clays from England and Georgia, feldspar from Abingdon's mines in the Black Hills of South Dakota, and ground silica sand from Illinois.

Abingdon's artware department was formed in 1934, but when it began making cookie jars isn't clear. Derwich and Latos give a lengthy and interesting accounting of Abingdon, in which they state handpainting of the company's pottery didn't begin until 1942. That would indicate Abingdon's handpainted cookie jars were made between 1942 and 1950, the year the artware department shut down.

In 1951, Briggs Manufacturing Company bought the plant and reconverted it back to a sanitary ware operation. Molds, however, were sold to the Pigeon Pottery, Barnhart, Missouri, later ending up with the Western Stoneware Company in Monmouth, Illinois. Some of the molds apparently made one more move, to the Regal China Company, of Antioch, Illinois, as several of Regal's cookie jars are near duplicates of Abingdon's.

The most common mark on Abingdon cookie jars is shown below. All other marks and paper labels the company used include the word Abingdon except two. One is an "A" inside a diamond. the other resembles a capital "H" with a curved horizontal bar, a "J" above the bar, and "R" below. "Made in U.S.A." is also included in this mark. To date, no cookie jars have surfaced with either of these marks.

It was always time for cookies at Abingdon. The jar is 9 inches high, marked with "Abingdon U.S.A." inkstamp on two lines and boxed as shown below, and "653" impressed. *Zera Collection.* $100

The same mold and same mark, but different color. Note that the entire lid is colored on this one whereas only the finial is colored on the other one. *Zera Collection.* $100

The two commas in "cookies" cleverly suggest a number instead of a word. The jar is 7-3/4 inches high, "Abingdon/USA" inkstamp. *Oravitz Collection.* $90

Nursery rhymes were a favorite theme with Abingdon designers. Is this Mother Goose? The jar, which also comes with light blue trim, is 12-1/4 inches high. "Abingdon/USA" inkstamp, "695" impressed. *Zera Collection.* $325

This windmill is 10-3/4 inches high, carries the Abingdon inkstamp, and has "678" impressed. *Oravitz Collection.* $225

Abingdon hippo, 8-1/4 high, "U.S.A./547" impressed on two lines. *Zera Collection.* $200

"Bo Peep" jar, 12 inches high, with "694" impressed. *Zera Collection.* $250

The locomotive is 7-1/2 inches high. Abingdon inkstamp, plus "651" impressed. *Courtesy of Jazz'e Junque Shop, Chicago, Illinois.* $150

The "Three Bears" cookie jar is marked with an impressed "969." Its height is 8-3/4 inches. *Courtesy of Jazz'e Junque Shop, Chicago, Illinois.* $110

The Abingdon "Fat Boy" is 8 inches high. It is not marked. *Zera Collection.* $300

Bases of the "Granny" jars. Note the recessed rim on the one on the right.

"Humpty Dumpty" is 11-1/2 inches high, with "663" impressed. Regal China made a nearly identical jar decorated in red. *Zera Collection.* $225

Marked with an "Abingdon/USA" inkstamp and "561" impressed, this jar is 11 inches high. *Zera Collection.* $250

"Granny" jar with hand decoration, 9-1/2 inches high. Mark is shown below. *Courtesy of Betty and Floyd Carson.* $240

This is an Abingdon "Granny" repainted to look like a mammy. The jar is 10 inches high, with an "Abingdon/USA" inkstamp and "401" impressed in base and lid. *Coughenour Collection.* $300

This Abingdon "Little Miss Muffet" jar is not marked. It is 11-1/4 inches high. *Courtesy of Betty and Floyd Carson.* $200

The Abingdon "Granny." The jar on the left is 9-1/2 inches high, and the jar on the right is 10 inches high. The bottoms are different, as shown in the next picture. Impressed in each lid is "471." Abingdon inkstamp mark on each bottom. This jar was also made with a green glaze. *Zera Collection.* $190 each

Inkstamp and impressed mark of above hand-decorated Granny jar.

# Chapter 10
## *Brush*

In business until 1982, this Roseville, Ohio, pottery made some of today's most desirable cookie jars.

The Brush Pottery Company came into being in 1925 when the McCoy family withdrew from the Brush-McCoy Pottery, which had existed since 1911, the year George Brush became a partner in the former J.W. McCoy Pottery. Brush had been general manager of the McCoy firm since 1909, following a 1908 fire that had wiped out his own fledgling ceramic operation.

Ross and Don Winton, twins who formed Twin Winton Ceramics, designed many cookie jars for Brush, most of which are marked with a "W" and a number, as shown below.

Most Brush cookie jars were airbrushed. Many have hand decorated details such as eyes. Most of the company's jars are multi-colored, a few are glazed with but one color.

A picture of Brush's first cookie jar, No. 344, which is the first mass-produced ceramic cookie jar known, appears in Chapter 1.

Several Brush Pottery marks are shown below, including those that incorporate the famous palette and brushes logo. Most difficult to recognize are Brush cookie jars that weren't marked, and those marked only "U.S.A."

The Collector's Encyclopedia of Brush-McCoy Pottery, by Sharon and Bob Huxford, is an excellent reference for Brush cookie jar collectors and Brush collectors in general.

The Brush clown, 12-1/2 inches high, which comes in several different color combinations, is marked "W22/Brush/U.S.A." on three lines. According to the Huxfords, the yellow pants indicate this jar was first made in 1964. *Zera Collection.* $250

Same clown but with pink pants and black buttons. It was made in 1965. *Bosson Collection.* $250

Another unmarked Brush jar, the "Hobby Horse" is 10 inches high. It was first produced in 1971. *Zera Collection.* $800

The "Happy Bunny" in gray was made in 1960, then the color was changed to white in 1965. It is 12-3/4 inches high, marked "W26/Brush/USA" on three lines. *Bosson Collection.* $200

Referred to as the Brush "Squirrel with Top Hat," this jar is 12 inches high. It was made in the early 1950s. The mark is "W15/USA" on two lines. *Oravitz Collection.* $250

While the brown cow with cat finial is much older (early 1950s) than the purple one (see Chapter 3), its value is quite a bit less. The height is 8-1/2 inches. The mark is shown. *Zera Collection.* $85

"Happy Bunny" in white. *Zera Collection.* $200

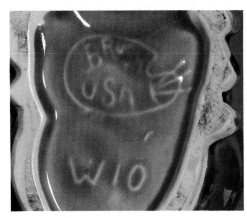

Mark of the brown cow.

The same jar as above, but in a different color. *Bosson Collection.* $250

Repainted Brush cow with cat finial. The size is the same, but the mark is different, "W10/USA" on two lines. *Courtesy of Jazz'e Junque Shop, Chicago, Illinois.* $90

The exact year of the "Circus Horse" is not known, but it is believed to be somewhere between 1950 and 1955. The unmarked jar is 9-1/2 inches high. It was made in different color schemes. *Bosson Collection.* $800

"Puppy Police," 9-1/4 inches high, marked "W39/Brush/ USA" on three lines. First made in 1966. *Bosson Collection.* $500

The panda made its debut in 1959. Its height is 10-3/4 inches, and its mark is "W21/Brush/USA" on three lines. *Oravitz Collection.* $200

Teddy bear, feet together version, from 1957. Like the previous example, it is 10-1/2 inches high. The mark, which is shown below, is somewhat different than the version with the feet apart. *Zera Collection.* $175

The "Formal Pig" in green, 11-1/4 inches high, is marked "W7/USA" on two lines. Production is believed to have started sometime in the early 1950s. *Courtesy of Jazz'e Junque Shop, Chicago, Illinois.* $225

This panda has subtle differences (whiter white, grayer black), but is considered a bona fide variation by some collectors. The size and mark are the same as above. *Coughenour Collection.* $200

Mark of Brush teddy bear, feet together version. It is one of the few Brush jars on which the mark is raised instead of incised.

Same color as the "Formal Pig" above, but gold lined. *Bosson Collection.* $375

Another rendition of the "Formal Pig." *Oravitz Collection.* $225

The teddy bear with feet apart stands 10-1/2 inches, is marked "W14/USA" on two lines, and was made in the early 1950s. *Zera Collection.* $225

"Smiling Bear," 11 inches high, has no mark but has a dry foot similar to the clown bust. It was first sold in 1969. Also made in yellow, brown, and possibly other colors. *Bosson Collection.* $275

Yellow is a rare color for Brush's "Formal Pig." *Bosson Collection.* $250

A simple and inexpensive way to give cookie jars an added measure of protection is to put a coffee filter over the opening, put on the lid, and cut to shape with shears. The filter was removed when the above picture was taken.

The "Elephant with Ice Cream Cone" is a good size jar, standing 13 inches high. On this example the ice cream cone has been broken off and glued back on, a common fate for this jar. It was made during the early 1950s and is marked "W8/USA" on two lines. *Zera Collection.* $400 if not broken

On the left is the sitting pig cookie jar, on the right the sitting pig bank. The heights are 11-1/4 inches and 11 inches, respectively. The jar is marked "W37/Brush/USA" on three lines, and the bank is marked "837/USA/Brush" also on three lines. The jars date from 1966. *Bosson Collection.* Left $375; Right $225

While the film didn't capture the difference in these two "nite" owls as well as it might have, the one on the left is finished in a gloss glaze, the one on the right a matte glaze. Both are 10-3/4 inches high, and neither is marked. According to the Huxfords, the gray nite owl is from 1967. *Oravitz Collection.* Gray $100; Yellow $125

The "Donkey with Cart" was made in the 1960s, and appears in different color combinations. It is 10-1/2 inches high, marked "W33/Brush/USA", on three lines. *Coughenour Collection.* $300

This stylized owl, 9 inches high, has no mark, but does have a U-shaped dry foot on the bottom. Also from 1967. *Coughenour Collection.* $325

The "Chick and Nest" is 11-3/4 inches high, marked "W38/Brush/USA" on three lines. Its first year was 1966. *Bosson Collection.* $300

The "White Hen on Basket" hails from 1969, stands 10-1/4 inches high, and is marked with a paper label on the bottom. *Bosson Collection*. $90

"Cloverleaf" cookie jar, 9-1/2 inches high, with matching salt and pepper shakers. A sugar and creamer were included in the same set, which was made in 1955. The jar is not marked. *Bosson Collection*. Jar $75; Salt & Pepper Shakers $25

The lighter version of the "Cookie House" appeared in the Brush line in 1965. The size and mark are the same as above. The line between the top and bottom is protective paper, as shown with the picture of the donkey and cart. *Coughenour Collection*. $100

These Brush crocks are marked "K26/USA" on two lines. The one on the left is 10-3/4 inches high, the one on the right 10-1/4 inches high. Besides the little girl praying and the duck, there is also one with a kitten finial. Believed to have been made in 1956, they were also finished in pink and possibly other colors. *Oravitz Collection*. $45 each

The "Three Bears" cookie jar is marked "K-2/Brush/USA/" on three lines. The jar is 9-3/4 inches high, and dates from the 1960s. *Bosson Collection*. $100

The "Old Clock," 10 inches high, marked "W-20/Brush/USA" on three lines, is from 1956. Verse on the back is shown below. *Oravitz Collection*. $150

The chocolate dollop is 9-1/2 inches high, has the Brush palette mark plus a "P30." The date is unknown. *Bosson Collection*. Value undetermined

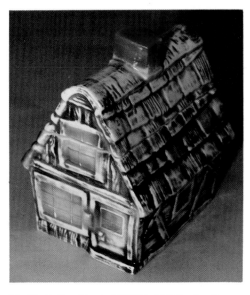

The "Cookie House," marked "W31/Brush/USA" on three lines, stands 10-3/4 inches high. This dark version was first offered in 1962. *Zera Collection*. $100

Verse on back of "Old Clock."

This puppy
*Collection*. $

A nice looking dog, 13 inches high. "905/USA" is impressed in the bottom on two lines, "905" impressed on the lid. *Bosson Collection.* $150

Given as a team leader gift by Avon in 1979, this unmarked bear has been identified as a California Originals. It stands 11-1/2 inches high. *Courtesy of Jazz'e Junque Shop, Chicago, Illinois.* $45

This Winnie is 11-1/2 inches high, and is marked "©Walt Disney Production." *Zera Collection.* $175

Unmarked rabbit, 13-1/2 inches high. *Oravitz Collection.* $60

Ears like a bear and nose like a pig, this jar is 11 inches high and has "2648" impressed. *Courtesy of Jazz'e Junque Shop, Chicago, Illinois.* $40

Tigger is 12 inches high and has two marks. "©Walt/Disney/Prod./902" is on each side of the tail, while "902" is impressed in the lid. *Oravitz Collection.* $225

Baby tiger, 8 inches high. While not marked, it was shown in the company's advertising. *Zera Collection.* $60

This jar has "907" impressed in the lid. One in another collection had "907/USA" impressed in the lid. It is 10-1/4 inches high. *Oravitz Collection.* $110

*Left:* Nearly the same but not quite. The surface detail is absent, and the unmarked jar is only 12-1/2 inches high. *Oravitz Collection.* $50

Superman is one of California Originals' more popular jars. More expensive, too. It stands 13-1/2 inches high, is marked "California Originals USA 846" on one side, "© DC Comics Inc. 1978" on the other. A similarly shaped jar, not shown, depicts Wonder Woman tying a burglar to a vault. Both jars were also made in an aluminum color. *Courtesy of Jazz'e Junque Shop, Chicago, Illinois.* $550

Donald's buddy, Mickey Mouse. The jar is 11-3/4 inches high and marked "©Walt Disney Productions" around the base. Part of the mark shows in the picture. *Courtesy of Jazz'e Junque Shop, Chicago, Illinois.* $400

A second Big Bird, this one 14 inches high, has two marks "976/USA" impressed on two lines and "© Muppets Inc./971/1977" impressed on three lines. *Bosson Collection.* $125

Donald Duck is 12-1/4 inches high. It is marked "©Walt Disney Productions 865" around the base. *Courtesy of Betty and Floyd Carson.* $300

Probably the most appropriate subject you could ever find for a cookie jar. Cookie Monster is 12 inches high and marked "©Muppets Inc. 970." In addition to the Muppets jars shown here, California Originals also made one of Bert, Ernie, and Cookie Monster all behind a counter with a platter of cookies sitting on the counter. *Zera Collection.* $50

Oscar is 11-3/4 inches high and marked "©Muppets Inc. 972." *Oravitz Collection.* $50

Ernie, 12-1/2 inches high. "©Muppets Inc. 973" is impressed on the back at bottom and also in the lid. *Zera Collection.* $50

Big Bird, 13 inches high, with "©Muppets Inc. 971" impressed in base. *Zera Collection.* $50

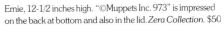

The Count is 12 inches high with "975" impressed. *Bosson Collection.* $800

Raggedy Ann. A few scratches on her stockings, but isn't her face nice and crisp. She is 13-1/2 inches high and has "859" impressed in the lid and base. *Courtesy of Betty and Floyd Carson.* $100

Here's the sheriff before the gunfight. An inch shorter than the above jar and unmarked, there is some controversy as to whether or not this one was actually made by California Originals. Still, this seems like the best place to put it. *Oravitz Collection.* $75

Humpty Dumpty California Originals style. The jar is 13 inches high with "884-USA" impressed in both bottom and top. *Oravitz Collection.* $120

Poor Eyore is a bit worse for wear. The jar is 9-3/4 inches high and marked "901/©Walt Disney Prod." on two lines. Two of these were photographed. It was a close race to determine the one in the best condition, which suggests they may have been manufactured with a defective finish. *Zera Collection.* $400

Little Red Riding Hood is 13-1/2 inches high and has "320" impressed in bottom. *Oravitz Collection.* $250

This lucky fellow is 13 inches high and has "726 USA" impressed in back. *Courtesy of Jazz'e Junque Shop, Chicago, Illinois.* $75

A young baseball player, 12-1/2 inches high. "875 USA" is impressed in lid. *Oravitz Collection.* $50

This juggler is 13 inches high. It is marked "876 USA." *Bosson Collection.* $75

The scarecrow with pumpkins is marked "871 USA." *Bosson Collection.* $75

This jar is 12-1/4 inches high and unmarked except for the rare California Originals paper label on the roof. *Oravitz Collection.* $60

Close-up of paper label on above jar.

Same elf school house jar as above but with a blue roof. *Bosson Collection.* $60

Another building, the "Cookie Bakery," is 9 inches high and has "863" impressed in base and lid. *Courtesy of Jazz'e Junque Shop, Chicago, Illinois.* $50

This is the same size as the bakery with the green roof, but is marked "863 USA." *Bosson Collection.* $50

The school house is 12-1/2 inches high and is marked "869 USA." *Bosson Collection.* $100

Except for the absence of the elves, this mold is the same as the two other school house jars. It is also the same size, 12-1/4 inches, and like the others is unmarked. The glaze and the gold trim seem inconsistent with California Originals' style. Another one of the many mysteries of cookie jar collecting. *Oravitz Collection.* $60

103

This school house is shorter than the green and red one, measuring 11-1/2 inches. The reason? The lid is made differently. Impressed in the lid is "869." *Oravitz Collection.* $100

The mark in this locomotive's lid, "2628," is somewhat of an exception for California Originals because it is composed of raised letters. The mark on the wheel is "2628 USA" impressed. The jar is 7-1/2 inches high. *Courtesy of Jazz'e Junque Shop, Chicago, Illinois.* $50

Circus wagon, 10-3/4 inches high. The top is marked "2631," the bottom "2631 USA." *Oravitz Collection.* $50

"Cookie Time Clock," 12-1/2 inches high. Impressed in both the top and bottom is "860." *Oravitz Collection.* $40

An ark, 12 inches high, is marked "881 USA." *Bosson Collection.* $60

This windup phonograph is 12 inches high. The mark is "891 USA." *Bosson Collection.* $175

The unmarked gumball machine is 12-1/2 inches high. *Courtesy of Jazz'e Junque Shop, Chicago, Illinois.* $85

# Chapter 12
## *Doranne of California*

Doranne's cookie jars can often be recognized by the company' distinctive mark, even though the mark doesn't state its name. Most marks on Doranne of California jars include the letters "CJ," plus a one-, two-, or three-digit number, and sometimes the letters "USA." For instance, "CJ 46 © USA" as on Pinocchio below. This won't identify all Doranne jars because sometimes the "C" was dropped, just the "J" remaining. Other times the jars were marked with "USA" in conjunction with a number.

Other telltale indicators of Doranne jars are the ochre, green, and brown glazes the firm favored, and Doranne's propensity toward using raised or incised designs on its solid color jars. Examples would be the raised palm trees on its camel, and the incised flowers on its elephant.

Doranne of California was started in 1951. The company was based in Los Angeles. It went out of business in 1991.

This clown is 13-3/4 inches high with the "Doranne of California" mark incised. *Zera Collection.* $70

An 11-inch high Doranne of California Pinocchio, marked "CJ46/©USA" on two lines. *Oravitz Collection.* $300

This clown is the same size as the previous one, but the impressed mark is simply "Doranne." *Courtesy of Betty and Floyd Carson.* $70

The "J-1 USA" marking on the bottom of this puppy identifies it as Doranne. It is 12-1/4 inches high. *Courtesy of Jazz'e Junque Shop, Chicago, Illinois.* $40

This bandit stands 11-1/2 high. No mark, but everything about it screams Doranne. *Bosson Collection.* $140

"Cow Jumped Over the Moon," 13-1/2 inches high. The mark is "USA" impressed on back of base. *Zera Collection.* $190

The same jar as above, but in a different color. The mark is also different, "J2," but impressed in the same place. *Courtesy of Jazz'e Junque Shop, Chicago, Illinois.* $190

Same pooch, same mark, different glaze. *Oravitz Collection.* $40

The dapper cat was also made in green, and in a yellow, white, and blue combination. It is 13-1/2 inches high, marked "J5 USA." *Bosson Collection.* $40

Another puppy, 13 inches high. It is marked "California USA/MM600" on two lines and shown in company advertising. *Oravitz Collection.* $60

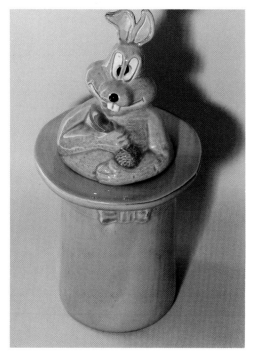

This jar is very tall at 16 inches. It is marked "CJ44/USA" on two lines. *Oravitz Collection.* $45

Note the palm trees decorating this camel, another clue to identifying Doranne jars. Quite often the company used this style of design on animal cookie jars. The camel is 9-1/4 inches high, marked "©USA J-8." *Zera Collection.* $100

This monkey is 12 inches high, unmarked. Often they are marked "CJ-21." *Courtesy of Jazz'e Junque Shop, Chicago, Illinois.* $50

This rabbit is 9-1/2 inches high. Its only marks are a written "P" and an impressed "4." *Zera Collection.* $45

Here is another example of Doranne decorating the body of an animal jar. The elephant is 12-1/2 inches high and has "USA" impressed in back. *Courtesy of Jazz'e Junque Shop, Chicago, Illinois.* $60

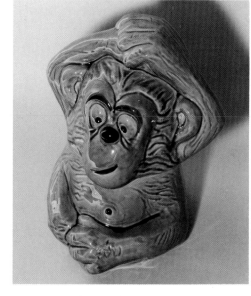

Another unmarked monkey of the same size as the brown one. *Oravitz Collection.* $50

Same rabbit, different glaze, and bigger—13-1/2 inches high. Unmarked. *Oravitz Collection.* $45

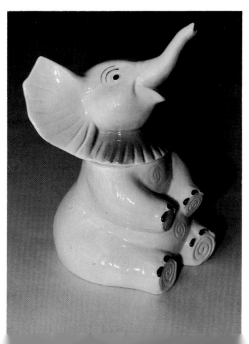

Pink and blue elephant, of the same size and mark as above. This jar is also seen in the palomino glaze. *Zera Collection.* $75

This baby bear is 12-1/2 inches high. While unmarked, the bees and the glaze color are dead giveaways of Doranne origin. *Oravitz Collection.* $50

During the 1980s, Doranne of California marketed a series of kitchen accessories called "Bear Essentials," which included canisters, napkin holders, cups, spoonrests, etc. Originally, this jar included a cloth bib. The bear is 11-1/2 inches high and not marked. *Oravitz Collection*. $25

Doranne of California standing elephant, 9-1/2 inches high. The mark is "©/Calif USA/CJ 15" on three lines. *Oravitz Collection*. $45

Frog, 10-1/2 inches high. The jar is unmarked but shown in Doranne advertising. *Zera Collection*. $75

An 11-1/2 inch high hen, marked "CJ 103©USA." This jar is part of Doranne's Farmyard Follies series from 1984. Others in the series included a rooster crowing, usually done in colors, a pumpkin, plus a duck, rabbit, bull, pig, and donkey, all sitting holding something similar to the basket of eggs this hen is holding. Like the hen, the other sitting jars were finished in clear (white) glaze with colored highlights. *Oravitz Collection*. $50

Standing elephant with the same size and mark. *Bosson Collection*. $45

This unmarked lion is 10-1/4 inches high. Note the ladybug on its nose. *Zera Collection*. $45

Don't those flowers and that lid look familiar. The turtle is 7 inches high and marked "Calif USA-CJ." *Zera Collection*. $40

The fish is 10-1/2 inches high and marked "J9/USA" on two lines on each side of the tail. *Bosson Collection*. $50

108

The mark on this mouse is "J53 Calif. USA." The jar is 12-1/2 inches high. *Bosson Collection.* $50

The sundae is 13-1/2 inches high, unmarked but shown in Doranne advertising. *Courtesy of Jazz'e Junque Shop, Chicago, Illinois.* $60

A cookie for cookies. It is 10-1/2 inches in diameter. While unmarked, it appears on company advertising sheets. *Courtesy of Betty and Floyd Carson.* $45

A very realistic looking three-lobe bell pepper, 10-3/4 inches high, with "U.S.A./CJ30" impressed on two lines. *Zera Collection.* $50

At 13 inches high, this is one very large cookie jar because of the way it flares toward the top. It is marked "USA" and is shown in Doranne advertising. With a small bag of ice set in the bottom, wouldn't this be a wonderful accessory from which to serve homemade ice cream. *Courtesy of Jazz'e Junque Shop, Chicago, Illinois.* $45

Perfectly at home in many kitchens, the Doranne brown bag is 10-3/4 inches high, unmarked. *Oravitz Collection.* $30

The fire hydrant stands 11-1/2 inches high. The jar is unmarked. *Bosson Collection.* $60

Ten inches high and marked "USA," original advertising shows this cupcake with a top similar to the sundae. Perhaps this is a married jar, the base of the cupcake and the top of the ice cream cone. *Courtesy of Jazz'e Junque Shop, Chicago, Illinois.* $40

Canning jar, 11-1/2 inches high and unmarked. Both this and the brown bag appear on Doranne advertising sheets. *Oravitz Collection.* $45

109

Although it doesn't show up well in the photo, "1971/Chianti" is impressed on the neck of this jar. The bottom is marked "USA/J73" impressed on two lines. *Courtesy of Betty and Floyd Carson.* $45

"Bean Pot," 11-1/2 inches high. Believed to be Doranne because of the glaze, its mark is shown below. *Courtesy of Jazz'e Junque Shop, Chicago, Illinois.* $30

Mark of "Bean Pot."

This mailbox is 10-1/2 inches high. The mark is "CJ-52/©USA" on two lines. *Zera Collection.* $80

# Chapter 13
## *Hull*

The oldest cookie jar in many collections is the Hull yellow and brown stoneware jar shown below. It was originally designated a pretzel jar. First made during the 1920s, by 1934 the wholesale price of this jar was $0.31 when purchased in lots of one dozen. Wouldn't it be wonderful to have a time machine.

Anchored in Crooksville, Ohio, the firm was organized by Addis E. Hull Sr. in July 1905, as the A.E. Hull Pottery Company. The date is sometimes given as 1903, the confusion existing because Hull later bought out the Acme Pottery Company, which did begin operations in 1903.

Although Hull made several styles of cookie jars, its Little Red Riding Hood jar attracts the most attention. The design patent for Little Red Riding Hood was issued to Louise E. Bauer, of Zanesville, Ohio, on June 29, 1943, with Hull Pottery listed as the assignor.

No doubt many collectors have noticed the uncanny similarity between the red glaze on Hull's Little Red Riding Hood, and the red glaze on Regal China's Van Tellingen peek-a-boo baby and other Regal jars. That's because they're one in the same. According to Brenda Roberts in *The Collectors Encyclopedia of Hull Pottery,* Hull manufactured the Little Red Riding Hood blanks, then shipped them to Regal, in Antioch, Illinois, to be decorated. Strictly a marriage of convenience between the two companies, it made for an excellent product because the jars are still popular nearly 50 years after they were first offered, and most of them that have survived are in very good condition.

Cookie jar collectors look at Little Red Riding Hood jars in much the same manner that philatelists look at postage stamps. While stamp collectors consider identical stamps that have different perforations, different printing methods, and other fairly insignificant variations to be entirely different stamps, so do cookie jar collectors consider Hull Little Red Riding Hoods to be different jars if they display only slight variations of decoration.

The only other company with whose jars this occurs to as great a degree is Shawnee Pottery, of Zanesville, Ohio, about 15 miles north of Hull's Crooksville location. A.E. Hull Jr., then president of the A.E. Hull Pottery Company, jumped ship to accept the presidency of Shawnee when that company was formed in 1937. Many of A.E. Hull's relatives remained at the Hull Pottery when he left, so perhaps constantly changing the decoration in little ways was a family inspired technique aimed at keeping otherwise tired designs fresh.

In 1950, 20 years after the death of Addis E. Hull Sr., a fire and flood destroyed the Hull plant. It was rebuilt from the ground up, reopened in 1952 as the Hull Pottery Company. Hull closed in 1986.

Most Hull cookie jars are marked by impression, inkstamp, or a gold stamp. Examples of several marks are shown below.

These are the two basic forms of Hull's "Little Red Riding Hood," one with a closed basket, the other with an open basket. Each is 13-1/4 inches high. The mark of the jar on the right is shown, mark of the jar on the left is similar. *Zera Collection.* Left - $350, Right - $300

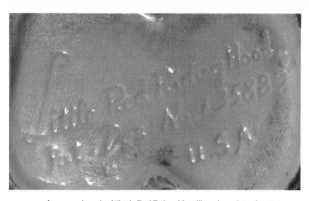

Impressed mark of "Little Red Riding Hood" on the right in the picture above.

At first glance these might appear identical to the two jars above. A closer look reveals larger flower decals, plus the absence of the extra flower on the closed-basket jar and a completely different flower pattern on the open-basket jar. Both jars are 13-1/4 inches high. The mark of one is shown below. *Oravitz Collection.* Left, $350; right, $300

The mark of the jar above, different than other mark shown.

Two more jars with subtle differences. Note the decal on the apron of the jar on the right. Same size as above, similar marks. *Zera Collection.* $300 ea.

Same jar, same size, but only one flower transfer. Mark is similar to the one above. *Oravitz Collection.* $300

More subtle differences. *Coughenour Collection.* $300

Yet another flower pattern, plus gold design on apron. Standard size and mark. *Courtesy of Hillary DiRenzo.* $375

Here is something really different: an entirely hand-decorated jar, believed to be a one-of-a-kind done by someone who worked at either Hull or Regal China. Marked "967/Hull Ware/Little/Red Riding Hood/Pat. App'd For/USA" on 6 lines. *Courtesy of Jazz'e Junque Shop, Chicago, Illinois.* $300

Another strange one, correct size and mark, but probably home decorated. *Courtesy of Betty and Floyd Carson.* $200

This Hull Little Red Riding Hood has only a coating of clear glaze. *Oravitz Collection.* $175

Stoneware pretzel jar, first made by Hull in the 1920s. It is 9-1/2 inches high and marked with an impressed "H" within a circle. *Courtesy of Dan Schneider.* $225

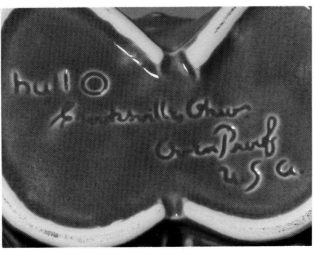

Mark of gray-blue gingerbread boy.

Tan gingerbread boy, 12-1/4 inches high, with the same mark as above. *Courtesy of Jazz'e Junque Shop, Chicago, Illinois.* $130

Reverse of Hull pretzel jar.

Brown gingerbread boy, 12-1/4 inches high, with the same mark as shown above. *Zera Collection.* $130

According to the Roerigs, this barefoot boy was made for Hull by Gem Refractories. It is 13 inches high. On the left side of the base is "Blessings on Thee" and on the right side, "Barefoot Boy." *Oravitz Collection.* $450

This is probably the second most popular Hull cookie jar. It stands 12-1/4 inches high. The mark is shown. *Zera Collection.* $200

The duck on the left is 11-3/4 inches high, the one on the right 11-1/4 inches high. Their marks are "Hull/966/USA" impressed. *Oravitz Collection.* $50 ea.

# Chapter 14
## *Metlox*

Looking over the Metlox cookie jars shown below—as benign as they are beautiful—it's hard to believe this pottery spent World War II making parts for B-25 bombers. Apparently it is not only politics, but also war that creates strange bedfellows.

The pottery was located in Manhattan Beach, California, where it was started by T.C. Prouty in 1927 as the Metlox Manufacturing Company. The original purpose was to make ceramic parts for neon signs. The name Metlox is an acronym derived from the words metal oxide, an ingredient used in neon sign production.

By 1934 Prouty had taken over the Malinite Corporation to produce dinnerware for department stores. Prouty sold Metlox to Evan K. Shaw in 1947. Eleven years later Shaw acquired the fixtures and design patents of Vernon Kilns. Over the years Metlox did some contract work, most notably for National Silver Company during the mid-1940s. Metlox went out of business in 1989.

According to Lehner, the pottery fired its bisque for 40 hours at 2100 degrees F., which is longer and somewhat hotter than most pottery is fired. The result is a fine quality ceramic product.

Unfortunately, not all Metlox cookie jars are marked, the Pinocchio jar below being one example. There are several jars in Chapter 34 whose look and feel strongly suggest Metlox made them, but because there was no definite proof, they haven't been placed here.

Metlox used a variety of marks and paper labels, some of which are illustrated below.

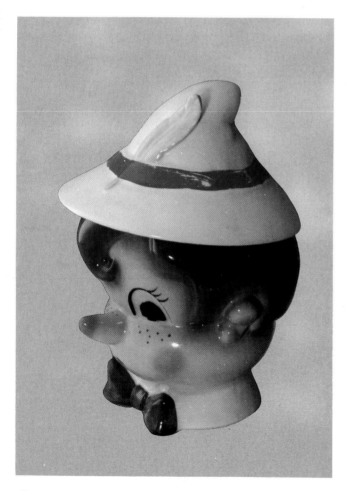

"Pinocchio" is an unmarked Metlox cookie jar, 11 inches high. *Blumenfeld Collection.* $450

This toy soldier is an exceptionally heavy jar. It is 10-3/4 inches high and is not marked. Metlox called it "Drummer Boy." *Blumenfeld Collection.* $500

The owl on the left is 10-1/2 inches high, and the one on the right is 9 inches high. The jar was also made in white. Each owl carries the Poppytrail mark shown below. *Oravitz Collection.* Blue - $75, Yellow - $65

Koala, 12-1/2 inches high, marked, "Metlox/Calif/USA" on three lines. *Oravitz Collection.* $120

The mark of the owls above.

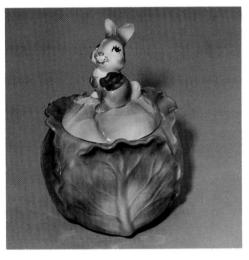

Rabbit on cabbage, 11-1/2 inches high, no mark. Note the lifelike veins in the cabbage and the hand finished detail on the rabbit's face, both typical of Metlox quality. *Zera Collection.* $140

This bear on roller skates is marked "Metlox/USA" and stands 12-1/2 inches high. *Courtesy of Jazz'e Junque Shop, Chicago, Illinois.* $110

Another Metlox bear. This one is 11-1/2 inches high and marked as the owls above. *Oravitz Collection.* $70

An unmarked Metlox mouse, 12 inches high. *Courtesy of Jazz'e Junque Shop, Chicago, Illinois.* $75

This unmarked Metlox cow head jar is 11 inches high. *Courtesy of Jazz'e Junque Shop, Chicago, Illinois.* $300

The cow is 10-1/4 inches high, marked "Metlox/Calif./ USA" on three lines. The jar was also made in purple, which is more popular. *Courtesy of Jazz'e Junque Shop, Chicago, Illinois.* Yellow - $250, Purple - $450

The noisemaker inside the lid of the lamb jar. Most aren't in nearly this good of a condition if they are present at all.

This dinosaur is 13 inches high, has two marks. One is "Metlox/California/USA" on three lines. The other is "©87/by Vincent" with Vincent in script. *Zera Collection.* $150

Squirrel on pine cone, 12 inches high and marked "Made/in/U.S.A." on three lines. *Courtesy of Mark Taylor.* $100

Poppytrail inkstamp mark of the lamb.

Remnant of the lamb's paper label.

Another cookie jar with sound, this kitten meows when its hat is tipped. The height is 9-1/2 inches, and the piece is unmarked. *Zera Collection.* $125

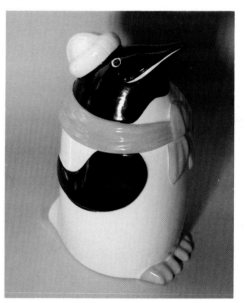

Penguin, 12 inches high. This jar is marked "Metlox/Calif./ USA" on three lines. $100

Here's "Granny Goose," not to be confused with "Mother Goose," which Metlox also made. This jar is 14-1/4 inches high and marked with an impressed "Metlox/Calif/USA." *Oravitz Collection.* $75

A 9-1/4 inch high lamb's head jar. It has the Metlox Poppytrail mark shown below. Turn the lid upside down and it bleats like a sheep. *Oravitz Collection.* $95

116

"Puddles the Duck," 11-1/4 inches high. *Oravitz Collection.* $60

Metlox grapes, 8-1/4 inches high. Note the paper label below the leaves. A close-up is shown below. *Taylor Collection.* $150

Strawberry, 9 inches high, with "Made in USA" impressed. *Courtesy of Jazz'e Junque Shop, Chicago, Illinois.* $90

Paper label of the Metlox grapes. Wording above Poppytrail is "Made in/California" on two lines.

This pelican is marked "Metlox/Calif/USA" impressed on three lines. It stands 10-1/2 inches high. *Coughenour Collection.* $200

Second paper label and pottery mark of the Metlox grapes.

Unusual in that the hoops are made of copper, this barrel of apples is 10-3/4 inches high. It is not marked. *Taylor Collection.* $75

The Metlox rose is an all time favorite. It is 7-1/2 inches high and has "Made/in/USA" impressed on three lines. *Courtesy of Betty and Floyd Carson.* $350

The orange blossom adds a nice touch to this 8-3/4 inch high jar. The bottom is marked "Made/in USA" on two lines. *Taylor Collection.* $100

This Metlox broccoli cookie jar carries the Poppytrail mark with the outline of California. *Oravitz Collection.* $100

This tomato is 7 inches high. Its mark and paper label are shown below. *Courtesy of Jazz'e Junque Shop, Chicago, Illinois.* $80

This clown also appears in yellow. It is 13-1/2 inches high and has the Metlox Poppytrail mark. *Oravitz Collection.* As shown - $175, Yellow - $125, Blue & White - $250

A 13-1/4 inch high Metlox Dutch girl. The jar is marked "Metlox/Calif./USA" on three lines. *Bosson Collection.* Girl - $275, Boy - $225

Paper label and partially obscured mark of the tomato. The mark reads "Made/in/USA" on three lines.

Raggedy Andy and Raggedy Ann, each 11 inches high. Andy has the Poppytrail mark, and Ann is unmarked. Metlox referred to the jars as "Rag Doll Girl" and "Rag Doll Boy." *Coughenour Collection.* Left - $225, Right - $175

This jar, 9-1/2 inches high, is part of a canister set. It is marked "Poppytrail by Metlox Made In USA" in a circle. *Courtesy of Dorothy Coates.* $40

Raggedy Ann in yellow, with her size and mark same as above. *Oravitz Collection.* $175

# Chapter 15
## *Red Wing*

The name of this pottery comes from its location, Red Wing, Minnesota, a Mississippi River town about 25 miles southeast of Minneapolis-St. Paul, and near which there are excellent clay deposits of the kind used in making stoneware.

The first successful commercial pottery in Red Wing was formed by a group of investors in 1878, who took their lead from several small independent potters who operated in the area during the 1860s and 1870s. But to give credit where credit is due, archeological digs in the area reveal that hundreds of years before the white man ever laid eyes on Minnesota, Native Americans had discovered the quality of the clay and took advantage of it by fashioning containers for both cooking and storage.

The firm formed in 1878 was called the Red Wing Stoneware Company. Through a series of mergers and acquisitions, it became known as Red Wing Potteries, Inc., in 1936. A strike drove the company out of business in 1967.

During the early years only stoneware crockery was manufactured. In the 1920s Red Wing began to include artware in its offerings, moving into dinnerware a few years later. By 1947 all stoneware production had ceased.

Besides the jars shown here, Red Wing also made a carousel, a flattened pumpkin with an elf on it that people call Jack Frost, and a crock jar in its familiar bob white dinnerware pattern. The Brush Art crock jar shown in Chapter 22 is a Red Wing blank.

Red Wing cookie jar marks are shown below, but not all of the company's jars are marked. Some were marked with paper labels.

Dutch girl in tan and brown, a rarer color combination that is more expensive on today's market. It is the same size and mark as above, but also has an inkstamp, "Red Wing/Pottery/Hand Painted" on three lines. *Zera Collection.* $125

These Dutch girls are typical of Red Wing—simple color schemes accompanying a texture that hints strongly of the firm's expertise in crockery. Height of the jars is 10-1/2 inches. Each is marked "Red Wing/USA" on two lines. Additionally, the yellow jar has a Red Wing inkstamp with a series of patent numbers: D-130-328, D-130-329, and D-130-330. These are sometimes present on other jars and are shown below with the yellow chef. *Zera Collection.* $100 ea.

This green and brown Dutch girl, like the tan and brown, commands a premium. Same size as the others, with an impressed mark and inkstamp like the tan jar. *Zera Collection.* $150

Most attractive of these more colorful jars, the white glaze and unpainted rings make for a cleaner appearance. Same size, no mark. Red Wing also made a wider, flatter jar of the same design. The flatter piece was probably sold as a casserole, but it is often collected as a cookie jar. *Zera Collection.* $75

Another chef, same size as the previous one, but marked differently as shown below. This jar was also made in at least two other colors, blue and green. *Courtesy of Rosa Sberna.* $90

This is commonly called the "Peasant Design." The unmarked jars are 10 inches high and date from the early 1940s. *Zera Collection.* $75 ea.

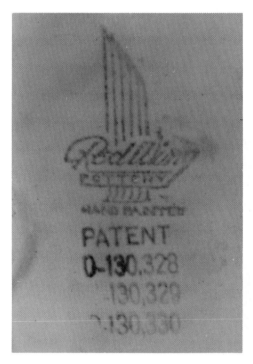

Inkstamp of the yellow chef. The color is different due to shooting the picture at an incorrect exposure.

Darker than the jar above, it is the same size and unmarked. *Zera Collection.* $75

Red Wing chef, 11-1/2 inches high. "Red Wing" impressed. *Zera Collection.* $125

Monk, 10-3/4 inches high. The jar carries Red Wing inkstamp on bottom. *Zera Collection.* $150

Same jar in beige, with the same height and mark. *Courtesy of Mary Huffman.* $150

This is called a fish, but it looks more like a composite aquatic creature, part snail, part fish. Maybe "snish" would be a better name. It is 6 inches high and marked "248/Red Wing/USA" on three lines. *Saxby Collection.* $75

Yellow bananas, with the same size and mark as above. *Bosson Collection.* $100

Perplexing. The jar on the left is definitely Red Wing, has "Red Wing/USA" impressed on two lines. The mark on the one on the right was apparently sponged off when it was cleaned, or it never received a mark. The decoration on the jar on the right isn't consistent with Red Wing, and the jar is somewhat smaller, too, but only by 3/8 of an inch. Possible solutions to this puzzle include it being a remolded jar, a jar made with a different clay mixture than the other, or a jar decorated at home by a factory worker or a decorating firm to which Red Wing sold bisque. *Zera Collection.* Blue - $150, Black - $200

This is the coveted Red Wing "King of Tarts" cookie jar. It is 10 inches high, has "Red Wing/USA" incised on two lines. This jar was also made in pink with a dark crown. The Roerigs show a splendid multi-color example. *Zera Collection.* As shown - $400, Multicolor - $600

Fruit is a major theme of Red Wing cookie jars. This hand of bananas is 9 inches high and marked "Red Wing/USA" on two lines. *Zera Collection.* $125

Grapes, 10 inches high, with "USA" impressed. *Courtesy of Jazz'e Junque Shop, Chicago, Illinois.* $125

Same size as the previous one, but marked with an impressed "Red Wing/USA on two lines. The grapes are also seen in yellow. *Zera Collection.* $150

The same size as the previous ones, but marked differently, with "Red Wing/USA" impressed on two lines. *Zera Collection.* $150 ea.

This apple is 8-1/2 inches high, with "Red Wing" impressed. *Zera Collection.* $75

Besides turquoise and yellow, the pineapple was made in a cobalt glaze, the same as the pear below. These jars are 9 inches high. Mark is shown below. *Zera Collection.* $100 ea.

Also 9-1/2 inches high, with "Red Wing/USA" impressed on two lines. *Zera Collection.* $150

Mark of turquoise pineapple.

Red Wing stoneware crock cookie jar, unmarked. The height is 8-1/2 inches. *Lilly Collection.* $40

The pears are 9-1/2 inches high, "Red Wing" impressed. The cobalt generally sells for more than any of the other colors shown. *Zera Collection.* Yellow - $150, Cobalt - $225

Same height as the jar above and also unmarked. *Courtesy of Jazz'e Junque Shop, Chicago, Illinois.* $40

# Chapter 16
## *Regal China*

The Regal China Company was apparently started sometime in the late 1920s, or perhaps 1930, since founder Herman Kravitz hired Catherine Miller, a top quality decorator, in 1930. Miller's name is on the Regal China Davy Crockett cookie jar, and other Regal jars, for copyright purposes.

Originally located in Chicago, the company moved approximately 50 miles north to Antioch, Illinois, in 1940. Sometime later during that decade Regal was bought by Royal China and Novelty Company, which acted as its distributor. In 1955 Regal made its first Jim Beam bottle, beginning a line that brought it fame and fortune. In 1968, the year Regal became a subsidiary of the James B. Beam Distilling Company, 60 percent of its output was lamps. By that time the company had grown to employ 275 people, and had a 140,000 square foot plant.

Regal decorated Hull Little Red Riding Hood cookie jars, also Hull vases and other decorative Hull pieces.

Several Regal cookie jars copy the designs of other companies. The Regal China cat cookie jar is a near clone of Shawnee's Puss'n Boots, while its majorette and churn boy closely resemble those of American Bisque. According to the Roerigs, the rocking horse and Little Miss Muffet made by Abingdon are Regal products if the mark on the bottom includes the name of the jar, for instance, "Little Miss Muffet, #705." The same is true of the Humpty Dumpty shown below. But marks on Regal cookie jars are the exception, not the rule.

Renowned children's illustrator and designer Ruth Van Tellingen did some work for Regal through Royal China and Novelty. The peek-a-boo cookie jar she designed for Regal is said to have had a production run of less than 1000. Regal China stopped manufacturing in 1992.

The unmarked Regal China majorette, 11-1/2 inches high, is one of the company's most popular cookie jars, a class act in every respect. Very similar to the American Bisque majorette pictured in Chapter 8. *Blumenfeld Collection*. $400

There's an old saying that goes something like "If it looks like a duck, walks like a duck and quacks like a duck—it probably is a duck." That's why this unmarked jar, commonly called "Harpo," is in this chapter even though Regal employees claim the company didn't make it. The Regal red glaze, the porcelain-like quality of the bisque, the feel of the bisque, and the grayish-white color of the bisque—not to mention the overall design quality of the jar—demand Regal attribution unless and until a catalog surfaces that can positively place it with another company. *Zera Collection*. $900

Another unmarked Regal jar that is typical of the fine design and workmanship for which this company is known. *Blumenfeld Collection.* $650

Like the majorette, the Regal China churn boy imitates an American Bisque cookie jar shown in Chapter 8. The boy faces to his right on both jars. There is also a third model circulating, possibly Japanese, on which the boy faces to his left. The Regal jar is 12 inches high and unmarked. *Coughenour Collection.* $250

Same as the previous one, but with a much lighter colored bottom. Possibly a married jar. *Courtesy of Jazz'e Junque Shop, Chicago, Illinois.* $350

This "Peek-A-Boo" was designed by Ruth Van Telligen, creator of the well-known "Snuggle-Hug" salt and pepper shakers, and is said to be the only cookie jar Van Telligen ever designed. A very rare jar, various sources state production numbers between 1000 and 1400. It is 11-3/4 inches high. Its mark is shown below. *Courtesy of Jazz'e Junque Shop, Chicago, Illinois.* $1100

Davy Crockett, 11-3/4 inches high. The mark is "Translucent/Vitrified China/©C.Miller/55-140." *Blumenfeld Collection.* $550

The Regal China baby pig is 12 inches high, with "404" impressed. *Oravitz Collection.* $400

Regal Dutch girl, 12 inches high and unmarked. *Courtesy of Betty and Floyd Carson.* $650

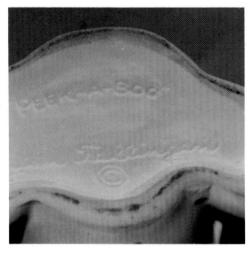

Mark of Regal China Van Telligen Peek-A-Boo jar.

Like the Shawnee "Puss'n Boots," this cat is 10-1/4 inches high. Subtle differences in addition to the bird on the hat being replaced by a fish, include the beaded area below the head, the texture of the fur, and a different ribbon. As far as is known, all Regal "Puss'n Boots" jars are unmarked. *Oravitz Collection.* $350

Goldilocks is 12-1/2 inches high. The bottom of the jar is marked "405" above and "Pat. Pend." below. *Courtesy of Betty and Floyd Carson.* $300

In the first edition I made quite a deal out of this "mystery" Goldilocks jar, so different from the others appearing here. Imagine my embarrassment when I received a note from cookie jar collector and future author, M.J. Giacomini (American Bisque, Schiffer 1994), informing me I had the base turned backwards. Make no mistake, it's marked the same, is the same. $300

Jar on the left is McCoy, jar on the right is Regal. The height of the McCoy jar is 10 inches, but Regal jar wasn't measured. McCoy jar is marked "USA" on bottom, and the Regal mark is shown. *Bosson Collection.* Left - $800, Right - $75

This Goldilocks, with blue hat and cape, is the same size as the one above but marked differently, "H405/'Goldilocks'/ Pat. Pending" on three lines. *Oravitz Collection.* $300

This chef is 12 inches high with "54-192" impressed in the bottom. *Courtesy of Jazz'e Junque Shop, Chicago, Illinois.* $300

Back of the Regal China Quaker Oats cookie jar.

The same mold, but did Regal pour it and decorate it? Probably not since it is not only unmarked, but also decorated entirely by hand, something that can't be said for any of the other jars in this chapter. Perhaps a factory worker took home a piece of bisque to finish. *Oravitz Collection.* $100

Close-up of Regal mark on back of Quaker Oats jar.

Kraft Marshmallows advertising cookie jar from 1982. It is 15 inches high and marked as shown. *Zera Collection.* $85

Regal barn cookie jar made for the same series as the canisters or to compliment it. The mark is "381/Pat. Pending" impressed on two lines; height is 9 inches. *Bosson Collection.* $275

The same barn with a clear glaze. *Courtesy of Betty and Floyd Carson.* $150

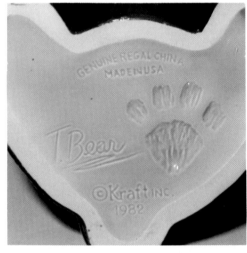

Mark of Kraft Marshmallows advertising jar.

Two pieces of an entire line of barrel canisters, spice jars, and other accessories made by Regal. Although only one was made with a "Cookies" sign, when the others are turned so the sign faces the rear, they make acceptable cookie jars and are often collected as such. The jar on the left is 11 inches high, marked with an impressed "387/Pat. Pending" on two lines. The right jar is 10-1/2 inches high and marked "389/Pat. Pending." *Courtesy of Betty and Floyd Carson.* $250 ea.

On the left is the Regal China version of Humpty Dumpty, with "Humpty Dumpty/707" impressed on two lines. On the right is the Abingdon version, with an "Abingdon/USA" inkstamp and "663" impressed. Both jars are 11-1/2 inches high. *Oravitz Collection.* Left - $300, Right - $225

Marks of the Humpty Dumpty.

One of the rarest and most expensive of Regal's cookie jars is "Alice in Wonderland," which I didn't run across. This is the sugar and creamer that were made as accessories for it. The green matches the grass that's behind Alice's feet on the cookie jar. The blue matches her dress, over which she is wearing a white apron. *Courtesy of Betty and Floyd Carson.* Creamer & Sugar - $375, Cookie Jar (not shown) - $2200

According to the Roerigs, this is not a Regal China cookie jar, but Regal made one almost exactly like it except the Regal jar was glazed instead of painted as this one is. Also, this jar is unmarked whereas the Regal jar is marked "Uncle Mistletoe Cookie Jar, Pat. Copyright 50028." Height of the above jar is 12 inches, height of the Regal jar may be different. If you see this jar with a Regal red glaze, be sure to pick it up because it is moderately rare. *Zera Collection.* Jar shown - $75, Uncle Mistletoe - $800

Mark of the creamer. The Alice in Wonderland cookie jar is marked in a similar fashion.

# Chpater 17
## Robinson-Ransbottom

The Robinson-Ransbottom Pottery Company, which is still in business today in Roseville, Ohio, was the result of a 1920 merger of Robinson Clay Products, of Akron, Ohio, and the Ransbottom Brothers Pottery, of Roseville. At that time the former was a brick producing operation. The latter was mainly devoted to stoneware jugs, reportedly outdistancing Red Wing in volume if not in reputation.

Because many of its products are marked in part with the word "Roseville," a lot of collectors, dealers, and auctioneers confuse Robinson-Ransbottom with the Roseville Pottery Company of Zanesville, Ohio. The two were not affiliated. It is an unfortunate situation because the average Roseville piece is worth several times more than the average Robinson-Ransbottom piece. The difference in value is not as great with cookie jars as it is with other lines of pottery. But to avoid any possible confusion, you might want to compare the jars below to the Roseville examples shown in Chapter 21.

Robinson-Ransbottom cookie jars are on a par with those of American Bisque, Brush, and other quality potteries, but for some reason their prices are often lower, making them a good area of exploration for beginning collectors, or collectors with limited finances.

According to a company spokeswoman, today Robinson-Ransbottom's focus is on stoneware crocks, garden ware, and very large flower pots.

Robinson-Ransbottom marks accompany the pictures. The round-bottom yellow bisque jars such as the cop and the brownie, long attributed to Robinson-Ransbottom, will be found at the end of Chapter 8, with an accompanying explanation. Robinson-Ransbottom Oscar jars are shown in Chapter 5.

Sailor with white hair. If you ever see this jar at a show or in someone else's collection, be extra careful when you handle it because the lid is extremely top heavy toward the rear. *Zera Collection.* $275

Although unmarked, these jars are attributed to Robinson-Ransbottom through a 1943 catalog. The jar on the left is 11 inches high, and the jar on the right is 11-1/4 inches high. *Blumenfeld Collection.* Left - $275, Right - $225

Some collectors call this cookie jar a "toy soldier," others say it resembles a Dutch boy. Whatever it is, its height is 12-1/2 inches. The mark is "R.R.P.Co./Roseville Ohio/No.423" impressed on three lines. *Blumenfeld Collection.* $200

View of mark on young lady cookie jar—"R.R.P.Co./Roseville, Ohio/No" on three lines.

This wise bird is 12 inches high and marked "R.R.P.Co./Roseville, Ohio/No. 359" on three lines. *Oravitz Collection.* $125

Same jar with gold trim. Same size and mark as above. *Zera Collection.* $275

This young lady is 12 inches high. The mark is shown. *Zera Collection.* $200

This snowman is 14 inches high. It is marked "Roseville Ohio/U.S.A./R.R.P.Co." on three lines. *Courtesy of Betty and Floyd Carson.* $450

The chef is 11 inches high. It is marked "R.R.P.Co./Roseville, Ohio/No. 411" on three lines. *Courtesy of Lisa Diane Golden.* $125

Here's "Jocko," Robinson-Ransbottom's banana-eating monkey. He is 11-1/2 inches high and marked "Roseville, O./USA/R.R.P. Co." on three lines. *Zera Collection.* $250

Sheriff Pig stands 12-1/2 inches high, is marked "R.R.P. Co./Roseville/Ohio/No. 363" on four lines. It is also seen with a gray hat. The hat strap is real leather. Also note the fringe on the jacket. Apparently a favorite with Robinson-Ransbottom, it's similar to that on the previous boy and girl. *Oravitz Collection.* $125

No lack of nursery rhyme characters at Robinson-Ransbottom says Old King Cole, that merry old soul. The jar is 10-1/4 inches high, its mark is shown. *Zera Collection.* $375

Old King Cole with blue legs and a yellow coat. It is the same size as the other but has a slightly different mark, "Roseville/Ohio/R.R.P. Co." on three lines. *Coughenour Collection.* $375

Mark of Old King Cole, different than most Robinson-Ransbottom marks, it reads "Roseville, 0/U.S.A./R.R.P. Co." on three lines.

Sheriff Pig with gold trim. Same size and mark as above. *Bosson Collection.* $150

"Cow Jumped Over the Moon," gold trim. The height is 9-3/4 inches, and the mark is "R.R.P.Co./Roseville, Ohio/No-411" on three lines. *Zera Collection.* $400 with gold, $250 without.

The Robinson-Ransbottom whale isn't easy to find, and it generally necessitates a fatter wallet to acquire it than most other R.R.P. cookie jars. It is 7-3/4 inches high, marked "RRP Roseville, Ohio." *Bosson Collection.* $600

Peter, Peter, Pumpkin Eater, had a wife and put her in a Robinson-Ransbottom cookie jar. This jar is 8-3/4 inches high; its mark is shown. *Oravitz Collection.* $275

This round jar is 8-1/2 inches high and marked "R.R.PCo./Roseville, Ohio/No-350." Westfall shows the same jar with aqua stripes. *Bosson Collection.* $40

Mark of Peter Pumpkin Eater. Note that the lettering is both raised and impressed.

A pair of similar jars, but one made of whiteware, the other yellowware. They are 8-1/2 inches high. The impressed mark is "R.R.PCo./Roseville, Ohio/312" on three lines. *Zera Collection.* $45 ea.

A pair of tiger kittens, 10 inches high. Mark is shown. *Courtesy of Jazz'e Junque Shop, Chicago, Illinois.* $60

Likely one of the earliest Robinson-Ransbottom cookie jars, this 8-1/4 inch high crock is marked "R.R.P/Roseville Oh/1500/USA" on four lines. *Bosson Collection.* $35

Mark of tiger kittens.

# Chapter 18
## *Shawnee*

This company operated in Zanesville, Ohio, from 1937 to 1961. According to Shawnee advertising, the plant was capable of turning out 100,000 ceramic items per day. Shawnee was housed in the former plant of American Encaustic Tiling Company.

As with Hull's Little Red Riding Hood, Shawnee cookie jars poured in identical molds will often exhibit major to minor variations in the way they are decorated. Most Shawnee cookie jar collectors pursue these variations. It's not uncommon to find several examples of the same jar in one collection, each decorated a bit differently. This is particularly true of Smiley pigs, Winnie pigs, Mugsey dogs, Puss'n Boots cats, and Dutch boys and girls.

The Smiley pig, designed by Rudy Gantz, was one of Shawnee's most successful products. The company was good at merchandising and made many spin-offs of its cookie jars, including Puss'n Boots creamers, and salt and pepper shakers to compliment Smiley, Cooky, Mugsey and other jars.

Many Shawnee pieces are marked with a simple and non-identifying, "USA," but this causes more of a problem for collectors of other Shawnee items than for collectors of cookie jars, as most Shawnee cookie jars are pretty well known. A few Shawnee cookie jars carry the marks, "Great Northern," and "Kenwood."

Shawnee Puss'n Boots jars bear a copyright notice. Puss'n Boots was a registered trademark of the Coast Fishing Company, of California, from 1934 until 1950 when Coast was purchased by the Quaker Oats Company. Quaker Oats is known to have favored cookie jar premiums (F & F mammy, F & F Ken L Ration pup) at that point in time, but thus far no connection has been found between Shawnee and Quaker, other than permission apparently had to be granted to use the Puss'n Boots name on the jar.

Terrace Ceramics Inc., which often used Shawnee cookie jar molds after Shawnee's demise, is discussed below.

### Terrace Ceramics, Inc.

When Shawnee closed its doors in 1961 then-general manager, John F. Boinstall, bought Shawnee's molds for Terrace Ceramics, Inc., a marketing firm he had started one year earlier. Bonistall then contracted with other companies to produce cookie jars for Terrace by using the Shawnee molds. Terrace Ceramics jars are easily distinguished from Shawnee jars, not only because they're usually marked, but also because the decoration is much different than that used by Shawnee.

Most Terrace cookie jars were made by the McNicol China Company, Clarksburg, West Virginia, a pottery that was mainly into hotel ware. A few were apparently made by either American Bisque or American Pottery Company, as covered in Chapter 8.

The mark of Terrace Ceramics, which is often unreadable due to glaze filling in the space between the letters, is shown below. Pictures of Terrace Ceramics cookie jars begin at the bottom of page 140.

Probably the most familiar of all the Shawnee cookie jars are the "Smiley" and "Winnie" pigs, which, like most Shawnee jars, was adorned with a variety of decoration. Smiley, on the left, is 11-1/4 inches high. Winnie, on the right, is 11-1/2 inches high. Both are marked with an impressed "USA". *Oravitz Collection*. Left - $325, Right - $350

Here's Winnie and Smiley in their bank forms, a slot having been cut in each of their heads. There are no bottom holes in the heads to get the money out. Winnie is 11-1/2 inches high, Smiley is 11-1/4 inches high. The mark of Smiley is shown. Winnie is marked "Patented/Winnie/Shawnee/USA/61" on 5 lines. *Oravitz Collection.* $450 ea.

Smiley and Winnie bank forms, but darker duds on both, plus gold trim on Smiley. Everything else same as previous ones. *Courtesy of Jazz'e Junque Shop, Chicago, Illinois.* $450 ea.

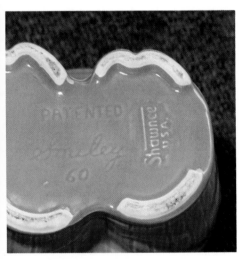

Mark of Smiley cookie jar/bank.

Same size as the other Smileys, but different flowers. The mark is "USA" impressed. *Smith Collection.* $325

Red clover, gold trim, 11-1/4 inches high. The mark is "Pat'd/Smiley/USA" in script on three lines. *Courtesy of Jazze's Junque Shop, Chicago, Illinois.* $425 w/gold trim.

Basically the same Smiley as in the first picture, but this one has gold trim, plus additional color on ears, cheeks, nose, and arms. Note "Smiley" written in gold below neckerchief. Some folks differentiate, calling those without the name written on them "Farmer Pig." *Zera Collection.* $425

Smiley with tulips, "USA" impressed mark, 11-1/4 inches high. Incidentally, Shawnee also made creamers and salt and peper shakers of many of its cookie jar patterns including this one. *Courtesy of Jazz'e Junque Shop, Chicago, Illinois.* $425

Red clover but no gold. Height and mark same as above. *Boson Collection.* $325

Smiley with green neckerchief, shamrocks, and gold trim, 11-1/4 inches high, "USA" impressed. *Courtesy of Jazz'e Junque Shop, Chicago, Illinois.* $475

Gold-trimmed Smiley with different transfer flowers. "USA" impressed, 11-1/4 inches high. *Courtesy of Jazz'e Junque Shop, Chicago, Illinois.* $450

And a blue neckerchief, also with gold trim. "USA" impressed, 11-1/4 inches. *Courtesy of Allan and Michelle Naylor.* $475

Same green neckerchief and shamrocks minus the gold trim. "USA" impressed, 11-1/4 inches high. *Zera Collection.* $375

Something really different, a yellow neckerchief. Note gold trim. Height is 11-1/4 inches, mark is an impressed "USA." *Smith Collection.* $375

Plain Smiley, 11-1/4 inches high, "USA" impressed. *Zera Collection.* $125

Small transfer flowers and gold trim decorate this Smiley. It is 11-1/4 inches high with "USA" impressed. *Courtesy of Betty and Floyd Carson.* $475

All paint, no flowers—unusual to say the least. Possibly Terrace Ceramics but not verified. *Bosson Collection.* $175 ea.

Winnie with both red and gold decoration. She is 11-1/2 inches high and "USA" impressed. *Zera Collection.* $475

Winnie with a beige collar, and blue and pink flowers. The height is 11-1/2 inches, and the mark is "Pat'd/Winnie/USA." *Zera Collection.* $325

Several differences here including the decals and the maroon bow. The jar is 10-1/2 inches high, and marked "Patented/'Puss N Boots'/USA" on three lines. *Smith Collection.* $500

The only difference here is the decoration surrounding top button. "USA" impressed, 11-1/2 inches high. *Smit Collection.* $500

Winnie in green with shamrocks. The height is 11-1/2 inches, and the mark is "USA" impressed. *Zera Collecti* $325

Blue collar, gold trim, 11-1/2 inches high, "USA" impressed. *Smith Collection.* $325

So much for pigs—on to cats, dogs, and elephants. Here is an exquisitely decorated example of "Puss'n Boots"—hand painting, transfers, and gold trim. It is 10-1/4 inches high, and marked "Patented/'Puss N Boots'/USA" on three lines. *Zera Collection.* $450

A much simpler "Puss 'N Boots," 10-1/4 inches high, same mark as above. *Zera Collection.* $175

A Mugsey dog with floral transfers and gold trim. The jar is 11-3/4 inches high and marked "Patented/Mugsey/USA" on three lines. *Bosson Collection.* $800

Similar to previous one but red flowers and highlights. Same size and mark as above. *Zera Collection.* $275

Different hat trim and different flowers, but size and mark the same as previous one. *Zera Collection.* $300

Red scarf, gold trim, and transfer flowers. Mark is "USA" impressed, and the height is 12-1/4 inches. $300

This jar is not as tall as the others—only 10-3/4 inches—because of the different bottom. Mark is "Great/Northern/USA" in raised letters on three lines, plus "1026" incised. All Shawnee cookie jars with this same base and top shown by the Roerigs and Westfall and by Mark E. Supnick in his book *Collecting Shawnee Pottery* have identical facial expressions, the girl's eyes cast to her right. Supnick pictures one finished in green both top and bottom. *Zera Collection.* $200

"Happy" with blue pants and patches, and gold trim. Height is 12 inches, "USA" impressed. *Smith Collection.* $325

Yellow pants, blue trim, no gold, 12-1/2 inches high and "USA" impressed. *Smith Collection.* $200

Plain Dutch boy, painted over the glaze with much of the paint chipped away. Same size and mark as above. *Zera Collection.* $100

Sailor, 11-3/4 inches high, "USA" impressed. Look closely and you'll *see* a star on the side of the cap. The hands behind the back on Shawnee's sailor jars hold a cookie. *Oravitz Collection.* $150

Where you find Dutch girls you usually find Dutch boys, the Shawnee Pottery Company is no exception. "Happy" (on pants) is 11-1/2 inches high, has "USA" impressed. *Zera Collection.* $300

Overall better condition and blond hair. The height is 12 inches, with "USA" impressed. *Smith Collection.* $140

This "Clown with Seal" is 9-1/2 inches high, and its mark is shown. The jar is also seen with gold trim. *Courtesy of Jazz'e Junque Shop, Chicago, Illinois.* $500

Mark of "Clown with Seal." This is exceedingly crisp for a Shawnee mark, many of which are barely readable.

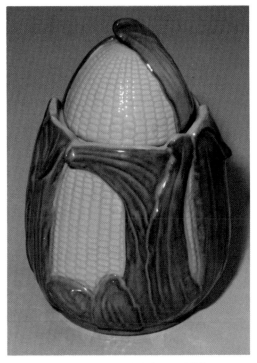

This jar, 10 1/2 inches high and marked "Shawnee/USA" in raised letters, is but one of many accessories for the company's famous corn pattern dinnerware. *Zera Collection.* $225

Sailor with gold trim, note "GOB" on left. The jar is 11-3/4 inches high, with "USA" impressed. *Smith Collection.* $600

Drummer boy, 10 inches high, with "USA" impressed. *Blumenfeld Collection.* $400

More produce from Shawnee, 8 inches high, and marked "Shawnee/USA" on two lines in raised letters with "84" impressed below. *Zera Collection.* $135

Here we're back to, "If it looks like a duck....." This jar is attributed to Regal China by some collectors, but the prima facie evidence pointing to Shawnee origin is overwhelming. The green and yellow match one of the "Cooky" Dutch girl jars above, while the transfer flowers can be found on the Smiley pigs. There is also the gold "Cooky" on the right shoulder, which is a carbon copy of the "Cooky" Shawnee used. Maybe Shawnee didn't make the jar, but clearly the company, or someone within it, had a hand in its decoration. The unmarked jar is 12 inches high. A mate that says "Cinderella" on it is shown in Chapter 34. *Courtesy of Jazz'e Junque Shop, Chicago, Illinois.* $275

Shawnee house cookie jar. It is 6 3/4 inches high, marked "USA/6" on two lines. This jar is quite rare. *Courtesy of Jazz'e Junque Shop, Chicago, Illinois.* $550

# Chapter 19
## *Treasure Craft*

Treasure Craft was founded in Gardena, California, in 1945 by Alfred A. Levin, and is one of the few American potteries that still produces cookie jars on a fairly large scale. Levin started the pottery in a single-car garage, using a 15 cubic foot kiln. The company is now located in Compton, California, in a 250,000 square foot complex, and employs between 500 and 600 people. It was sold to Pfaltzgraff Pottery, of York, Pennsylvania, in 1988. Pfaltzgraff retained Treasure Craft management.

If potteries had cheers as football teams do, Treasure Craft's would probably go something like, "Dark brown, light brown, ivory and white; our favorite glazes, fight, fight, fight!" Those colors dominate the company's output. The muted earth tones probably account for the failure of Treasure Craft cookie jars to capture the fancy of many collectors. It seems probable they will gain respect at some point inthe future, because Treasure Craft's molds are quite often more detailed than those of many other companies.

When Twin Winton Ceramics was sold in 1977, Treasure Craft purchased its molds. According to Alfred Levin, Treasure Craft has used some of the molds, making "technical changes the average person wouldn't recognize."

Most Treasure Craft jars are marked inside the lid, as shown below. Paper labels, also shown below, have been used, too.

This cookie chef and several jars following it are from the predominantly ivory colored line spoken of above. This one is 12-1/2 inches high, "Treasure Craft/©Made in USA" impressed in lid on two lines. *Courtesy of Lisa Diane Golden.* $65

Marked "Treasure Craft/©Made in USA" on two lines in lid, this jar stands 12 inches high. *Oravitz Collection.* $80

The mouse is 11-1/2 inches high, and is marked "Treasure Craft/©USA" on two lines inside lid. *Oravitz Collection*. $60

Also made in brown, this rocking horse is 13-1/4 inches high. The mark "Treasure Craft/©Made in USA," is shown in the lid. *Courtesy of Jazz'e Junque Shop, Chicago, Illinois*. $75

As his sign says, this puppy is actually part of a canister set. But the same jar was made as a cookie jar, too. The cookie jar model has a top hat about the same size as the hat on this jar. Possibly the heads were interchangeable. The jar is 10 inches high and carries the Treasure Craft paper label shown below. *Oravitz Collection*. $50

A cookie trolley, 9-1/2 inches high. The mark is "Treasure Craft/©/Made in USA" impressed under lid on three lines. *Courtesy of Betty and Floyd Carson*. $70

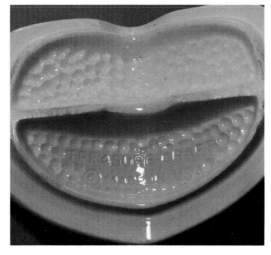

Mark of Treasure Craft rocking horse.

Paper label from puppy coffee canister.

Different mode of transportation, 8 inches high. This jar is unmarked. If it isn't Treasure Craft, someone certainly did a fine job of imitating it. *Oravitz Collection*. $55

This monk also appears in light tan. He is 12 inches high and marked "Treasure Craft/© Made in USA" on two lines inside the lid. *Oravitz Collection*. $50

The lamb is 11-1/2 inches high and marked Treasure Craft/19©68/Comptom, Calif." on three lines on side of base. *Oravitz Collection*. $40

# Chapter 20
## *Twin Winton*

Here is a typical Twin Winton cookie jar—cute, wood tone, matte glaze, and hand-painted details. The jar is 12-1/4 inches high, was offered in Twin Winton's 1975 catalog. It was also made for the Collectors' Series, some examples of which are shown elsewhere in this chapter. The inkstamp mark is shown. *Zera Collection.* $60

Inkstamp mark on bottom of the bear.

Twin brothers Don and Ross Winton began producing ceramics while attending high school in Pasadena, California, during the 1930s. Following hiatus of several years for World War II, the brothers formed Twin Winton Ceramics upon returning to Pasadena in 1946. Another brother, Bruce Winton, participated by overseeing the business end of the enterprise. The first cookie jars were made in 1951.

Operations were moved to San Juan Capistrano, and El Monte, California, sometime in the early 1950s. The El Monte plant closed in 1964, but the San Juan Capistrano plant remained open until 1977 when it was sold to William F. Bowmaster. Molds were sold to Treasure Craft.

Twin Winton specialized in kitchen artware, making things such as cookie jars, salt and pepper shakers, napkin rings and other fancies. For its cookie jars, the company favored a wood tone matte glaze the majority of the time. Wood tone type finishes were applied in three different shades, light, medium and dark, all illustrated below. The Collectors' Series, which encompassed 18 jars, was initiated in 1974. All Collectors' Series jars are marked as such.

Despite the commercial success of Twin Winton Ceramics, collectors tend to hold in higher esteem the cookie jars the Wintons designed for the Brush Pottery Company, of Roseville, Ohio, from the mid-1940s through 1971.

Similar in style to the above jar, but a police chief is 11 inches, and the mark is "Twin Winton/©/ Calif.USA" on three lines. *Oravitz Collection.* $70

This Twin Winton swashbuckler is 12 inches high and has two marks. Impressed is "Twin Winton made in California/ ©(two unreadable numerals)." The accompanying inkstamp proclaims "Twin Winton/©/California, USA" on three lines. This design was included in the Collector's Series. *Oravitz Collection.* $75

The Wintons made this fellow a lot more ambitious than the squirrel on a log they designed for Brush, which is shown in Chapter 10. The jar is 11-1/2 inches high and marked "Twin Winton/Calif. USA" on two lines. It was offered in the company's 1965 catalog. *Oravitz Collection.* $50

Twin Winton jars that are basically one color appear plain at first glance, but a closer look reveals nice detailing such as the collar and ear on this horse. The jar is 14-1/4 inches high and has an inkstamp mark "Twin Winton/San Juan Capistrano/Calif. USA" on three lines. Some examples also include the year 1962. *Courtesy of Betty and Floyd Carson.* $80

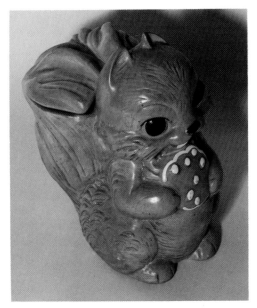

Squirrel, 10-3/4 inches high, appeared in 1965 catalog. The mark is the inkstamp "Twin Winton ©/ San Juan Capistrano/Calif." on three lines. Apparently the same work was carried on at both Twin Winton plants as the Roerigs show this jar with a similar mark, except that it reads "El Monte, Calif." *Oravitz Collection.* $50

This pretty lady is 13-1/2 inches high and marked "Twin Winton ©/Calif. USA" on two lines. *Oravitz Collection.* $70

Some might say the biggest difference between this jar and the McCoy "Mouse on Clock" in Chapter 7 is the time, 11:50 as opposed to 9:34. This one came first, at least in the production phase, as it is shown in Twin Winton's 1965 catalog. McCoy's didn't appear until 1968. The jar is 14-1/2 inches high and the mark is shown. *Oravitz Collection.* $40

The cow is 8-1/2 inches high and is marked with a simple "Twin Winton" on one line. *Courtesy of Betty and Floyd Carson.* $55

Impressed mark of above jar showing the design was copyrighted in 1960.

Both rabbits are 13-1/2 inches high. The mark of the one on the left is shown. The mark of the one on the right is "Twin Winton ©/Calif. USA" on two lines. *Oravitz Collection.* Left - $150, Right - $75

This lion is 13-1/2 inches high and is also seen in wood tone and in reddish brown. Impressed mark reads "Twin Winton©/Calif. USA" on two lines. *Oravitz Collection.* $60

Mark of the ivory rabbit.

The lamb on the left is not marked. The lamb on the right carries the Twin Winton inkstamp. Both jars are 12-1/4 inches high. A very similar jar is sometimes seen with a mark that takes up nearly the whole bottom and says "Lamb, World Wide, P.O. Drawer L, Lafayette, Louisiana." One of the main differences between that jar and these two is that the lettering on the front of the jar with the "Lamb" mark does not appear wavy as it does on both of these. *Oravitz Collection.* Left - $70, Right - $45

Owl, 11-3/4 inches high. The mark is shown. The jar was also made in wood tones. *Zera Collection.* $50

Mark of the gray owl.

Each is 11-1/2 inches high, marked Twin Winton. *Oravitz Collection*. $50 ea.

Collectors' Series jar, 13 inches high. The impressed mark reads "Twin Winton©/California USA" on two lines, and the inkstamp states "Twin Winton Collectors' Series/©/California USA" on three lines. *Courtesy of Betty and Floyd Carson*. $100

Standing 13 inches high, the elf on the right is 1/4 of an inch taller than the one on the left. Both are stamped "Twin Winton." The brown elf was in 1965 catalog. *Oravitz Collection*. $45 ea.

This jar is virtually identical to the brown jar but 1/4 of an inch taller at 11-1/2 inches. It has strange marks: an "EA" carved in the lid and a "W" inkstamp on both the lid and base. *Oravitz Collection*. $95

Mother Goose, 13-3/4 inches high. The mark is shown. *Bosson Collection*. $80

This little guy showed up in the company's 1975 catalog. The jar is 11-1/4 inches high. A mark is present but unreadable. *Oravitz Collection*. $70

This lovely Dutch girl is 13 inches high and has two marks. "Twin Winton" is impressed on one line while an accompanying inkstamp reads "Twin Winton/©California USA" on two lines. The jar was included in the company's 1965 catalog. *Courtesy of Betty and Floyd Carson*. $70

Mark of Mother Goose.

Appearing in Twin Winton's 1965 catalog, this jar is 10-1/2 inches high, and is marked "Twin Winton©/Calif. USA." *Courtesy of Jazz'e Junque Shop, Chicago, Illinois.* $45

The ark is 11 inches high and has a Twin Winton mark. The Roerigs show it in white with greenish-yellow antiquing. *Bosson Collection.* $50

This jar stands 12-1/4 inches high, has a Twin Winton inkstamp. It was shown in a 1965 company catalog. *Oravitz Collection.* $65

The bird in the chimney adds a nice touch to this 12-inch high jar. The mark is "Twin Winton©/Calif. USA" impressed on two lines. *Courtesy of Jazz'e Junque Shop, Chicago, Illinois.* $60

The cookie jar is 12 inches high, and the accompanying salt and pepper shakers are 6-1/4 inches high. The jar is marked "Twin Winton Calif. USA©60." *Courtesy of Joyce Hollen.* Cookie Jar - $70, Salt & Pepper - $60

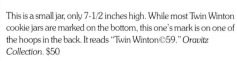

This is a small jar, only 7-1/2 inches high. While most Twin Winton cookie jars are marked on the bottom, this one's mark is on one of the hoops in the back. It reads "Twin Winton©59." *Oravitz Collection.* $50

This elephant found a place in Twin Winton's 1965 catalog. It is 11-1/2 inches high and unmarked. *Oravitz Collection.* $50

# Section IV: Other American Producers

This section covers pottery cookie jars that were made in the United States by companies other than those listed in Sections II and III. If you can't find a particular company in this section, it will probably show up in Section V "Cookie Jar Handlers," which encompasses decorators, distributors, importers and retailers. For instance, Ransburg, familiar to many for its crock jars, was a decorating and distributing firm that did not manufacture pottery. And Pottery Guild, also familiar to many collectors as a company that made quality cookie jars, was in reality a sales organization that marketed ceramic products made by the Cronin China Company, of Minerva, Ohio.

# Chapter 21
# *Potteries*

### Bauer Pottery

The Bauer Pottery, of Los Angeles, California, was started shortly after the turn of the century by J.A. Bauer as a family run organization. It lasted until the late 1950s or early 1960s.

It is believed Bauer used California clays nearly exclusively. Cheerfully colored mix-and-match dinnerware, made famous by Homer Laughlin's Fiesta Ware, is said to have been a Bauer innovation of the 1930s.

Apparently more into table service than cookie jars, Bauer, along with Gladding McBean, Pacific Clay Products, Vernon Kilns, and Metlox was rated by Jo Cunningham (*The Collector's Encyclopedia of American Dinnerware*) as one of California's "big five" of dinnerware.

### California Cleminsons

Called California Clay during its first two years, 1941 to 1943, this El Monte, California, pottery was run by George and Betty Cleminson. She handled the creative side of the venture, he took care of the commercial end. Like many successful potteries of that year, the Cleminsons began as an in-home business, soon outgrew their garage facilities, and eventually employed 165 people. The pottery lasted until 1963.

California Cleminsons cookie jars are unusual in that they were slip-decorated, a process by which colored liquefied clay is used to adorn pottery. The difference between slip decoration and glaze decoration, although slight, can be determined by running your fingers over it. Glaze decoration will be smooth, slip decora-

## BAUER POTTERY

This Bauer Pottery swirled jar, perhaps a poke, is 9 inches high. The mark is "Bauer/Made in Calif./823" on three lines. *Courtesy of Betty and Floyd Carson.* $125

## CALIFORNIA CLEMINSONS

This "Cookie Book" stands 9-3/4 inches high and is marked "Cleminsons/Hand Painted" on two lines. *Oravitz Collection.* $140

Brown bear, 12-1/4 inches high. The mark is the same as the polar bear, which is shown. *Bosson Collection.* $100

The "Bartender" in blue and green. The jars are 10-1/2 inches high and marked "USA." Long credited to Fredericksburg, the bartender was recently found with a Pan-American art paper label, according to Joyce Roerig. Perhaps this explains why the mark on the "Bartender" doesn't include the words "FAPCO," or "FAP." as other FAPCO jars do. Other Pan-American Art cookie jars appear on page 170 under the heading "San Jose Potteries." *Bosson Collection.* $225 ea.

FAPCO polar bear, 12-1/4 inches high, with mark shown. *Oravitz Collection.* $100

Dutch windmill, 10 inches high, marked "F.A.P.co." *Zera Collection.* $60

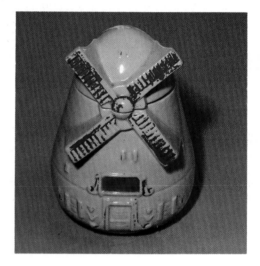

Windmill with red trim, the same size as the previous example, but marked a bit differently: "F.A.P." Besides the colors shown, the windmill was also made with blue, yellow, and gray blades. *Zera Collection.* $60

Reversed mark of FAPCO polar bear. You see the same thing with other potteries occasionally, particularly with Niloak of Benton, Arkansas.

## Gilner

Very little is known about Gilner, including exactly what it was. It might have been a pottery, distributor, importer, or line. It might even have been a department store.

Here's what is known: Gilner was located somewhere in California, and was active in 1951. The information comes from Fred Strunk and Denise Dakoulis, well known cookie jar collectors who have a Gilner spoon holder marked "Gilner Calif./©1951" on two lines.

Gilner was somehow connected to Triangle Studios, of Los Angeles and El Monte, California, which made cookie jars marked "Vallona Starr." The Peter Pumpkin Eater cookie jar below is often seen with a Vallona Star mark.

In addition to the jars shown below, Gilner is known to have made or marketed a crowing rooster, sitting bear, and a goose commonly referred to as Mother goose. While it appears all Gilner cookie jars were of very high quality, it is the mammy head jar that excites collectors the most.

Although this 11-inch high jar is unmarked, the spoonrest that was mentioned previously holds a companion shaker. *Blumenfeld Collection.* $1500

This Peter Pumpkin Eater, 8-1/4 inches high, is marked "Gilner/ Potteries/Design Pat./©" impressed on four lines. Interestingly, the Roerigs photographed an identical jar that was marked "Vallona Starr Design Pat. copyright 49 California." *Courtesy of Betty and Floyd Carson.* $225

### Gladding, McBean & Company (Franciscan)

This California firm was started in 1875 by transplanted Chicagoans Charles Gladding, Peter McGill McBean, and George Chambers. Original product was sewer tile from clay deposits near its Lincoln plant in Placer County, about 20 miles north of Sacramento. Terra-cotta ceramics for the construction industry followed about 10 years later. After a series of acquisitions—including, most notably, the Tropico Pottery in 1923 and the west coast facilities of American Encaustic Tiling Company in 1933—Gladding, McBean began producing dinnerware and art pottery in 1934. Frederick J. Grant served as the first art director. He was the former Weller Pottery president who had left that position one year earlier upon his divorce from Ethel Weller, daughter of the founder. Artware and dinnerware were made at plants in Los Angeles, and Glendale, California.

In 1962 Gladdening, McBean merged with Lock Joint Pipe Company, the name being changed to Interpace Corporation in 1963. Concentrating primarily on construction products, Interpace proved to be more than a casual dabbler in ceramics by acquiring the Shenango China Company, of New Castle, Pennsylvania, in 1964, and Alfred Meakin, of Tunstall, England, in 1974. In April 1979, Josiah Wedgewood and son, Ltd., of Barlston, Stoke-on-Trent, England, bought Interpace's Franciscan Division. Wedgewood closed the plant five years later.

With a heritage so rich in pottery royalty, you would expect Gladdening, McBean cookie jars to be truly spectacular. Unfortunately, it appears the company restricted production to rather mundane canister type jars as additions to canister sets, and to complement lines of dinnerware.

As far as is known, all marked Gladdening, McBean cookie jars include the word, "Franciscan," as shown below. Jars that evaded marking can often be identified by comparing them to Franciscan dinnerware patterns.

This Franciscan cookie jar, or canister as the case may be, is 10-1/2 inches high. *Zera Collection.* $75

Mark of the canister jar.

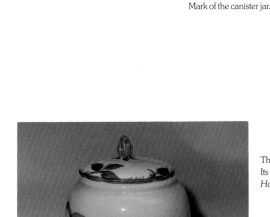

This canister jar is 11 inches high. Its mark is shown. *Courtesy of Homer and Bev Simpson.* $250

### Haeger Potteries, Inc.

The Haeger Potteries began as a brickyard in Dundee, Illinois, in 1871, the same year of the Chicago Fire. It's still in operation today.

Always stronger in artware than kitchenware or dinnerware, Haeger has made few cookie jars. Besides those shown below, it also made a 12-1/2 inch high cookie barrel with the words "Cooky Barrel" on the front, and possibly other jars.

Two of Haeger's many marks are shown below.

# HAEGER POTTERIES, INC.

The jar on the left was made by Haeger, the jar on the right by McCoy. The heights are 10-1/2 and 9-3/4 inches. The Haeger jar is unmarked, while the McCoy version is generally marked "USA/350" on two lines. The easiest way to tell them apart is by the elf, which is molded (three-dimensionally) on the Haeger jar, but is a flat decal on the McCoy jar. In *Collecting Royal Haeger*, co-author Lee Garmon cites a letter received from Haeger Potteries indicating the Haeger jar was made sometime prior to the McCoy jar, which was introduced in 1986. *Bosson Collection*. Left - $60, Right - $30

A canister jar, 9-1/2 inches high. The mark is shown. *Courtesy of Jazz'e Junque Shop, Chicago, Illinois.* $25

This jar is 11-1/2 inches high. Its mark is shown. *Oravitz Collection*. $225

## Hall China Company

The Hall China Company, of East Liverpool, Ohio, was set up in August, 1903 by Robert Hall, who died the next year. The business was than carried on by his son, Robert Taggart Hall.

Hall China Company took an unsuccessful stab at dinnerware from 1908 to 1911, long before the concept of the cookie jar was ever thought of. Hall reentered the dinnerware market in 1936, and this time latched on to the brass ring, making lines for major retailers such as Montgomery Ward and Sears, and also providing restaurant-type ware, not only for restaurants but also for railroads and, later, airlines.

During World War I, Hall became the largest maker of teapots in the world, thanks in part to a well run advertising campaign aimed at educating the public about tea and the proper method of brewing it. Had the company pursued the same course when cookie jars were beginning to gain popularity 15 years later, there's no telling what might have been possible.

# HALL CHINA COMPANY

This owl is 12-1/2 inches high and can easily be identified by its Hall backstamp. *Zera Collection*. $250

Inkstamp mark of Hall owl.

Mark of the Haeger canister jar.

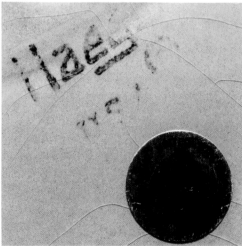

Inkstamp mark of above jar.

On the right is the autumn leaf pattern made for Jewel Tea. Both jars are 9-1/2 inches high, with marks showing. *Zera Collection*. Left - $85, Right - $150

Instead, it followed a path similar to Gladdening, McBean and Company (Franciscan), for the most part limiting cookie jar production to canister-type jars to be sold as accessories to its dinnerware and kitchen utility lines. Every so often a surprise will pop up, such as owl shown below, which Hall apparently made for itself and Carbone, Inc. a Boston distributor listed in Chapter 22. Best known of the Hall jars is the Autumn Leaf pattern, made exclusively for the Jewel Tea Company from 1933 until 1976.

Hall is still in business today.

Hall used many, many back stamps to mark its pottery. Several are shown below.

Mark of Hall autumn leaf cookie jar that was also used on other pieces in the Jewel Tea line.

Hall Flare Ware jar, 9 inches high. The mark is shown. *Zera Collection.* $85

This jar, and the other three of the same shape, are 8-1/2 inches high. The mark is shown. *Courtesy of Jazz'e Junque Shop, Chicago, Illinois.* $60

Unmarked Hall jar with geranium transfer. Probably part of a canister set, the jar stands 8-1/2 inches high. *Zera Collection.* $50

Mark of Hall Flare Ware jar.

Hall jar with poppy transfer. The height is 6-3/4 inches. The Hall backstamp is shown. *Zera Collection.* $175

Mark of the green Hall jar.

Same as the geranium jar but a solid color. This jar is also unmarked. *Zera Collection.* $50

Mark of the Hall jar with poppy transfer.

This jar is also 8-1/2 inches. The mark is very similar to that of the green jar, but is done in gold. *Courtesy of Jazz'e Junque Shop, Chicago, Illinois.* $85

157

Another jar like that above. *Courtesy of Charles Kidd.* $50

A slightly different story here. The jar is 9-1/2 inches high, poured very heavy, and is marked by a gold "Hall" stamp with a circle around it. The mark is found inside the lid. *Courtesy of Betty and Floyd Carson.* $50

## William H. Hirsch Manufacturing Company

Although manufacturing is in this company's name it was actually a sales organization, not a pottery. Aside from that little is known other than that it was active by 1946, and trade journals from that time place it in Hollywood, California. The mark shown below, however, very clearly states Los Angeles. It also shows that the company lasted until at least 1958. Hirsch is said to have made florist ware, figurines, miniatures, and other ceramic products.

While most collectors are aware of the monk cookie jar, those interviewed did not know of any other jars the company might have made.

### WILLIAM HIRSCH MANU-FACTURING COMPANY

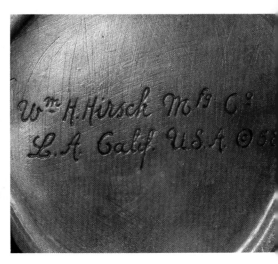

This monk is 12-1/4 inches high. It is a fairly common jar in the midwest, having shown up in several of the collections photographed. *Courtesy of Betty and Floyd Carson.* $60

Mark of the Hirsch monk. Some of these jars were marked by an inkstamp.

## Hoening of California

All that was found on Hoenig is what you see below—that it made a nice pumpkin jar, somewhat in the Art Deco style, and that the firm was apparently located in California. While the possibility exists that Hoenig might have been an importer, the inclusion of California in its name suggest a domestic pottery. Hoenig of California console sets that are seen have a definite late-1950s or early-1960s flavor.

### HOENIG OF CALIFORNIA

A Hoenig pumpkin, 7-1/2 inches high. The mark is "Hoenig/of/California/660" on four lines. *Taylor Collection.* $40

## Holiday Designs, Inc.

Holiday Designs, located in Sebring, Ohio, was established in 1964, but today functions as an arm of Designer Accents, the same parent company that bought Nelson McCoy Ceramics. Kitchen artware is its main output. Many of its products have been marketed through Sears, and other major retailers. The pottery is made in the same plant that was used by Spaulding China Company, the maker of Royal Copley, which is now just beginning to be fully appreciated by collectors.

Some Holiday Designs cookie jars are marked with its name, but many are not. However, a lot of the company's jars can be identified by an inkstamped, "22222."

### HOLIDAY DESIGNS, INC.

The owls are 12-1/4 inches high. Their marks indicate Holiday Designs. *Oravitz Collection.* $50 ea.

Due to its glaze and design, if this cat cookie jar wasn't marked one would probably tend to think it was Doranne of California. It is 12 inches high, and its mark is shown. *Courtesy of Jazz'e Junque Shop, Chicago, Illinois.* $45

A 12-inch high panda is marked "Holiday Designs/USA" on two lines on the bottom. Another example photographed was marked "Holiday Designs" on one line inside the neck of the lid. *Oravitz Collection.* $45

The little red schoolhouse is 9-1/2 inches high, with a "22222" inkstamp. *Lilly Collection.* $35

Mark of the Holiday Designs cat. The change in color resulted from a combination of the critical nature of lighting in close-up photography, and the writer's noncritical approach to it.

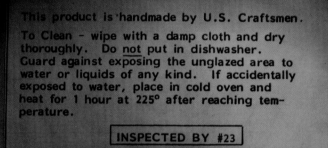

This product is handmade by U.S. Craftsmen.

To Clean – wipe with a damp cloth and dry thoroughly. Do <u>not</u> put in dishwasher. Guard against exposing the unglazed area to water or liquids of any kind. If accidentally exposed to water, place in cold oven and heat for 1 hour at 225° after reaching temperature.

INSPECTED BY #23

Refer to inspector number in correspondence.

These instructions were packaged inside the little red schoolhouse jar.

Snoopy is 12-1/4 inches high and has "22222" stamped on bottom along with "USA©Holiday Designs." *Courtesy of Betty and Floyd Carson.* $75

This jar is called a "Dawg," according to Holiday Designs. It is 12 inches high. The mark is a simple "USA" impressed in the head. However, the advertising on the original box is "4193 Dawg, Almond, ©Holiday Designs, USA, Sebring, OH, Ph 216-938-2194." *Oravitz Collection.* $40

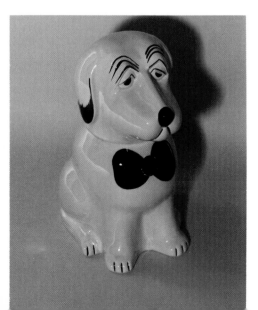

Obviously the king of beasts, this jar is 12 inches high, with "©Holiday Designs/USA" impressed on two lines and a "22222" inkstamp. *Bosson Collection.* $45

A 12-1/2 inch high pear, with a "22222" inkstamp. *Oravitz Collection.* $40

This orange is 8-1/2 inches high and has a "22222" inkstamp. *Lilly Collection.* $40

Canister, 13 inches high. The bottom of the jar is inkstamped "22222." *Lilly Collection.* $25

## House of Webster Ceramics

House of Webster cookie jars are not marketed as such, but are used as containers for gifts of honey, jam, jelly, etc. The jars are made by Eastland Ceramics, Eastland, Texas, but are filled at, and shipped from, Rogers, Arkansas. In the past, House of Webster is said to have shipped as many as 200,000 pieces of pottery per year.

One House of Webster mark is illustrated below. Another shows a similar cabin with a fence in front, a tall pine tree at each end, and a mountain in the rear, but no wording.

## HOUSE OF WEBSTER

The telephone is 8-3/4 inches high, the coffee grinder 8 inches high. Both have House of Webster inkstamps. *Courtesy of Jazz'e Junque Shop, Chicago, Illinois.* Left - $40, Right - $25

There's a real bell in the bell tower of this 8-1/2 inch high House of Webster jar. The mark is shown opposite. *Zera Collection.* $30

House of Webster mark.

An unmarked House of Webster raspberry, 6-1/2 inches high. *Zera Collection.* $25

Shock of wheat, 7-1/4 inches high, with the House of Webster inkstamp. This design is very similar to a jar made by Metlox. *Oravitz Collection.* $25

The basket of strawberries is 7-1/4 inches high and has the House of Webster backstamp. *Taylor Collection.* $15

Liberty Bell, 6 inches high, with House of Webster inkstamp. *Courtesy of Jazz'e Junque Shop, Chicago, Illinois.* $25

Unmarked House of Webster wishing well, 7 inches high. *Oravitz Collection.* $25

## Imperial Porcelain Corporation

This company was located in Zanesville, Ohio. It was established by three doctors in 1946, remained in business until 1960 when it was sold to Denzil Harding, who changed the name to Imperial Pottery. A fire claimed the plant in 1967, by which time a change in Zanesville's zoning code is said to have prevented rebuilding.

Imperial Porcelain is best known for its Paul Webb figures. These included the Al Capp "Dogpatch" series, Americana Folklore Miniatures, and the Paul Webb Mountain Boys series. They were the joint effort of artist Paul Webb, who developed Li'l Abner for Al Capp, and Imperial ceramic designer, Paul Genter. The Paul Webb characters are said to have made and broke the pottery. They were the firm's most popular pieces, but the high cost of royalties paid to Capp and Webb made them unprofitable.

The two jars shown below do not contain a recognizable Imperial mark. But one does have a Daisy Mae copyright, and both jars reek of the various Paul Webb lines. They were photographed in Zanesville at a shop whose owner is somewhat of a historian on Zanesville potteries, and for those reasons they are *assumed* to be Imperial Porcelain. It is hoped that in they future concrete evidence will surface to prove their origin one way or another.

## Judy of California

No information was found on this company. All of the jars below were copyrighted in the 1970s. Obviously from canister sets, they are often collected as cookie jars.

JUDY OF CALIFORNIA

This jar, commonly referred to as "The Bum," is 13 inches high. It is marked "USA." *Courtesy of Elvin R. and Frances (Jerry) Culp.* $500

"©Daisy Mae" is marked inside the lid of this jar. It stands 13 inches high. A collector from New Jersey sent me a picture of this same base with a plain flat lid. However, the color of the glaze on the lid did not exactly match that of the base, so I hesitate to say Imperial made a third jar until other examples surface. *Courtesy of Elvin R. and Frances (Jerry) Culp.* $600

This coffee house is 10-1/2 inches high, marked "Judy/of California/©1977 USA C841" on three lines. *Courtesy of Jazz'e Junque Shop, Chicago, Illinois.* $30

161

The bake shop is marked "Judy/of California/©1977 USA BS-4" on three lines. *Courtesy of Jazz'e Junque Shop, Chicago, Illinois.* $30

The mill is 12-1/2 inches high. The mark is the same as the bake shop. *Courtesy of Jazz'e Junque Shop, Chicago, Illinois.* $30

## Los Angeles Potteries

Started in 1940 by the owners of a company that made brass plumbing fixtures, the original intent of this Lynwood, California, firm was to make sanitary ware. Equipment limitations kept it from doing so, and forced the pottery down the path of artware and figurines.

The N.S. Gustin Company, of Los Angeles, distributed its products. According to Derwich and Latos, at least one cookie jar became a staple of Sperry & Hutchinson (S & H green stamps). As far as is known, all of Los Angeles Potteries' cookie jars were hand decorated.

In 1970 Los Angeles Potteries liquidated and sold its molds to N.S. Gustin which used them at Designcraft, a pottery it owned in West Los Angeles, California. Designcraft is still operating in West Los Angeles, but its name has been changed to Los Angeles pottery. It is now owned by David Gustin, grandson of Nelson Sage Gustin, founder of the Gustin company. The pottery makes ceramic products, including cookie jars, for the N.S. Gustin Company, of which David Gustin is vice president.

## LOS ANGELES POTTERIES

This jar is called the wedding pineapple. It is 11-1/2 inches high and marked "L.A. Potteries ©'65/89 Calif. USA" on two lines. *Courtesy of Jazz'e Junque Shop, Chicago, Illinois.* $65

The height of this little porker is 10 inches. It is marked "Los Angeles/84/Potteries/hand Decorated/Calif. USA" impressed on five lines. *Oravitz Collection.* $35

## Maddux of California

The company was established by William Maddux in Los Angeles in 1938. Louis and Dave Warsaw purchased it in 1948. Morris Bogdanow bought Dave Warsaw's share in 1956 and later bought out Louis Warsaw, too. A new plant was built in 1958, pottery was no longer made after 1974, and Maddux of California went out of business in 1980, four years after Morris Bogdanow's son, Norman, had taken over the business. Add that Maddux acquired two other potteries over the years, Hollywood Ceramics and Valley Vista Pottery, and you have its 42-year story in a nutshell.

Perhaps best known for the many flamingo figurines it made during the earlier years, Maddux isn't believed to have begun making cookie jars until the late 1950s or early 1960s. Besides the jars shown below, Maddux also did a series that included a rabbit, cat, and bear, each carrying a basket and an umbrella. The bottoms of three jars are identical, only the tops being different.

As far as is known, all Maddux cookie jars are marked.

## MADDUX OF CALIFORNIA

Tall at 15-1/4 inches, this particular Raggedy Andy is marked "USA©2108" but other examples include the Maddux name. *Zera Collection.* $200

Squirrel or chipmunk, 13 inches high, marked "Maddux of /Calif.©/Romanelli 2110" on three lines. The Romanelli is possibly for Carl Romanelli, a Los Angeles sculptor known to have worked for Metlox and, apparently, other potteries. *Oravitz Collection.* $175

Humpty Dumpty, 11 inches high. The mark is "2113/ Maddux of California/©USA" on three lines. The jar is also seen with a white collar and, sometimes, a white vest. *Oravitz Collection.* $225

## Marcia Ceramics of California

According to Derwich and Latos, this Los Angeles firm started about 1940, and was run as a family business. In the early 1980s it was being operated by Gerald and Michael Siegal, and their father, George Siegal.

## MARCIA CERAMICS OF CALIFORNIA

This bear is very much like one made by Metlox. It is 12-1/4 inches high and marked "Marcia Ceramics©84" around the base in back. *Oravitz Collection.* $45

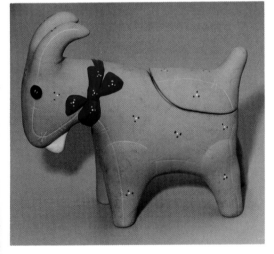

Goat, 12-1/2 inches high. The mark is "GKJ8©1987/NAC/USA" on three lines. *Zera Collection.* $25

An 8-legged reindeer, 11-1/2 inches high. The mark is "DCJ-19©1985©/NAC" on two lines. *Zera Collection.* $30

The same size and mark as the above jar, but without the lavender trim. *Courtesy of Jazz'e Junque Shop, Chicago, Illinois.* $30

The dinosaur is 8 inches high, marked "CJ-50©1986/NAC USA" on two lines. *Coughenour Collection.* $65

The black cat is 6-1/2 inches high. It is marked "DCJ 18©1985/ NAC" on two lines. *Zera Collection.* $40

163

### Maurice Ceramics of California

This company is located in Los Angeles, and is run by Maurice Peckman. It was in business by 1967, perhaps earlier.

In addition to the jars shown below, Maurice is also known to have made a large rooster, a brown sitting bear with a drum, brown sitting monkey, a brown, sitting puppy with a pink "Love me" sign, a chef head, an elephant, an Indian with a bow and arrow, and a locomotive.

One Maurice mark is shown below. A second mark is similar but incised in script.

## MAURICE CERAMICS OF CALIFORNIA

Pair of cats, 10-1/2 inches high. Westfall shows this jar in yellow. The mark is pictured below. *Courtesy of Mercedes DiRenzo.* $40

The clown is 13-1/2 inches high. Its mark is "JD 19-Maurice©California USA" on one line. Sometimes it is seen unmarked. *Oravitz Collection.* $225

Mark of the Maurice cats.

The frog is 11 inches high and marked "Maurice Ceramics/MP21" on two lines. *Bosson Collection.* $145

## MORTON POTTERIES

Morton coffee pot, 11-3/4 inches high, marked "USA-3721." *Bosson Collection.* $45

### Morton Pottery Company

The Morton Pottery Company has a long and involved history that is far too complicated to cover in a book on cookie jars.

In a paragraph, what collector's generally refer to as the Morton Pottery was incorporated in Morton, Illinois, near Peoria, on December 8, 1922. The first kiln of pottery was fired seven months later on July 7, 1923. Incorporators of the company were William Rapp, Dan W. Rapp, and J.E. Gerber. The Rapps were sons of Andrew Rapp, the oldest of six brothers who founded the Rapp Brothers Brick and Tile Company in Morton in 1877. Several other sons of Andrew Rapp were also involved in the new pottery.

The company was sold to William York and Ronald Cowan in 1969, after which it underwent several changes in name and ownership before the kilns cooled permanently in 1976. The building was razed in 1979.

Morton made utility ware, and later expanded to giftware and figurines. According to the Roerigs, it was one of the earliest players in the cookie jar game, making the hen jar with chick finial in 1930. It also made a similarly designed turkey. All known Morton jars are either unmarked, or have a non-attributing mark such as that on the coffee pot below.

Unmarked Morton hen, 8-3/4 inches high. *Zera Collection.* $80

This Morton jar is 9-3/4 inches high and unmarked. It is very heavy. *Oravitz Collection.* $110

Mosaic Tile mammy, 13-1/4 inches high, unmarked. *Zera Collection.* $375

Yellow mammy, the other most common color for Mosaic's only cookie jar. *Coughenour Collection.* $375

## Mosaic Tile Company

Mosaic Tile Company was organized in 1894 in Zanesville, Ohio, by American Encaustic Tiling Company renegades, Herman Mueller and Karl Langenbeck, and several other partners. Throughout the years it bought out several other tile companies. These acquisitions included Atlantic Tile and Manufacturing Company (Matawan, New Jersey) 1920, Carlyle Tile Company (El Segundo, California) 1937. Mosaic Tile Company was a large operation that had branch offices, sales agencies, and warehouses scattered across the country. By 1925 it employed 1250 people. The company was dissolved in 1967.

The mammy shown here is the only cookie jar Mosaic Tile is known to have made. The design of the jar was patented by Kenneth Gale in 1943 or 1944. Gale was Mosaic's director of design. He was 16 years old in 1923 when he began working in Mosaic's design department during summer vacation. He started full-time with the company upon graduating from high school. Mosaic sent him to Chicago to study art for a year, and to Europe to study for another year. Gale retired when the company closed in 1967. He died in December 1990 at age 83.

According to Roy Greene, a designer who spent 31 years with the company, and who was Gale's assistant, the mammies were made and decorated at the Mosaic plant. But they were not made as a sales item. Greene said they were given as gifts, primarily to architects. This was during World War II when the demand for tile was low and the competition among building material manufacturers was stiff, if not cutthroat. At the end of the war, production was halted, he said. How many mammies were made is not known.

It is known, however, that prototypes or limited production examples were made in at least six additional colors.

## Pacific Stoneware, Inc.

Pacific Clay Products Company, of Los Angeles, California, used a mark that included the words "Pacific Stoneware, Inc.," so it is likely that Pacific Clay made the jars illustrated below.

The company was established in Los Angeles in 1881 as a brick and tile manufacturer. It made products of red clay, another point toward attribution. In 1932 Pacific Clay switched to dinnerware and made quite a name for itself in the field. During World War II it dropped dinnerware to make radio insulators. What happened after that is uncertain, but it apparently remained in business for some years later.

Attempts to reach Pacific Stoneware and Pacific Clay Products were unsuccessful.

### PACIFIC STONEWARE

Mark on the side of the orange pig. If you look closely at the picture of the jar, you'll see the lavender also appears between the pig's feet.

This pig is 14-1/2 inches high. The Roerigs picture it with the colors reversed, green with orange trim, but the orange is very muted. Its marks are shown. *Oravitz Collection.* $50

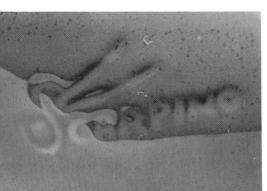

Bottom of orange pig.

Pacific Stoneware cat, 13-3/4 inches high. The mark is shown. *Zera Collection.* $70

Mark of the cat, somewhat different from that of the pig.

## Pearl China Company

Pearl China was owned by George Singer, possibly in partnership with his brother, Dennis Singer. It was located in East Liverpool, Ohio, in a plant leased from the Hall China Company. George Singer was a jobber who is said to have opened the pottery as a means of acquiring additional inventory. The company employed about 165 people during the mid-1940s, was bought by Craft Master Corporation, Toledo, Ohio, in 1958.

The only cookie jars thus far associated with Pearl China are the Cooky and Mammy shown below, a watermelon mammy in the same color, and a sitting bear. The bear appears in the light yellow glaze of the Cooky and Mammy, and also in a light blue glaze.

All known Pearl China jars are trimmed with gold.

## PEARL CHINA COMPANY

"Cooky" and "Mammy." *Left*: 10-3/4 inches high. *Right*: 10-1/2 inches. The mark of Cooky is shown below. Salt and peppers in range size and table size were made to accompany these jars. *Courtesy of Jazz'e Junque Shop, Chicago, Illinois.* Left - $500, Right - $800

Mark of Pearl China Cooky. There is also "639" impressed in another area of the bottom.

## PENNSBURY POTTERY

Red barn Pennsbury cookie jar, 8-1/2 inches high. The mark is shown. *Courtesy of Jazz'e Junque Shop, Chicago, Illinois.* $75

Reverse of Pennsbury jar.

## Pennsbury Pottery

The Pennsbury Pottery was started in Morrisville, Pennsylvania, in 1950, by husband and wife team Henry and Lee Below who were natives of Germany. Both had worked for the Stangl Pottery, of Trenton, New Jersey, directly across the Delaware River from Morrisville. Pennsbury Pottery was named for the nearby Bucks County estate of Pennsylvania founder William Penn.

The company filed for bankruptcy in 1970, two years after the death of Lee Below, and 11 years after Henry Below had passed away. An April, 1971 fire claimed the building that had housed the pottery.

In her book, *Pennsbury Pottery*, Lucille Henzke presents a Pennsbury catalog that refers to the jar shown below as the red barn cookie jar. Four others of the same shape are illustrated on the same page—"Red Rooster," "Black Rooster," "Harvest" depicting an Amish man and woman carrying a litter of vegetables, and "Hex" showing a Pennsylvania Dutch hex sign. The same designs were used on pitchers, plates, and other Pennsbury pieces.

As far as is known, all Pennsbury cookies jars are marked. In the event some did slip through unmarked, the pottery is distinctive enough that identifying them should not pose a problem.

Mark of Pennsbury jar.

## The Pfaltzfraff Company

Those whose collections include a Pfaltzgraff cookie jar have the pleasure of owning a jar made by the oldest pottery in the United States to make cookie jars. The company was founded in 1811 by German immigrant George Pfaltzgraff, whose initial efforts encompassed utilitarian redware and stoneware. Pfaltzgraff is still in business, a subsidiary of Susquehanna Pfaltzgraff Company, which is owned by the descendants of George Pfaltzgraff. Treasure Craft and Syracuse China Corporation are also subsidiaries of Susquehanna Pfaltzgraff.

The Derby Dan Muggsy jar below is an accessory for a line of mugs with names such as Sleepy Sam and Pickled Pete. Lehner dates the mugs (and presumably the cookie jar) in the 1940s, while Derwich and Latos place them in the 1950s. They probably overlapped both decades. Dates of the other jars are unknown.

Pfaltzgraff pig, 7 inches high. The mark is a "P" in a keystone. *Oravitz Collection.* $60

## PFALTZGRAFF POTTERY COMPANY

Here's old "Derby Dan," 8-1/2 inches high. The mark is "Derby Dan/Muggsie/the Pfaltzgraff Pottery Co./York, Penn/Designed by Jessop" on five lines. *Zera Collection.* $200

This locomotive is 9 inches high and marked "USA." The Roerigs show it unmarked with a white body, the Derby Dan colors for trim, and a face painted on the front. *Oravitz Collection.* $150

The clock is unmarked, 10 inches high. *Zera Collection.* $150

## Purinton Pottery Company

On the same day that the Japanese air force destroyed our navy at Pearl Harbor—December 7, 1941—the Purinton Pottery Company, of Shippenville, Pennsylvania, fired its first kiln load of ceramics.

The company was named for its president and principal investor, Bernard S. Purinton, of Wellsville, Ohio. It remained in business until 1960. Most of the company's products, including cookie jars, were slip decorated. Dark red, close to but not quite burgundy, was a predominate color at Purinton Pottery. Many Purinton pieces are unmarked.

For those who would like a more detailed view of the Purinton Pottery Company and its products, *Purinton Pottery,* by Jamie Bero-Johnson and Jamie Johnson (Schiffer) is an excellent source.

Unmarked Purinton Humpty Dumpty, 11 inches high. This is a heavy jar. *Coughenour Collection.* $350

Purinton Howdy Doody, 9-3/4 inches high and unmarked. *Courtesy of Jazz'e Junque Shop, Chicago, Illinois.* $550

Canister type cookie jar, 10 inches high, unmarked. *Zera Collection.* $90

## PURINTON POTTERY COMPANY

Same as the jar previously but 9-3/4 inches high. *Oravitz Collection*. $100

Unmarked apple, 9 inches high. It is believed to be Purinton because of the color and the brush strokes in the apple. *Zera Collection*. $100

### Roman Ceramics

Roman Ceramics was located in Mayfield, Kentucky, a city about 25 miles south of Paducah in the western part of the state. It was owned by Harold Roman, who also owned California Originals beginning in 1979. Production at Roman Ceramics is said to have started prior to World War II. It ended in 1982.

Roman Ceramics referred to its line as Cumberland Ware, which accounts for its mark, a "C" through a "W," as shown below. In addition to the two jars illustrated, the company is known to have made a mouse sailor jar, monk, koala, and head jars of W.C. Fields, Stan Laurel, and Oliver Hardy.

## ROMAN CERAMICS

Smokey the Bear, 13-3/4 inches high. The mark is shown. *Oravitz Collection*. $100

R2-D2 from the Star Wars movie series. When photographed this jar had a white plastic liner. It fit perfectly, and prevented cookies from falling down into R2-D2's feet where they would have been accessible only by turning the jar upside down and letting them fall out. The height is 12-1/2 inches and the mark is shown. *Zera Collection*. $175

Mark of R2-D2. Marks such as this show only the year of the copyright, which is often different than the year the jar was manufactured.

Mark of Smokey the Bear.

Smokey with blue bow tie and red buttons. *Bosson Collection*. $100

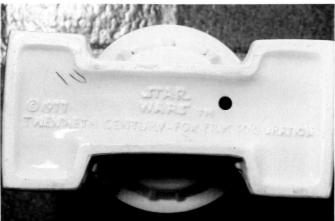

## Roseville Pottery, Inc.

For 56 of its 64 years in business, Roseville Pottery's name was a misnomer. The company made a permanent move to Zanesville, Ohio, in 1898, eight years after being founded in Roseville, about 15 miles to the south. The original name was Roseville Pottery Company, which was changed to Roseville Pottery, Inc. in the early 1930s.

Breaking the stereotypical image many have of 1890s businessmen and business practices—gray hair and mustache, wire-rimmed glasses, scowl, stogie, and a conservative approach—the company hired George Frank Young in 1891, at the tender age of 27, to serve as secretary and general manager. Young guided Roseville on a path that eventually led to it being recognized as one of the foremost art potteries in the United States. Along the way, he bought up shares of stock until he owned the company outright.

The flowered cookie jars shown below were made in the 1940s. Note that the jars comprise four different shapes, the handles being the most variable feature. Sharon and Bob Huxford, in *The Collector's Encyclopedia of Roseville Pottery*, show another shape, known as No. 5. It's a slightly more rounded form, with handles to match; the line is Zephyr Lilly.

Most Roseville cookie jars are marked. A couple examples of Roseville's many marks are shown below.

## ROSEVILLE

Two more "Clematis" colors. Same size and similar mark to others on page. *Zera Collection.* $300 ea.

Two Magnolia jars. Both are 10-1/2 inches high. The blue jar has same mark as the rust Water Lily; the green jar's mark is the same as the Freesia cookie jar but with the numbers "2.8." *Zera Collection.* $300 ea.

Roseville "Clematis" cookie jar, 10-1/2 inches high. Mark is shown. *Zera Collection.* $300

Roseville "Freesia" cookie jar, 10-1/2 inches high. Same mark as above but the number is "4.8." *Zera Collection.* $300

Rust with "Water Lily," same mark but the number is "1.8." *Zera Collection.* $350

This is from Roseville's "Glossy Utility" line from the 1950s. It is 10 inches high, and the mark is shown. Jar was also made in green and possibly other colors. *Zera Collection.* $65

Mark of blue "Glossy Utility" cookie jar.

Mark of Roseville "Clematis" jar.

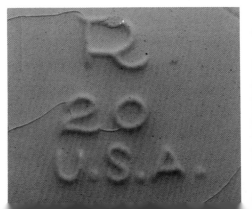

## San Jose Potteries

This pottery was located in San Antonio, Texas. It is known to have been in business by 1945, perhaps earlier. San Jose Potteries was owned by James M.A. Cassel, who was manager of a New York firm called Michaelian and Kohlberg, Inc., which was listed in trade journals as operator of the pottery. In all probability, Michaelian and Kohlberg was a distributor that decided to open a pottery, or buy an already existing one, in order to have more control over its product lines. San Jose made dinnerware, art pottery, and decorative accessories.

The two cookie jars shown below are the only ones known to date that were made by San Jose. Both are marked, "Pan American Art." San Jose is known to have used a paper label with its name on it, possibly an incised mark with its name on it, too, so it wouldn't be surprising if a jar marked San Jose showed up in the future.

Another jar by San Jose is shown on page 154.

### SAN JOSE POTTERIES

Clown, 11-1/4 inches high. Marked "Pan-American/Art" impressed on two lines. *Zera Collection.* $50

Often called "Southern Belle," this jar is 11-1/2 inches high. The mark is shown. *Courtesy of Jazz'e Junque Shop, Chicago, Illinois.* $50

Mark of "Southern Belle." Somewhat light, the mark "©Pan-American/Art" appears on two lines.

"Southern Belle" in lighter bisque, 11-1/2 inches high. "Pan-American/Art" incised on two lines. *Zera Collection.* $50

## Sierra Vista Ceramics

By most accounts, Sierra Vista Ceramics was founded in Sierra Vista, California, in 1942 by the father and son team of Reinhold and Leonard R. Lenaburg. Also, by most accounts, the elder partner retired in 1951, where upon the younger partner moved the company to Phoenix, Arizona, where it is assumed to have died a natural death some years later.

Generally left unexplained is the many Sierra Vista cookie jars marked "*Pasadena*, California," that show copyright dates as late as 1958. A recent article in *Crazed Over Cookie Jars*, however, stated Walter Starnes bought some of Sierra Vista's molds in 1952 and used them through at least part of 1954. Lending credibility to this statement is that Sierra Vista jars are often found carrying Starnes paper labels. But it still doesn't account for the later dates.

Sierra Vista is said to have relied on California clays to produce the cookie jars, lazy Susans, and other utility pieces and giftware for which it was known. The company made its own glazes but not always its own molds. Because it sometimes purchased molds from established mold companies, the possibility remains open that you may occasionally encounter homemade jars that are normally credited to Sierra Vista.

The cookie jar is 11 inches high, the bank 5-1/2 inches. The jar is marked "Sierra Vista/California" impressed on two lines. Westfall shows this jar with an earth-tone brown finish similar to Twin Winton or DeForest of California. *Blumenfeld Collection.* Left - $100, Right - $45

### SIERRA VISTA POTTERY

The locomotive is 9-3/4 inches high. The smoke is the handle of the lid. The mark is "Sierra Vista/California" impressed on two lines. *Oravitz Collection.* $100

The locomotive is only 9-1/2 inches high here and a has different mark, too, "California/SC" impressed on two lines. *Bosson Collection*. Value not determined.

Sierra Vista owl with Starnes paper label. The height is 10-1/2 inches and the mark is shown. *Oravitz Collection*. $70

Humpty Dumpty, 11-3/4 inches high. Impressed mark is "Sierra Vista/Ceramics/Pasadena Calif." on three lines. *Bosson Collection*. $300

The rooster is 12 inches high and marked with an impressed "Sierra Vista/California" on two lines, plus a Starnes paper label. Was also made in earth-tone brown. *Taylor Collection*. $80

Mark of Sierra Vista owl.

The 10-1/2 inch high squirrel is marked "Sierra Vista/Ceramics/Pasadena Calif." on three lines. *Bosson Collection*. $140

"Tuggle" is 9-1/4 inches high, marked "Sierra Vista/California" impressed on two lines, and also carries the remnant of a Starnes paper label. *Oravitz Collection*. $120

Close-up of Starnes paper label on Sierra Vista rooster.

Same jar, same size, but no mark or paper label. The smokestack and mouth may have been remodeled. *Bosson Collection*. $120

Great cookie house, 8-1/2 inches high. Impressed mark is "Sierra Vista/Ceramics/Pasadena Calif./©1958 USA" on four lines. *Courtesy of Betty and Floyd Carson*. $95

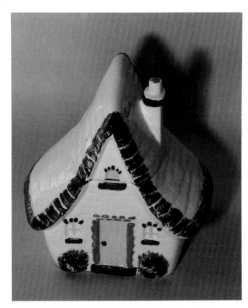

House, 9 inches high, with "Sierra Vista/©53/California" impressed on three lines. *Bosson Collection.* $80

The telephone is 11-1/2 inches high. It is marked "Sierra Vista/Ceramics/Pasadena, Calif." impressed on three lines. *Courtesy of Jazz'e Junque Shop, Chicago, Illinois.* $90

This telephone cookie jar is 11-1/2 inches high, just as the other one, but has different decoration and is also unmarked. The bank is 5-3/4 inches high. Note the three bars under the cookie jar. These are often a sign of a jar being made by Sierra Vista and also appear on the unmarked "Tuggle" boat on the previous page. *Bosson Collection.* Left - $90, Right - $50

### Southeast Minnesota Pottery

In the fall of 1986, Kellogg, Minnesota, residents Peter and Debbie Preussner decided they needed a change. After 20 years on the job, Peter had had enough of tool and die making, and Debbie wanted something more challenging than sending the kids off to school each morning and waiting for them to return in the afternoon. So, with no background, experience or training, the couple bought a ceramics business and set about making flower containers to wholesale within the Minneapolis-St. Paul metropolitan area, about 100 miles north of Kellogg.

The Indian head shown below is the only cookie jar they've made. It is from an old mold Peter Preussner purchased after discovering it in the basement of a ceramics shop that was going out of business. The mold is not marked, so at this time it is not known which mold company made it. The Preussners did not used the Indian mold, or any of several thousand they acquired with their business, until they opened a storefront for retail sales in 1989. At that time only four of the jars were poured, after which they were decorated by Patricia Wiech, an artistically inclined former employee. Debbie Preussner said none of the Indian heads are identical due to being hand decorated.

After the publication of this book in 1991 the Preussners made more jars for collectors who requested them.

### Stanford Pottery, Inc.

Located in Sebring, Ohio, this pottery was founded by George Stanford, Sr., George Stanford, Jr., and two other partners in 1945. The Stanfords were also involved in the founding of the Spaulding China Company, in Sebring, in 1939, and the Pilgrim Pottery Company, of Fredericksburg, Ohio, in 1949.

Stanford Pottery is said to have employed about 150 people. It was another of many companies that made products for National Silver Company. The plant was destroyed in a fire in January 1961, but the company remained in business for several years as a selling agency.

As far as is known, the corn cookie jar shown below is the only one Stanford made that can be identified. It may have made others under the names of distributors.

## STANFORD POTTERY

Standford Pottery ear of corn cookie jar, 10 inches high. The mark is shown. Note the leaf closely resembles the letter C. Cookies? *Zera Collection.* $85

## SOUTHEAST MINNESOTA POTTERY

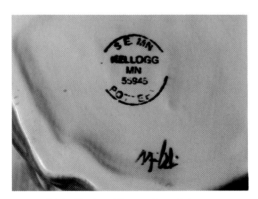

Mark of Southeast Minnesota Pottery Indian.

The Indian head is 10 1/4 inches high. The mark is shown. *Blumenfeld Collection.* $150

Mark of Stanford corn jar.

172

## Starnes

Starnes was listed in trade journals as a pottery in the early 1950s. It was located in Los Angeles. Not much more is known about it, except that it bought some molds from Sierra Vista. Jars marked Sierra Vista often have Starnes paper labels.

STARNES

Starnes paper label on ABC bear.

Rag doll, 11 inches high. There is no mark, but it has the Starnes paper label on front. *Oravitz Collection.* $150

This 11-3/4 inch high bear raises some questions. The only mark is the Starnes paper label shown on this page. The Roerigs show the same jar as Marsh (a Los Angeles pottery) and give a catalog number and a date, 1967. The brown glaze is exactly the same as that on Sierra Vista's owl. What could have been the link between the three companies? *Courtesy of Betty and Floyd Carson.* $250

TRIANGLE STUDIOS
(VALLONA STARR)

## Triangle Studios (Vallona Starr)

Trade journals show Triangle located in Los Angeles in 1945 and 1948, El Monte, California, in 1949, a name change to Vallona Starr Ceramics in 1951, and no listing after 1953. Owners of the company in 1945 were Valeria de Marsa and Everett S. Frost. Besides cookie jars, they are said to have made salt and pepper shakers, sugars and creamers, bowls, boxes and vases.

For more extensive information, *Vallona Starr Ceramics,* by Bernice Stamper (Schiffer 1995) is recommended.

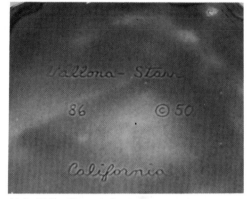

Mark of Vallona Starr squirrel on stump.

Vallona Starr squirrel on stump. The mark is shown. *Courtesy of Jazz'e Junque Shop, Chicago, Illinois.* $50

## Weller Pottery

Samuel A. Weller began throwing pots in a one-room log cabin in Fultonham, Ohio, in 1872, graduated to a small pottery in Zanesville in 1882. By the early 1900s he had one of the largest ceramics operations in the country. The Essex Wire Company of Detroit, Michigan, purchased the pottery in 1947, shut it down one year later.

While Weller was one of the most important 20th Century potteries in the United States, it's forte was art pottery for rooms other than the kitchen. Consequently, its impact on cookie jar collecting is minimal, other than it's mammy with watermelon jar, which is highly prized and commands a premium price.

WELLER

Mark of Weller Pierre cookie jar.

This basketweave cookie jar is from the Weller Pierre line, a product of the mid-1930s. It is 10 inches high, was also made in blue green. The mark is shown. *Zera Collection.* $110

"Watermelon Mammy" from Weller's Decorated Novelty Utility line. The jar is 11 inches high. The line included a teapot and syrup, each with the mammy on top, a batter bowl, and creamer and sugar. The bowl, creamer, and sugar have black children for handles: two on the sugar and one each on the bowl and creamer. The pieces were introduced in 1935. The mark is shown. *Bosson Collection.* $3800

## Western Stoneware Company

Many collectors refer to this company as the Monmouth Pottery because in many cases its familiar maple leaf mark says "Monmouth," the city in Illinois were the pottery was located. There was a Monmouth Pottery Company in Monmouth at one time, but in 1906 it merged with six other potteries to form the Western Stoneware Company. Western Stoneware went out of business in 1985.

The company is probably best remembered as the last producer of the now popular and expensive Old Sleepy Eye pottery. Primarily blue and white, Old Sleepy Eye depicted a Sioux Indian chief, and was made as premiums for the Sleepy Eye Milling Company, of Sleepy Eye, Minnesota.

As you can see below, "Stoneware" belonged in the firm's name, that being the type of ceramic in which it specialized. The clay the pottery used was mined near Colchester, Illinois, a small town about 30 miles south of Monmouth, which in turn is an equal distance south of the Davenport-Moline area. Western Stoneware made stoneware for Marshall Burns, a Chicago distributor. These pieces were marked Mar-Crest. While Western Stoneware used many different marks, all that are known, aside from Marcrest, incorporate the word "Monmouth," or the name of the company.

Mark of Weller "Watermelon Mammy."

Stoneware crock by Western Stoneware. The jar is 8-1/2 inches high. The mark is shown. *Courtesy of Homer and Bev Simpson.* $30

Monmouth mark of Western Stoneware crock cookie jar.

Lenell advertising jar, 9-1/4 inches high, with Monmouth mark. *Courtesy of Jazz'e Junque Shop, Chicago, Illinois.* $45

Bean pot, 8 inches high. The mark is shown. *Courtesy of Jazz'e Junque Shop, Chicago, Illinois.* $20

Mark of the bean pot. Note that the wording is different.

# Section V: Cookie Jar Handlers

This section presents American and foreign cookie jars that have been identified not by the companies that made them, but by the American firms that handled them at one point or another along the road from manufacturer to consumer. These firms include decorators, distributors, importers, and consumer outlets.

Foreign cookie jars that have been identified only by country of origin appear in Section VIII. American jars that have not been traced to a specific company, along with foreign jars that have not been positively identified by country, are shown in Section IX.

# Chapter 22
## *Decorators, Distributors, Importers and Retailers*

Decorating companies buy bisque cookie jars from potteries, then apply either glaze, paint or transfer decorations, or a combination of those techniques, before passing the jars on to distributors, or selling them through their own marketing departments. An example of a decorating firm would be the Harper J. Ransburg Company, of Indianapolis, Indiana, which was well known for its crock cookie jars. Ransburg acted as its own distributor.

Distributors sell cookie jars produced by other companies, sometimes obtaining their items from potteries, sometimes from decorators. While it was common for many potteries to market their jars through distributors, the jars shown here are only those that don't include the name of the manufacturer. Cardinal China Company, which bought cookie jars made by American Bisque but had them marked with the Cardinal name, is an example of a distributor.

Until the late 1940s, most pottery distributors specialized in American wares. Since the end of World War II, however, nearly all distributing firms have become mainly importers due to the large amount of ceramics generated form overseas.

Importers obtain their cookie jars in three ways, by contracting with overseas potteries, by contracting with foreign exporters (often owned by the same parent company as the importing firm), or by setting up their own potteries in foreign countries where labor costs are usually more attractive than at home. Some importing companies—Fitz & Floyd and Lefton to name two—offer only the highest quality wares, while others settle for merchandise that would be hard to categorize as anything but second class.

Sometimes retail chains contract with potteries to buy cookie jars, eliminating the markup charged by a distributor. The cookie jars may be marked with the name of the retailer, as in the case of the Sears strawberry, or with the name of a line the retailer has registered, such as Grantcrest, which was sold exclusively by the W.T. Grant Company.

### Accents Unlimited
If you have a jar marked Accents Unlimited, you have something rather unusual—a cookie jar made of plaster. The company makes molded plaster objects, sells them in kit form for people to decorate at home. Accents Unlimited is based in Milwaukee, Wisconsin. It was founded in 1970. According to a company spokeswoman, in recent years the firm has shown a preference toward working with items that are quite a bit smaller than cookie jars.

Owl cookie jar, 11-1/2 inches high. The marks are "Accents/Unlimited, Inc./1976" impressed on three lines inside the jar, "2131" impressed at base, and "L. Cross" incised on side. *Oravitz Collection.* $20

## Arcadia Export-Import Corporation

Very little is known about Arcadia and it probably wouldn't even deserve a mention except for one thing. The Shenango China Company, of New Castle, Pennsylvania, and Jackson China, Inc. of Falls Creek, Pennsylvania, made products for it, presumably for export. But since import companies act as their own distributors, it's possible some of the American-made items may have been sold here.

Arcadia is known to have been in business during the 1950s. The only known mark that implies its location includes the words "Newark" and "New York," in that order. There is a Newark, New York, just north of the finger lakes about halfway between Rochester and Syracuse. Whether the mark stands for this city, or whether it means the company had offices in Newark, New Jersey and New York City, has not been determined.

## ARCADIA EXPORT-IMPORT CORPORATION

German garden scene, 8-1/2 inches high. The mark is "Arcadia/C-6672" on two lines. *Zera Collection.* $35

## George Borgfeldt Corporation

Borgfeldt was a long time New York importer and distributor that, according to Lehner, was in business prior to 1891. The date makes sense because Borgfeldt is well known among collectors of Limoges porcelain for marketing decorative Limoges plates under the name Coronet, during the American china painting fad of the late Victorian era. The company remained in business into the 1950s, possibly longer.

The mark of "Thumper" was lightly impressed on a light colored surface, so it will be explained in addition to being shown. It basically looks like a spoked wheel complete with a tire. A seven-point crown emerges from the top of the tire. Around the bottom of the tire is the word "Celebrate." Over the crown is "Reg. U.S. Pat. Off.," Below the tire is "Made in U.S.A." All of the words in the mark are written in block letters.

## GEORGE BORGFELDT CORPORATION

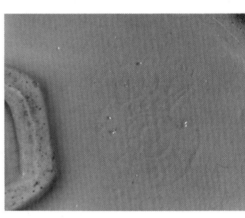

Mark of Thumper.

Often called "Thumper" but never displaying a Disney copyright, this jar is 11-3/4 inches high. Mark is shown. *Zera Collection.* $75

## Avon Products, Inc.

Avon Products, originally called the California Perfume Company, was founded in New York by David Hall McConnell about 1886. The name was changed to Avon Products, Inc. on October 6, 1939.

On occasion the company has used cookie jars as sales awards for its representatives.

## AVON PRODUCTS, INC.

Mark of Avon bear.

Avon bear cookie jar, 10-1/2 inches high. Mark is shown. *Oravitz Collection.* $40

Avon house canisters. *Left:* 6-1/2 inches high. *Right:* 9-3/4 inches high. Mark is shown. *Bosson Collection.* Left - $60, Right - $80

Mark of Avon canisters.

## Brush Art

Apparently a decorating company, nothing was found on Brush Art. The crock jar shown below is Red Wing bisque, identified by Delores Simon in *Red Wing Pottery with Rumrill*.

BRUSH ART

Brush Art crock cookie jar, 8-1/2 inches high. The Brush Art signature appears above the grape vine on the right side above the handle. *Zera Collection.* $75

Brush Art signature.

## Cardinal China Company

The Cardinal China Company was formed in 1946 in Carteret, New Jersey, a suburb of Newark. Early on it manufactured its own pottery but somewhere along the line, presumably quite early, switched to being a distributor.

During the late 1950s Cardinal marketed cookie jars made and decorated by American Bisque, which explains why the bottoms of Cardinal jars have the wedges that are usually found on American Bisque jars.

Still in business, the firm's name has been changed to Cardinal, Inc. During the late 1980s its offices were moved a few miles away to Port Reading, New Jersey. Today Cardinal functions as an importer and distributor.

CARDINAL CHINA COMPANY

Cardinal soldier, 12-3/4 inches high. Most are marked, but this one isn't. *Bosson Collection.* $225

This jar is 9-1/2 inches high. The mark on back is "©Cardinal/USA" impressed on two lines. In the shadow at the left of the cap is "For Smart Cookies." *Zera Collection.* $90

## Carbone, Inc.

Look in Chapter 21 under Hall China Company, and you'll find a white owl identical to the one shown below. That's because Hall was one of several American potteries that made products for this Boston, Massachusetts, distributor. Two others were Taylor, Smith, and Taylor, and Zanesville Stoneware Company.

Exact dates for Carbone aren't known, but suffice it to say it was around a long time. It registered a trademark (Castelli) in 1926, claiming use since 1920. At that time the company is believed to have been strictly a distributor of American pottery. By 1967 it was calling itself an importer in the trade journals. It was listed in *Trade Names Directory* as late as 1982, showing a Norwood, Massachusetts, address, but attempts to contact it there in 1991 were not successful.

CARBONE, INC.

Each of the owls is 12-1/2 inches high. Mark is shown. *Oravitz Collection.* $200 ea.

Mark of Carbone owls.

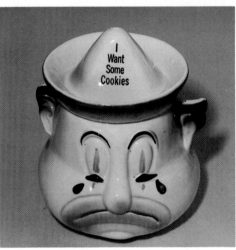

This Cardinal cookie bag is 10 inches high. It is marked "USA/#4200" on two lines. *Zera Collection.* $65

The cookie jar is 8 inches high, but the height of the jam jar was not recorded. The mark of the cookie jar is shown below. *Blumenfeld Collection.* Left - $90, Right - $40

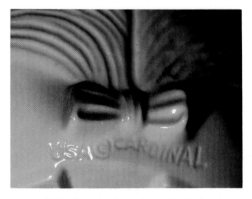

Mark of the smiling boy cookie jar. Note the American Bisque wedges.

Sad clown, 9-1/2 inches high, marked "©Cardinal/USA" on two lines. *Zera Collection.* $100

Cookie safe, 10-1/2 inches high, marked "Cardinal 309©USA" on one line. *Oravitz Collection.* $80

French chef, 9 inches high. The mark is "©Cardinal/USA" on two lines. *Zera Collection.* $130

Telephone, 11-1/2 inches high. The mark is "Cardinal©/311/USA" on three lines. *Zera Collection.* $75

Cookie garage, 6-1/2 inches high, unmarked. *Bosson Collection.* $120

The pig is 7-1/2 inches high. It is not marked. *Zera Collection.* $75

Cardinal cookie castle, 11-1/2 inches high. The mark is "Cardinal/301©USA" on two lines. Cardinal's numbering system was apparently inconsistent. On this jar the number is 301. The Roerigs show it as 307, Westfall 3100. *Oravitz Collection.* $150

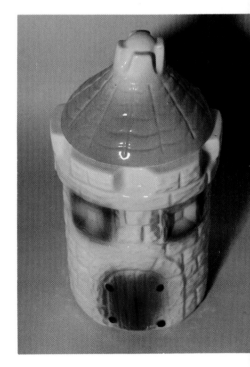

## China and Glass Distributors

This is the New York distributor that sold cookie jars marked "Pantry Parade," the example shown below being the only shape currently known. The Stanford Pottery, of Sebring, Ohio, did some contract work for China and Glass Distributors around 1949, but it has not been established whether or not it made cookie jars for them. Another well known line of China and Glass Distributors was Charm House.

## CHINA AND GLASS DISTRIBUTORS

Pantry Parade tomatoes, 8-1/4 inches high. The mark is shown below. *Zera Collection.* $35 ea.

Same tomato but unmarked. *Bosson Collection.* $35

Another unmarked tomato, 8-1/2 inches high. *Zera Collection.* $35

Mark of red Pantry Parade tomato.

## Dayton Hudson Corporation

This corporation resulted from the 1969 merger of the J.L. Hudson Company, a Michigan retail chain, and The Dayton Corporation, a similar chain based in Minnesota. The company is headquartered in Minneapolis. In June, 1990 it acquired Marshall Field's the Chicago-based retailer. With that acquisition, Dayton Hudson now has 61 stores in 11 states. (Marshall Field's is treated separately later in this chapter.)

The Hudson stores were started by Joseph Lowthian Hudson in Detroit in 1881. George D. Dayton opened his first store in Minneapolis in 1902.

Although the cookie jars below have marks showing "Dayton Hudson," the stores have retained their own names. People in Michigan, Indiana and Ohio shop at Hudson's, while folks in Minnesota, North Dakota, South Dakota and Wisconsin patronize Dayton's.

Due to these stores having a limited geographical area, there may be a tendency on the part of collectors outside the upper midwest to consider Dayton Hudson cookie jars rare finds, but that's not the case.

## DAYTON HUDSON CORPORATION

B.W.Bear is 11-1/2 inches high. Its mark is shown. *Zera Collection.* $45

The dog is 10-1/4 inches high. Mark is "©1986 Dayton Hudson" on one line. *Oravitz Collection.* $40

Mark of B.W. Bear. A tad light, it reads "B.W.Bear/©1986/Dayton Hudson" on three lines. Paper label indicates the jar was made in Taiwan.

## Demand Marketing

Though this is obviously a marketing firm based in Henderson, Kentucky, attempts to reach the company have not been successful. It is believed to have been in business during the 1970s. As the pictures show, it sold very nice Sesame Street jars.

DEMAND MARKETING

Mark of Oscar.

Oscar the Grouch, 12-3/4 inches high. The mark is shown. *Courtesy of Jazz'e Junque Shop, Chicago, Illinois.* $60

Big Bird is 13-1/2 inches high. This one is not marked, but the Roerigs found it with the same mark as the one to the left. *Courtesy of Jazz'e Junque Shop, Chicago, Illinois.* $60

## Dept. 56

Dept. 56 is an importer and distributor located in Eden Prairie, Minnesota, in the Minneapolis-St. Paul metropolitan area. The firm has been in business since the mid-1970s. It handles giftware in all price ranges, and imports from many different countries. The majority of its merchandise relates to Christmas. According to a company spokesman, Dept. 56 acquired its unusual name, "Because it was the next number in the computer."

Dept. 56 has handled many cookie jars over the years, but never as single items. The company deals strictly in groupings of coordinated accessories. The chef head jar below is from a line called "Le Chef," which included a garlic jar, potholders, and other coordinated kitchen items. The other jar, "Peasant People," was accompanied by things such as matching vases and serving bowls.

Most of Dept. 56's giftware is designed by an in-house staff of artists, but it also works with freelancers.

DEPT. 56

Dept. 56 peasant woman cookie jar, 12 inches high. The mark is shown. *Oravitz Collection.* $90

Mark of the peasant woman.

Paper labels on Le Chef cookie jar.

"Le Chef" head jar, 10 inches high. Impressed mark is "Le Chef Cuisine/©Dept. 56" on two lines. Paper labels are shown. *Blumenfeld Collection.* $110

180

# ENESCO

ENESCO is an import company headquartered in Elk Grove, Illinois, a Chicago suburb. To say it handles a lot of giftware would be an understatement, the Elk Grove complex consisting of 455,000 square feet of warehouse space, and another 33,000 square feet of office space. Additionally, it has showrooms in 12 major cities. ENESCO designs the products it markets.

The company was formed in 1959 as an import division of the N. Shure Company, the acronym being derived from that name (N.S. Co.). As with many import companies of that era, its early merchandise did not draw rave reviews. In recent years its lines have been upgraded, and now it markets much higher quality pieces, often unique such as the Mickey Mouse jar with leatherette ears and the penguin with textile cap and scarf.

All known ENESCO paper labels bear the company name.

ENESCO

Garfield, 8-3/4 inches high. Paper and cellophane labels are shown. *Zera Collection.* $125

Garfield labels.

Mark of ENESCO house.

The cat jar is 11-3/4 inches high. Its cellophane label is shown. *Courtesy of Jazz'e Junque Shop, Chicago, Illinois.* $30

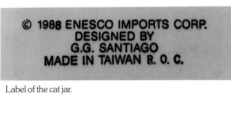

Label of the cat jar.

This jar, unmarked and 9-3/4 inches high, has been repainted. Originally the main body of the jar was red, feet and bells were gold. The Roerigs show it with an ENESCO paper label. Unusual jar in that it has a glass bezel. *Zera Collection.* $300

Back of repainted Mickey Mouse clock.

The house is 7-3/4 inches high. Its marks are shown. *Courtesy of Jazz'e Junque Shop, Chicago, Illinois.* $40

Mickey Mouse with leatherette ears. The mark is "©Walt Disney Productions." The jar has an ENESCO paper label. *Blumenfeld Collection.* $300

181

These jars are commonly called "Prunella the Pig" and "Pomeroy the Pig." Prunella is 11-1/4 inches high, while Pomeroy is 10-1/2 inches high. Both have the "Styled by/Lorraine Elam" mark shown below, and Pomeroy has an ENESCO paper label. *Oravitz Collection.* $45 ea.

Betsy Ross, 9 inches high, unmarked, but shown by the Roerigs with ENESCO label. *Courtesy of Jazz'e Junque Shop, Chicago, Illinois.* $200

Penguin with textile scarf and cap believed to be original. The jar is 11 inches high, ENESCO paper label. *Bosson Collection.* $40

Designer's mark on Prunella and Pomeroy.

### Ethan Allen, Inc.

Ethan Allen is a furniture company headquartered in Danbury, Connecticut. Besides producing what is generally acknowledged as the finest furniture made in America today, it also sells decorative accessories. Several calls to the corporate offices resulted in very little information, other than that the company was founded in 1936 by Ted B. Ancell.

It was apparently named for the Revolutionary War figure, Ethan Allen, who with his Green Mountain Boys captured Fort Ticonderoga on May 10, 1775, shortly after the start of the war. Allen is featured on the company's logo.

The age of the cookie jar shown below is not known, other than that it was purchased several years prior to Ethan Allen's 1991 television advertising campaign that spotlighted accessories.

ETHAN ALLEN, INC.

### Fitz and Floyd

Fitz and Floyd is a ceramics importing company in Dallas, Texas. It was started by Pat Fitzpatrick and Bob Floyd in the late 1950s. Although its cookie jars are made by Pacific-Asian potteries, Fitz and Floyd supplies its own designs. On the quality scale, Fitz and Floyd cookie jars ride far above the vast majority of imports.

Marks of the company are shown below.

FITZ AND FLOYD

Fitz and Floyd's "Rio Rita," 10-3/4 inches high. The mark is shown. *Courtesy of Jazz'e Junque Shop, Chicago, Illinois.* $100

Bottom of Rio Rita, with a warning about cleaning.

Marks of Ethan Allen beehive jar.

Somewhat unsettling perhaps, but nicely modeled with excellent mold detail. The jar is 11 inches high, with marks showing. *Zera Collection.* $50

182

Nicely painted granny, but the bonnet makes her head look too small. The jar is 11-1/2 inches high. The mark is shown. *Courtesy of Jazz'e Junque Shop, Chicago, Illinois.* $70

Raccoon, 9-3/4 inches high. The mark is shown. *Oravitz Collection.* $90

Marks of Fitz and Floyd Santa.

The mark of the Fitz and Floyd granny.

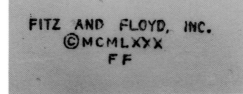

Inkstamp mark of the raccoon.

This jar is 10 inches high. Its mark is "©FF" impressed, with a Fitz and Floyd paper label. *Courtesy of Jazz'e Junque Shop, Chicago, Illinois.* $95

The elephant is 10-1/2 inches high. Its mark is "Fitz & Floyd Inc./©MCMLXXVI/FF" on three lines. *Oravitz Collection.* $110

This jar is 9-1/2 x 16 inches. Santa and his deer are removable, so if you see one on which they're missing, it is not necessarily a different jar. It isn't, however, worth as much. The marks are shown. *Courtesy of Jazz'e Junque Shop, Chicago, Illinois.* $450

## Grantcrest

Grantcrest is a mark that was used by the W.T. Grant Company prior to its sale to Ames Department Stores in 1985. The mark was stamped on china produced for Grant by domestic potteries such as the Salem China Company, of Salem, Ohio, and, as shown below, by foreign potteries also.

William Thomas Grant was born in 1876, opened his first "25-cent store" in 1906 at a Y.M.C.A. in Lynn, Massachusetts. The premise was to adhere to a 25-cent cap on all merchandise,

which cut about halfway between the 5-and-10 cent stores of F.W. Woolworth, and the nominal 50-cent minimum common to department stores of that era. The ceiling was raised to $1 following World War I, and was discontinued in 1940. By the time Grant died in 1972 at the age of 96, his chain had multiplied to 1190 outlets covering 43 states, and generating annual sales of $1.5-billion.

Mark of the cat jar.

Both of these biscuit jars are assumed to be Grantcrest, but only one, the cat, is so marked. The dog has a Japan inkstamp. Perhaps it was originally marked with a paper label. The height of the dog is 8 inches, and the height of the cat is 7-1/2 inches. Neither measurement includes the handle. The mark of the cat is shown. *Oravitz Collection.* $35 ea.

### Great American Housewares

The only currently known information about this company is that shown on its mark, that it was located in New York. Directory Assistance could not find it listed. The jar shown is fairly recent; perhaps the company merged with another, or is operating under a different name.

### Green Products

No information was found about Green Products, but several aspects of the two jars below may be more than coincidental.

Before it was broken up and sold in pieces during the 1980s, Durkee Famous Foods, Inc. was located in Cleveland, the same city where Green Products was located. According to old trade journals, at one point Durkee sold a margarine called Kook-E-Special Margarine. While there is no explanation for the difference in spelling, both jars could easily be related to using margarine, so maybe there's a connection.

GREAT AMERICAN HOUSEWARES

GREEN PRODUCTS

Transformers jar, 8-1/2 inches high. The mark is shown. *Courtesy of Betty and Floyd Carson.* $100

Kooky-Kook, 13 inches high. The mark is shown. *Zera Collection.* $100

Mark of Kooky-Kook.

MANUFACTURED BY:
GREAT AMERICAN HOUSEWARES INC.
NEW YORK - N.Y. 10003
© HASBRO BRADLEY INC.
All rights reserved
MADE IN PORTUGAL

Mark of Transformers jar.

"Kooky-K-Egg" is 11 inches high. Its mark is shown. *Zera Collection.* $90

Mark of Kooky-K-Egg—"Kooky-K-Egg©/by Newhauser/Pat Pending/Green Products/Cleveland O." on five lines.

## N.S. Gustin

Nelson Sage Gustin founded the N.S. Gustin Company in Los Angeles, California, in 1941. According to David Gustin, grandson of the founder and current vice president, the company has the distinction of being one of the few pottery distributors that still deals mainly in domestic wares. Only two of its lines are imported.

Gustin distributed the products of Los Angeles Potteries until that firm was liquidated in 1970, at which time its molds were acquired by Gustin for use at Designer-Craft, a West Los Angeles pottery the distributor owned. Today Designer-Craft is owned by David Gustin, but the name has been changed to Los Angeles Pottery. It is still located in West Los Angeles, and still produces cookie jars. Some of them are marked Los Angeles Pottery; others are marked N.S. Gustin.

Currently, the main thrust of N.S. Gustin's business is supplying ceramic giftware to mom-and-pop franchise operations such as Hallmark Card stores, and other quality gift shops.

N.S. GUSTIN

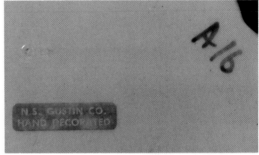

Paper label and mark of the N.S. Gustin sitting cat.

This cat is 13 3/4 inches high. Its mark is shown. *Oravitz Collection.* $25

## HIMARK Enterprises

HIMARK is a giftware importer located in Hauppauge, New York, a city on Long Island about 40 miles from Manhattan. A company spokesperson declined to give any further information.

HIMARK ENTERPRISES

## Hoan, Ltd.

Apparently an importer that has dealt in Walt Disney products in the recent past.

HOAN LTD.

HIMARK cat, 8 inches high. Its paper label is shown. *Courtesy of Mercedes DiRenzo.* $30

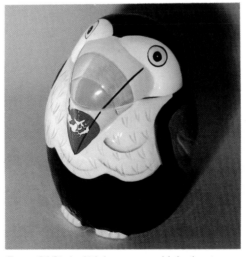

Toucan, 9-1/2 inches high, has same paper label as the cat. *Oravitz Collection.* $90

Mickey Mouse, 11 inches high. The mark is "©The Walt Disney Co./By/Hoan Ltd" on three lines plus a "Made in Taiwan" paper label. *Oravitz Collection.* $75

Paper label of HIMARK cat.

185

Donald Duck is 12-1/2 inches high and has the same mark as Mickey Mouse. *Oravitz Collection*. $75

## Holt Howard

Holt-Howard was founded in 1949 in New York City by A. Grant Holt and John Robert Howard. At first the company's focus was strictly on Christma items.

After a few years it expanded to kitchenware such as cookie jars, salt and pepper shakers, creamers and sugars, etc. Favorite among today's collectors is Pixieware but to my knowledge no Pixieware cookie jar was produced. It did make cookie jars for lines such as Cozy Kitten and the popular Red Rooster dinnerware.

In 1968 Holt-Howard was sold to General Housewares Corporation, of Hyannis, Massachusetts. Holt and the two Howards stayed on for a while but all of them left after a few years. In 1990 Charles Donnell and Richard Rakauskas, former vice presidents of General Housewares, formed Kay Dee Designs in Hope Valley, Rhode Island, and bought the company.

HOLT HOWARD

Holt Howard Santa jar broken down.

Three-piece Holt Howard Santa Claus candy and cookie jar, 8-1/2 inches high. Holt Howard paper label. *Oravitz Collection*. $125

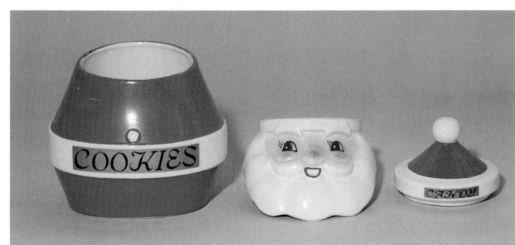

## International Artware Corporation (INARCO)

The history of INARCO is sketchy at best. It was apparently in business as early as 1961, because in 1965 it filed a trademark registration claiming use since May 1961. All known INARCO paper labels show Cleveland, Ohio. But officials at National Potteries Corporation (NAPCO) say the company was operating out of Twinsburg, Ohio, about halfway between Cleveland and Akron, when NAPCO purchased it in 1985. Perhaps its main offices were located in one city, its warehouses in the other. One year after NAPCO took over INARCO, it moved the company to Jacksonville, Florida.

In the field of ceramics, INARCO is best known for knickknacks, and probably didn't handle a lot of cookie jars. While there's nothing particularly outstanding about the jar shown below, the workmanship is adequate, and nuts are an unusual theme for a cookie jar.

INTERNATIONAL ARTWARE CORPORATION (INARCO)

INARCO nut cookie jar, 9 inches high. The mark is "E-2981/INARCO" on two lines. *Bosson Collection*. $35

186

## M. Kamenstein, Inc.

Although the two cookie jars shown below are quite recent (1984), this firm dates all the way back to 1893 when a man named M. Kamenstein started it as a housewares company. It has always been based in the state of New York, moving to its present location in White Plains during the early 1970s. The company is both an importer and manufacturer, making some plastic and wooden products.

### M. KAMENSTEIN, INC.

M. Kamenstein paper label on pencil and light bulb.

Like the pencil, the light bulb is 12-1/2 inches high and has the same paper label. *Courtesy of Jazz'e Junque Shop, Chicago, Illinois.* $35

One big pencil, 12-1/2 inches high. Its paper label is shown. *Courtesy of Jazz'e Junque Shop, Chicago, Illinois.* $35

## Laurel Sales

While no information was found on Laurel Sales, it must have been in business during the early 1950s. The Romper Room was a one-hour children's television program that was syndicated in 1953.

### LAUREL SALES

Romper Room jar, 7-1/2 inches high. The mark and paper label are shown. *Zera Collection.* $175

Mark and paper label of Romper Room cookie jar.

## Leeds China Company

The Leeds China Company was a Chicago distributor. All references consulted agreed that Leeds was licensed to produce Walt Disney products from 1944 to 1954. According to Lehner, Leeds contracted with Ludowici Celadon, of New Lexington, Ohio, to produce Disney turnabout cookie jars between 1941 and 1945. But Heide and Gilman (*Cartoon Collectibles - 50 Years of Dime-Store Memorabilia*), state these jars were made only from 1947 to 1949. Either could be right as all of the characters depicted on turnabout jars - Jose Carioca, Donald Duck, Dumbo, Mickey and Minnie Mouse, and Pluto - made their debut prior to 1945.

Beginning and ending dates for Leeds are not known.

Other jars in the Leeds turnabout series appear in Chapter 8.

### LEEDS CHINA COMPANY

Turnabout Dumbo, 13-3/4 inches high, believed to have been marketed by Leeds China. It is marked "Patented/Turnabout/4 in 1/Walt Disney" on four lines. *Zera Collection.* $150

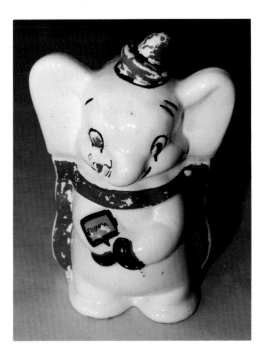

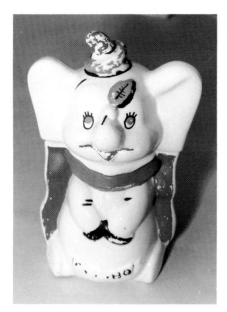

Reverse of Dumbo.

187

## George Zolton Lefton China Company

In recent years some import companies, ENESCO for example, have considerably upgraded the quality of their ceramics to the point that there is little doubt they will become the collectibles of tomorrow. Lefton has not because there was no need to. Ever since this Chicago-based importer began operations in 1940, its wares have been superior to those of most other importers, and now both early and later pieces appear to be rising significantly in price. Many of Lefton's ceramic products that appear to be poured thin are made out of porcelain.

Still in business, Lefton has showrooms in several cities across the nation. Lefton marks often display a crown. All known Lefton marks include the word "Lefton" except one that has only a crown with a cursive "L" above. Some early pieces that would be impossible to attribute without old catalogs were simply marked "Made in Occupied Japan."

For more on this company see *Lefton China,* by Ruth McCarthy (Schiffer 1998).

## GEORGE ZOLTON LEFTON CHINA COMPANY

A pair of pretty young ladies, each 7-3/4 inches high. The mark is shown. *Blumenfeld Collection.* Left - $150, Right - $175

This Lefton duck is 11 inches high. Its mark is shown. *Courtesy of Jazz'e Junque Shop, Chicago, Illinois.* $50

Mark of above Lefton head jars.

The Bluebird is 7-1/2 inches high. It has a "©Geo.Z.Lefton/289" inkstamp and Lefton paper label. *Oravitz Collection.* $300

A partner for the duck, the cow is 12 inches high. Mark is shown. *Bosson Collection.* $50

This jar is 9 inches high and has a Lefton paper label. *Zera Collection.* $80

Miss Priss cat head jar, 8 inches high, with "1502" inkstamp and Lefton paper label. *Oravitz Collection.* $140

Impressed Lefton mark of the duck and the cow.

Canister, 9 inches high. It is marked Lefton, but details of the mark were not recorded. *Courtesy of Jazz'e Junque Shop, Chicago, Illinois.* $25

Tree stump canister, 9-1/2 inches high. The paper label reads: "©Geo.Z.Lefton/1970/6353" on three lines. *Courtesy of Jazz'e Junque Shop, Chicago, Illinois.* $20

## MARSHALL FIELD & COMPANY

### Marshall Burns & Company

Marshall Burns was a distributor out of Chicago that marketed dinnerware, kitchenware and ovenware made of stoneware. The company filed for a Marcrest trademark registration in July 1959, stating it had used the mark since August 1954, but how long it was active on either side of these dates has not been determined.

The Hull Pottery Company, of Crooksville, Ohio, and Western Stoneware Company, of Monmouth, Illinois, both made pieces for Marshall Burns that were marked Marcrest. It is possible that other potteries did, too.

## MARSHALL BURNS & COMPANY

Marcrest stoneware crock cookie jar, 9 inches high. The mark is shown. *Courtesy of Jazz'e Junque Shop, Chicago, Illinois.* $35

Mark of stoneware crock jar.

### Marshall Field & Company

The retail chain that became known as Marshall Field's was founded in 1852 when a man named Potter Palmer opened a dry goods store in downtown Chicago. Marshall Field bought into the business in 1865, became chief proprietor in 1891, and changed the name to reflect his ownership. By 1900 Marshall Field's was the largest wholesale and retail dry goods firm in the world. As of 1989, the company had 24 stores in Illinois, Wisconsin, Ohio, and Texas. In June 1990, Marshall Field's was acquired by the Dayton Hudson Corporation, of Minneapolis, Minnesota.

According to the Roerigs, the original box in which the Frango Mint Chip Cookies jar shown below was packed, indicated the jar was a product of Italy.

Marshall Field Frango Mint Chip Cookies jar, 12 inches high. No mark except the advertising. *Zera Collection.* $95

The unreadable writing on the face of the clock is "Marshall Field & Company." The jar originally held milk chocolates. It is 8-1/2 inches high. *Zera Collection.* $70

## National Potteries Corporation (NAPCO)

According to a company spokesperson, this importing firm was founded by three investors in Cleveland, Ohio, in 1939. For many years it operated out of Bedford, Ohio, a Cleveland suburb. In 1984 the company was moved to Jacksonville, Florida.

NAPCO bought out International Artware Corporation (INARCO), another Cleveland area importer, in 1985, and moved the company to Jacksonville in 1986. In recent years NAPCO has severely scaled back its giftware sales, choosing instead to cater to the florist trade.

Marks of several of the jars shown below indicate they were made in the 1950s. Most that do not show dates are assumed to be from the same period. While this was a time during which many imported cookie jars were of inferior quality, the pictures show very clearly that NAPCO's jars were always a cut above those of the great majority of its competitors.

NATIONAL POTTERIES
CORPORATION (NAPCO)

NAPCO "Miss Cutie-pie," 8-1/2 inches high. This jar was also made in yellow and in blue. Its mark is shown. *Blumenfeld Collection.* $200

Little Red Riding Hood, 9-1/2 inches high. Its mark and paper label are shown. *Oravitz Collection.* $250

Mark of Cinderella, same as Little Red Riding Hood except that the copyright symbol is missing. You would normally expect them to have different numbers.

The "Cookie Corporal." He is 8 inches high with mark showing. *Blumenfeld Collection.* $200

Inkstamp mark of Miss Cutie-pie with NAPCO paper label.

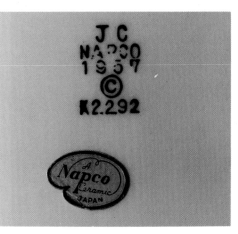

Inkstamp mark and paper label of Little Red Riding Hood.

Mark of the cookie corporal.

This spaceship is 10 inches high and was also made in yellow and maybe other colors. The mark is shown. *Bosson Collection.* $375

Cinderella, 9-3/4 inches high. Its mark is shown. Others in this series include Goldilocks and Little Bo Peep. *Zera Collection.* $250

Mark of the NAPCO spaceship.

Drum, 8 inches high. The mark and paper label are shown. *Oravitz Collection.* $45

C-5919
©NATIONAL POTTERIES
BEDFORD, OHIO

Mark and paper label of the drum. Note the different location on each label.

This is a sucker jar, a typical addition to many cookie jar collections. It is 7-1/4 inches high and has a "NAPCO" paper label plus a "K4546" inkstamp. *Oravitz Collection.* $50

A real cookie jar. It is 10 inches high and marked with a NAPCO paper label. *Courtesy of Jazz'e Junque Shop, Chicago, Illinois.* $35

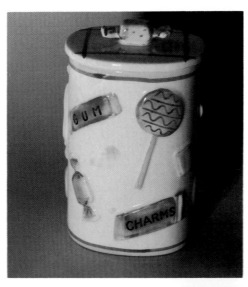

## NATIONAL SILVER COMPANY (NASCO)

National Silver chef and mammy. Mammy is possibly repainted. The chef is 10-1/4 inches high, the mammy 9-1/2 inches. Chef is marked "U.S.A./N.S.Co." impressed on two lines, similar to the apple on the following page. Mammy is marked, but the mark is unreadable. *Coughenour Collection.* $275 ea.

### National Silver Company (NASCO)

The National Silver Company was a New York distributing firm that depended upon several potteries around the country to make the wares it marketed. Among them were the Canonsburg Pottery Company (Canonsburg, Pennsylvania), Fredericksburg Art Pottery (Fredericksburg, Ohio), French Saxon China Company (Sebring, Ohio), Gladdening, McBean and Company (Los Angeles, California), W.S. George Pottery (East Palestine, Ohio), Santa Anita Pottery (Los Angeles, California), and Southern Potteries (Erwin, Tennessee). There may have been more.

National Silver, which often used the acronym "NASCO," started in business no later than 1934, but it might have been much earlier. The head jar shown below seems to indicate it remained in business until the 1970s or 1980s. Recent attempts to locate National Silver in New York, and other places, have been unsuccessful.

The best known and most sought National Silver cookie jars are the chef and mammy. They are assumed to have been made in the 1930s or the 1940s.

National Silver chef and mammy but of a different bisque and unmarked. Molds and sizes are the same as those above. *Zera Collection.* Price not determined.

Apple, 6-1/2 inches high, mark shown. *Zera Collection.* $35

This jar is 9 inches high. Its paper label is shown. *Blumenfeld Collection.* $50

Mark of National Silver apple.

Black and gold paper label from above NASCO jar.

The bunny with carrot is 11-3/4 inches high. Paper label showing. *Oravitz Collection.* $35

Black and silver NASCO paper label on bunny with carrot.

## Neiman-Marcus

Neiman-Marcus is a retailer based in Dallas, Texas, that has become well known for having one of the most expensive lines of giftware in the country. As of 1999, the company had 31 retail outlets.

### NEIMAN-MARCUS

Taxi, 7-1/2 inches high. "Neiman-Marcus" on back license plate, no other identifying marks appear. *Courtesy of Jazz'e Junque Shop, Chicago, Illinois.* $150

Kitty, 7-1/2 inches high. The mark is "©Otagiri/Handpainted" impressed on two lines with a "1980" inkstamp below. *Courtesy of Jazz'e Junque Shop, Chicago, Illinois.* $30

## Otagiri

James Otagiri was a Japanese immigrant who attended the Berkeley School of Commerce after graduating from the Berkeley Public Schools. This was prior to World War II. Upon the United States entering the war with Japan, Otagiri was interned by the federal government, during which time he taught Japanese at the University of Colorado Language School.

Shortly after being freed he founded Otagiri, a San Francisco importing firm. The year was 1946. James Otagiri passed away about 1976, but the company remains in business, still based in San Francisco. It wholesales house and giftware items, including cookie jars, to upscale department stores.

According to the company, 100 percent of its cookie jars are made in Japan.

### OTAGIRI

The pig is 8 inches high, with "©Otagiri 1979" impressed. *Oravitz Collection.* $40

192

Trolley with people, 7-1/4 inches high, marked "©Otagiri 1980." Yellow banner across the front of the vehicle reads "Municipal." *Oravitz Collection.* $50

The Victorian house is 10-3/4 inches high. The mark is "©Otagiri" impressed. *Courtesy of Mercedes DiRenzo.* $50

## PIPPIN

Pippin apple, 6-3/4 inches high. The mark is "USA/Pippin" impressed. Pippin is a variety of apple. The jar was made by American Bisque. *Oravitz Collection.* $45

## Over and Back, Inc.

An importer-wholesaler, Over and Back is located in Ronkonkoma, New York, a city on Long Island about 35 miles east of Kennedy International Airport. The firm, which was founded in 1976, caters to specialty shops and department stores. Over and Back describes itself as a trendy company that regularly changes its merchandise based on what's hot at any given time. As a result, it sold many different cookie jars from 1986 through 1990, but in 1991 was offering but one model to its customers.

## OVER AND BACK

Original container of Country Quilt Series bear.

This duck is 8-1/2 inches high. Its paper label is shown. *Oravitz Collection.* $25

Over and Back "Country Quilt Series" bear. The mark is "©1987/Over & Back, Inc." on two lines, plus a "Made in Taiwan" paper label. *Courtesy of Jazz'e Junque Shop, Chicago, Illinois.* $35

Over and Back paper label of duck cookie jar. The jar also had a "Made in Taiwan" paper label.

Close-up of Country Quilt Series container.

## Pittman-Dreitzer and Company, Inc.

A New York distributor, obviously in business as early as 1942, as shown on the mark below. Sometime prior to 1966 it became a division of Lancaster Colony Corporation, the same company that owned McCoy for a time. How long Pittman-Dreitzer remained active has not been determined. Albert Apple and Stella Strawberry are the only two cookie jars the company is known to have distributed. There were also figures made in the likeness of the cookie jars, plus other figural characters with names such as Lee Lemon and Priscilla Pineapple.

PITTMAN-DREITZER COMPANY, INC.

Albert Apple is 12-1/4 inches high. Same mark as shown except with "Albert Apple" across the bottom. *Zera Collection.* $60

Stella Strawberry, 12 inches high, marked "©FKR—PD & CO." *Courtesy of Betty and Floyd Carson.* $60

Longer mark of another Stella Strawberry that was photographed. It reads "©FKR 1942 PD & Co. Inc./Stella Strawberry" on two lines. *Zera Collection.*

## Pomona

At this time no information is available on Pomona.

POMONA

Three little pigs jar, 9-1/2 inches high. "Pomona" inkstamp under the glaze. *Zera Collection.* $80

Reverse of Pomona three little pigs jar.

## Pottery Guild of America

The Cronin China Company, of Minerva, Ohio, made semi-porcelain marketed by Pottery Guild of America. Pottery Guild incorporated in New York County on August 10, 1937. It was dissolved by proclamation on March 8, 1946. The founder of Pottery Guild was J. Block. After Pottery Guild went out of business, Block and other members of his family formed and ran several New York distributing firms including J & I Block Company, Rosenthal-Block China Corporation, and Block China Company.

Ivory and pink Pottery Guild Dutch girls, marked as shown, 12-1/4 inches high. *Zera Collection.* $100 ea.

POTTERY GUILD OF AMERICA

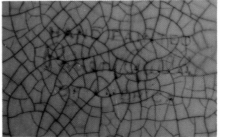

Sometimes you really have to look close to see a mark, such as this one on the Dutch girls.

As you might expect, Pottery Guild sold more than just cookie jars. Platters, pitchers, mixing bowls, casseroles, salad sets, custard cups, waffle sets and other pieces were marketed by the company. In addition to the jars shown below, it is known to have made a Dutch boy, and a jar similar to McCoy's round ball shape, but with flat handles on the sides and a recessed round knob in the lid. A 1939 Wards catalog shows the round jar in a pattern called calico fruit, in which the leaves of fruit were made to resemble cloth. The jar was on sale for $1.19.

Cronin China was located in New Cumberland, West Virginia, prior to 1934 when it moved into the Minerva plant of the defunct Owen China Company. Owen was founded by Ted Owen in 1902, went belly up in 1931. Cronin lasted until 1956 when it was taken over by the United States Ceramic Tile Company, of Canton, Ohio.

This pot shaped cookie jar is 7 inches high. Its mark is shown. *Zera Collection*. $25

Mark of pot shaped jar.

Blue Dutch girl, 12-1/4 inches high and unmarked. *Zera Collection*. $100

Unmarked Pottery Guild balloon lady, 12 inches high. *Courtesy of Jazz'e Junque Shop, Chicago, Illinois*. $130

Peach Dutch girl, the same size as the blue and also unmarked. *Bosson Collection*. $100

Balloon lady with a lighter skirt. Same size as the unmarked example featured above. *Zera Collection*. $130

The girl stands 11-1/4 inches high. The mark is shown. *Courtesy of Jazz'e Junque Shop, Chicago, Illinois*. $100

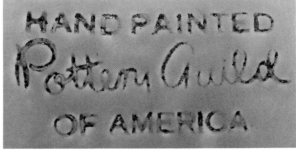

Mark of the girl.

Vandor specializes in a mixture of giftware and home decorations, which includes cookie jars and salt and pepper shakers among other things. Over the years it depended largely on freelance designers until Sadler was hired in 1990. All of its products are made overseas.

As evidenced by the jars shown, Vandor imports only the highest quality ceramics.

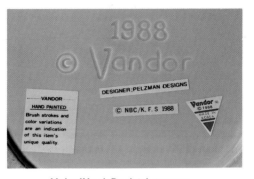

Marks of Howdy Doody in bumper car.

The standing Fred Flintstone is marked with an impressed "Vandor©1989" and two paper labels that read "Vandor Made in Korea" and "Pelzman Designs." *Courtesy of Jazz'e Junque Shop, Chicago, Illinois.* $140

This Howdy is 10 inches high, has a Vandor paper label. *Courtesy of Jazz'e Junque Shop, Chicago, Illinois.* $275

The Vandor Popeye is 8-1/2 inches high and unmarked. *Blumenfeld Collection.* $350

Sitting Fred Flintstone, 10 inches high, with "©1989 Vandor" impressed in bottom. *Courtesy of Jazz'e Junque Shop, Chicago, Illinois.* $225

Commonly called "cowmen Moo-Randa, "this jar is 9-3/4 inches high. Its mark is "© Vandor 1988." *Courtesy of Mercedes DiRenzo.* $150

The cookies toaster is 8 inches high. Its paper label reads "Vandor/©1985/ Made in/Japan" on four lines. *Courtesy of Jazz'e Junque Shop, Chicago, Illinois.* $65

*Whip Me...Beat Me...Don't Let Me Down*, by The Egg whites, plus 19 other songs for your listening pleasure on the Vandor jukebox.

"Select-A-Cookie" jar, marked "Vandor." *Zera Collection.* $75

Dishwasher warning card packed inside every Vandor jukebox.

# Section VI: Character Cookie Jars

Character cookie jars fall into two main categories, those that are copyrighted and those that are not. Woody Woodpecker and Hopalong Cassidy are examples of copyrighted characters. A company wanting to reproduce them must get permission from the copyright holder in order to do so legally. A copyright notice is generally an integral part of the mold, though sometimes it is communicated by a paper label. Humpty Dumpty and Little Boy Blue are characters in the public domain. No permission is needed to make them. There is, of course, a prohibition on copying any character cookie jar which is currently protected by a design patent, whether or not the character it is based on is copyrighted.

Sometimes character copyrights get a little cloudy. Consider Davy Crockett. No cookie jar portraying Walt Disney's 1955 movie hero carries a Disney copyright notice, the natural assumption being that because Davy Crockett was an actual historical figure, he was free game to manufacturers. Yet Scott Bruce, in his book, *The Fifties and Sixties Lunch Box*, writes that when American Thermos began distributing a Davy Crockett lunch box, Disney lawyers came down hard, forcing the company to halt production and recall all of those already on the shelves. Perhaps the attorneys felt the Davy Crockett cookie jars were more generic in nature, none of them closely imitating the face of Crockett actor Fess Parker. Or perhaps they felt the jars were less of a threat than lunch boxes, and not worth a court battle.

Many of your favorite characters are absent from this section as it includes only those that haven't been pegged to a specific manufacturer or distributor.

# Chapter 23
## Santa Claus

Probably everyone's favorite character, at least when he brings all those goodies at Christmas, Santa Claus is as American in origin as the cookie jar on which he is often portrayed. Early Dutch settlers in New Amsterdam (now New York) celebrated St. Nicholas Feast Day each December 6, but referred to the 4th Century Turkish bishop as Sinter-Klass. Later, English settlers changed the name to Santa Claus, and the character gradually became associated with Christmas.

The modern image we have of Santa Claus—so aptly perpetuated by cookie jar designers—evolved in large part from two sources, the 1822 publication of Clement C. Moore's classic poem, "A Visit from St. Nicholas," and drawings by political cartoonist, Thomas Nast, in *Harper's Illustrated Weekly* in 1863, and again in 1866. Nast, incidentally, is the illustrator who first showed Uncle Sam as a bearded figure wearing striped pants.

Most Santa Claus jars have appeared fairly recently on the cookie jar time line, and the subject has also been a popular one with hobby ceramists over the years.

This Santa Claus head cookie jar stands 9 inches high and is not marked. *Bosson Collection.* $85

Wider and shorter than the example to the left, this unmarked jar is 8 inches high. *Zera Collection.* $70

As you can see, these jars are identical with the exception of the height. The example on the left is 8-1/4 inches high, and the example on the right is 8-3/4 inches high. Both jars are unmarked, but the one on the left has stilt marks on the bottom, while the one on the right was dry footed. The Roerigs show this jar with a Mallory mark, probably a ceramic mold company. *Blumenfeld Collection.* $45 ea.

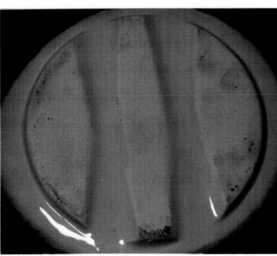

Bottom of Santa Claus jar shown at bottom left.

This is the same as the Santas in the above picture, but the top is turned, and the glazing is different. It is probably a home ceramic jar since some of the skin is white instead of flesh color, a mistake generally not made by skilled decorators. The height of the unmarked piece is 8 inches. *Courtesy of Jazz'e Junque Shop, Chicago, Illinois.* $45

This one is 9-1/2 inches high, unmarked. *Courtesy of Jazz'e Junque Shop, Chicago, Illinois.* $35

An 8-1/2 inch high Santa, unmarked. The bottom, which is shown, is similar to McCoy, but the jar is not believed to be McCoy. *Blumenfeld Collection.* $60

Unmarked Santa holding a bell, 10 inches high. *Bosson Collection.* $50

Marked inside the lid of this 14 inch-high Santa is "Original Sculpture By Don Winton." As shown on next page, the back of this jar is just as interesting as the front. *Courtesy of Betty and Floyd Carson.* $150

Back of 14-inch Santa on previous page.

Standing Santa, with "Made in Taiwan" paper label, 12-1/2 inches high. *Oravitz Collection.* $35

These must be some of Santa's helpers. The jar is 8-1/4 inches high and unmarked. *Oravitz Collection.* $30

Another Santa loaded down with gifts. The height is 9 inches, the paper label reads "Made in Taiwan," and inside the lid is a light-sensitive music box. *Courtesy of Jazz'e Junque Shop, Chicago, Illinois.* $40

A teddy bear Santa, 12-1/2 inches high. Marked with "B & D©" impressed, "1986" raised, and a "Made in Taiwan" paper label. *Courtesy of Jazz'e Junque Shop, Chicago, Illinois.* $40

A 12-inch high Santa, marked "1986 George Good Corp. Calif." No information was found on this company. *Courtesy of Jazz'e Junque Shop, Chicago, Illinois.* $80

# Chapter 24
## *Walt Disney*

The 1928 release of Chicago-born Walter Elias Disney's animated film, *Steamboat Willie*, featuring Mickey Mouse and Donald Duck, began a marketing mania that eventually spread worldwide. It has kept cookie jar makers and other manufacturers busy ever since. Disney made *Steamboat Willie* as a silent film, but failed to get it released commercially until adding a sound track. Walt Disney went on to win 30 Academy Awards - still a record - before his death in 1966 at age 65.

According to Derwich and Latos, since 1972 molds for licensed Disney characters have been made by a subsidiary of Walt Disney Productions. Prior to that time manufacturers were given model sheets from which their designers worked.

Unfortunately, few of the popular Walt Disney cookie jars carry the mark of the manufacturer. Some of the potteries and distributors licensed to produce Disney characters over the years are said to be Brayton Laguna, Laguna Beach, California 1938-40; Hagen-Renaker, San Dimas, California 1955-60; Leeds China Company, Chicago, Illinois 1944-54; National Porcelain, Trenton, New Jersey 1939-42; Salem China, Salem, Ohio, 1932-34; Vernon Kilns, Los Angeles, California 1940-42; Eleanor Welborn Art Productions, Seaside, California, 1955.

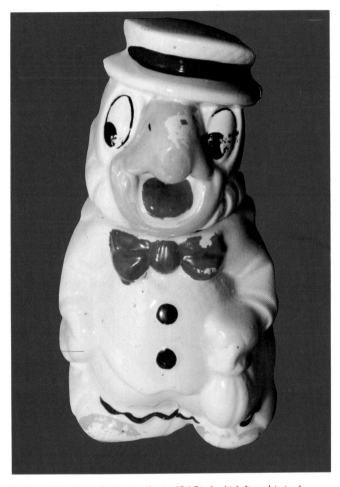

This Donald Duck—Joe Carioca turnabout is 13-1/2 inches high. Its mark is simply "Walt Disney Productions," though some have a longer mark explaining the characters are from the movie *The Three Caballeros*, a 1945 animated feature film. The jar was marketed by the Leeds China Company, a Chicago distributor. *Zera Collection.* $175

Reverse of the Donald Duck—Joe Carioca turnabout. Because Leeds commissioned several potteries to make its wares during the years it held a Disney license (1944—1954), it is uncertain as to which pottery made this jar. Based on the appearance of the bisque and the feel of the jar, however, it seems the Ludowici Celadon—American Pottery—American Bisque triumvirate is a reasonable bet. A repainted example of this cookie jar is shown in Chapter 4.

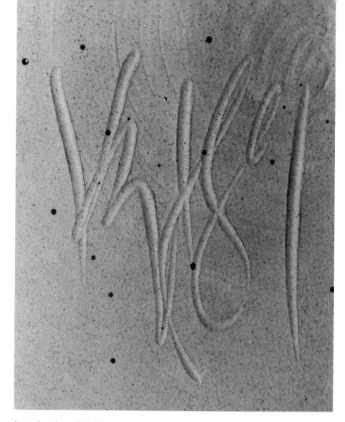

Incised mark on all Herklotz cookie jars.

Herklotz cookie jar, 8-1/8 inches high. *Courtesy of Down to Earth Ceramics Studio.* $40

This jar is 8-1/4 inches high. *Courtesy of Down to Earth Ceramics Studio.* $40

# Section VIII: Foreign Cookie Jars

Identified foreign cookie jars have been divided into two categories, those from Pacific-Asian countries, which account for the majority of the imports, and those from other areas of the world.

Cookie jars made outside the United States are similar to cookie jars made within the United States in that they exhibit varying degrees of workmanship running from crude to sophisti-cated. At one time most collectors excluded foreign jars on general principles. While some still do, the trend today appears to be that people include foreign cookie jars in their collections based on the merits of the individual jars. As American cookie jars become less and less available, it seems almost certain that the popularity of foreign jars will continue to rise.

# Chapter 30
## *Pacific-Asian Cookie Jars*

Following their devastating defeat in World War II, the Japanese literally rebuilt their industries from the ground up, clay for the pottery industry being their most accessible material. Initial efforts produced figurines, salt and pepper shakers, and other knick-knacks.

The majority of Japanese cookie jars apparently came somewhat later, from the early 1950s through the 1960s and beyond. If they had been made earlier, more would have been marked Occupied Japan, but this mark on a cookie jar is rare, if it exists at all. The Japanese were not necessarily required to use the mark during the American occupation, which lasted from 1945 until the spring of 1952. But it seems some jars, actually a great many, would have the occupied stamp had the country been producing them in quantity prior to 1952.

Japanese, and other Pacific-Asian cookie jars, are generally much lighter in weight than American jars, probably more a testament to the high cost of overseas shipping than to a lack of skills or poor workmanship.

During the 1950s American potteries complained about the Japanese pirating their designs. Ironically, as far as cookie jars are concerned, it appears this practice was more prevalent between American potteries than it was between Japanese and American potteries. There are some Japanese examples of this, such as the imitation Regal China churn boy, but as you leaf through this book, you will find much more evidence of American manufacturers imitating other American manufacturers, than you will find of Japanese manufacturers imitating the Americans.

The collecting community's feeling toward Japanese cookie jars is currently in a state of transition. At one time the jars were summarily rejected by collectors. Today they have gained acceptance to the point where they are included in the majority of collections, though most people appear to be somewhat uncomfortable about owning them. A common phrase heard when expressing interest in a collector's Japanese cookie jar is, "That's a Japanese jar," said in a tone of voice that implies "That's *just* a Japanese jar." Based on the current trend, it seems probable that in the future more and more Japanese jars will make their way into collections, and they will eventually be accepted at face value with no stigma attached.

When Japan moved on to cameras, steel, electronics, and automobiles, Taiwan served importers as the pottery road to riches. More recently, Korea and Malaysia have begun developing their ceramics industries. To the collector's advantage, when new countries jump onto the pottery bandwagon, they tend to enter the market at the current level of sophistication, instead of beginning at the bottom and working up as Japan had to do. Many Pacific-Asian countries have not yet made the inevitable change from agricultural- to industrial-based economies, so the region will probably continue to be a hotbed of cookie jar production for some time to come.

Isn't this guy great! The jar is 9 inches high, marked "Japan." On top of the hat is a windup music box. *Blumenfeld Collection.* $150

This clown has a more complicated mark than most Pacific-Asian cookie jars: a "PY" in a circle above "Japan" with a "C" superimposed on a "N" below. The jar is 9-1/2 inches high. *Blumenfeld Collection.* $100

A somersault clown, 11-1/4 inches high, marked "Japan" in raised letters. *Oravitz Collection.* $45

Old King Cole is 12-1/2 inches high and has a "Japan" inkstamp. *Bosson Collection.* $45

The jar is 9-1/2 inches high. The paper label reads "Made in Taiwan/R.O.C." on two lines. *Courtesy of Jazz'e Junque Shop, Chicago, Illinois.* $35

Peter Pumpkin Eater, 12 inches high, with "Japan" impressed. *Oravitz Collection.* $35

Humpty Dumpty, 13-1/4 inches high, marked "Japan." *Coughenour Collection.* $45

The jar on the left is 10-1/2 inches high, and the jar on the right is 10-1/4 inches high. The left jar is marked with an impressed "Japan," while the right jar has no mark. *Oravitz Collection.* $30 each.

This elf is 12-1/4 inches high and has "Japan" impressed. *Oravitz Collection.* $40

Mark of "Gnome on Stump." The paper label reads "From the Gift World of/Gorham/Made in Japan" on three lines. Gorham is a giftware company based in Providence, Rhode Island. It was founded in 1831 and is known primarily for its sterling silver flatware, though it also markets kitchenware, Christmas ornaments, dolls, crystal, and collector's plates, among other things.

A real hunting dog. *Bosson Collection.* $50

More elves, 10 inches high, with "Japan" inkstamp. *Oravitz Collection.* $40

All six jars in this occupation/avocation set are 13 inches high and marked "Japan" in raised letters. *Bosson Collection.* $50 ea.

"Gnome on Stump." The mark is shown. *Oravitz Collection.* $30

The elephant is 12 inches high with "Japan" impressed. *Oravitz Collection.* $35

Bought at a discount store in 1990, this jar is 10 inches high. It has a Taiwan paper label. *Oravitz Collection.* $30

Although the bottoms appear to be interchangeable, they're not because of details such as the rope on the bear and suspender buttons on the cow. *Bosson Collection.* $50 ea.

A fishing hippo. *Oravitz Collection.* $50

A girl hippopotamus, 9 inches high. The paper label reads "Made in Taiwan/ROC" on two lines. A boy (minus the bow) was also made. *Oravitz Collection.* $45

This jar and the elephant on page 231 seem to have a lot in common. Perhaps they were created by the same designer or made by the same pottery. The height is 12-1/2 inches, with "Japan" impressed. *Courtesy of Jazz'e Junque Shop, Chicago, Illinois.* $35

With the "C" on his sweater, there seems little doubt this teddy bear attends Cookie College. The jar is 10-3/4 inches high, and it has "Japan" impressed. *Oravitz Collection.* $45

This jar is 10-1/2 inches high with "Japan" impressed. *Oravitz Collection.* $40

Teddy bear, 10-1/2 inches high, with "Japan" impressed. *Oravitz Collection.* $30

This miss is 13 inches high and has a "Japan" inkstamp. *Oravitz Collection.* $30

The elephant is 10 inches high with a "Made in Japan" paper label. *Oravitz Collection.* $20

Time to stop drinking. The pink elephant is 10 inches high. The paper label is shown. *Oravitz Collection.* $20

Paper label of the pink elephant.

This jar is 10-1/2 inches high with a "Japan" inkstamp. *Courtesy of Jazz'e Junque Shop, Chicago, Illinois.* $30

The jar on the left is 10-3/4 inches high with "Japan" impressed. The jar on the right is 11 inches high with "Japan" in raised letters. The one on the left looks very much like the jar above, but close inspection reveals it isn't. *Oravitz Collection.* $25 ea.

Two more jars that might have come from a single pottery. *Left:* 8-1/2 inches high. *Right:* 9-1/2 inches high. "Japan" in raised letters is on both. *Oravitz Collection.* $25 ea.

Butterfly puppy, 7-1/2 inches high. Its "Japan" paper label is shown. *Oravitz Collection.* $40

The mark and paper label of butterfly puppy. The bottom line of paper label reads "Crafted in Japan."

Both of these jars are 8 inches high. The one on the left has a "Made in Taiwan" paper label. The one on the right is unmarked but is assumed to be of Pacific—Asian origin, probably the same company. *Oravitz Collection.* $15 ea.

"Mr. Cookie," 10-1/4 inches high, with "Taiwan" impressed. *Oravitz Collection.* $65

Mark of the blue and white animal jar.

These little guys are all 7-1/2 inches high, and all have "Made in Taiwan/ROC" written on two lines on a paper label. In 1990, they sold for $5 each at discount stores. *Oravitz Collection.* $15 ea.

Another blue and white animal jar of questionable species. Its height is 6-1/4 inches. The paper label reads "Made in Taiwan." *Oravitz Collection.* $25

The owl on the left, apparently in elementary school, is 11-3/4 inches high. The owl on the right, obviously at graduation, is 12-1/4 inches high. While neither of these two jars is marked, identical jars have marks indicating Japanese origin. *Courtesy of Jazz'e Junque Shop, Chicago, Illinois.* $35 ea.

Dog or cat? It is 10-3/4 inches high. Its mark is shown. *Courtesy of Jazz'e Junque Shop, Chicago, Illinois.* $25

This owl is 10 inches high. The inkstamp is "Japan."
*Bosson Collection.* $25

An Indian owl, 9 inches high, with "Japan" impressed.
*Oravitz Collection.* $25

Granny duck, 12 inches high. The paper label reads
"Fabrique à Taiwan." *Oravitz Collection.* $30

The height here is 10-1/4 inches. The mark is shown.
*Oravitz Collection.* $25

Chicken chef, 13 inches high. It has an Omnibus paper label.
*Courtesy of Jazz'e Junque Shop, Chicago, Illinois.* $30

This jar is 10-1/2 inches high and has a "Made in
Japan" paper label. *Oravitz Collection.* $40

Mark of the owl clock.

The penguin on the left is 11 inches high. It has "Made in
Taiwan/ROC" impressed on two lines, and a paper label that
indicates the jar was copyrighted in 1985. The penguin on the
right is 12-1/2 inches high and unmarked. *Oravitz Collection.*
$25 ea.

Another house, 9-1/2 inches high, has "Japan" impressed. *Oravitz Collection.* $25

This house is 9-1/2 inches high, with "Japan" impressed. *Oravitz Collection.* $25

Another clock, also 10-3/4 inches high, with "Japan" impressed. *Courtesy of Jazz'e Junque Shop, Chicago, Illinois.* $30

Lots of action here: a mouse being chased by a cat being chased by a dog. The jar is 10 inches high with "Japan" impressed. *Courtesy of Jazz'e Junque Shop, Chicago, Illinois.* $25

A little girl at her playhouse. Note the nice detail such as the bird on the chimney and the dog by the girl. The jar has an impressed "Japan" mark and is 10-1/2 inches high. *Oravitz Collection.* $25

A stove with tea kettle, 10 inches high, with "Japan" impressed. *Courtesy of Jazz'e Junque Shop, Chicago, Illinois.* $25

A cookie house, 9-1/2 inches high. It has a "Japan" inkstamp. *Oravitz Collection.* $20

This clock is 10-3/4 inches high. "Japan" is impressed along with additional letters that are unreadable. *Oravitz Collection.* $25

The drum is 10 inches high, and its mark is shown. *Zera Collection.* $20

Mark of the silver drum.

Just about the best subject you could get for a cookie jar. It is 9-1/2 inches high, "Japan" impressed. *Courtesy of Jazz'e Junque Shop, Chicago, Illinois.* $25

Just about the worst subject you could get for a cookie jar. This one is 9 inches high. The mark is an impressed "Japan." *Oravitz Collection.* $35

This barrel jar is 9 inches high. It is unmarked but another that was photographed has "Japan" impressed. Does anyone understand the theme? *Bosson Collection.* $30

Both jars are 10-1/2 inches high. Raggedy Ann is inkstamped "Japan," and Raggedy Andy is unmarked. *Oravitz Collection.* $40 ea.

The shoe on the left is 9-3/4 inches high, has the Brinn's paper label "Made in Japan." The shoe on the right is 13 inches high. It had felt glued to the bottom so it is unknown whether or not it is marked. *Oravitz Collection.* $25 ea.

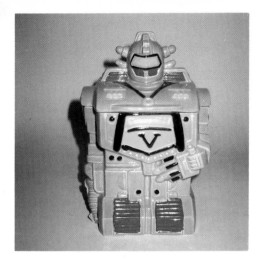

Robot, 10-1/4 inches high, marked with "Japan" impressed. *Saxby Collection.* $75

Yellow robot, 10-1/4 inches, with "Japan" impressed. *Saxby Collection.* $75

This 9-1/2 inch high cookie jar is unmarked. Original box says "JASCO, Made in Taiwan, Item no. 189." *Oravitz Collection.* $25

Robot in white, with the same size and mark as above. *Saxby Collection.* $75

This jar has a light-sensitive music box in the lid. The height is 9-1/2 inches, and the mark is "Made in Taiwan." *Courtesy of Jazz'e Junque Shop, Chicago, Illinois.* $30

Many biscuit jars were made in Japan during the postwar ear. More a fixture of the British kitchen than of the American kitchen, they were nevertheless imported to the United States. This one is 7-1/4 inches high, inkstamped "Made in Japan." On all biscuit jars the measurement is for the pottery only, which does not include the handle. *Oravitz Collection.* $35

Blue robot, same as above. *Saxby Collection.* $75

The snowman with gift is 11-1/2 inches high and has a "Made in Taiwan" paper label. *Oravitz Collection.* $25

The height of this jar is 6-1/4 inches with the inkstamp "Made in Japan." *Courtesy of Jazz'e Junque Shop, Chicago, Illinois.* $25

The jar on the left is 5-1/2 inches high and not marked. The jar on the right is 5-1/4 inches high, mark is shown. *Oravitz Collection.* $40 ea.

From *left* to *right* the sizes are: 5-3/4 inches, 6-3/4 inches, and 6-1/2 inches. The marks from *left* to *right* are: "10052" inkstamp, no mark, "Japan" paper label. *Oravitz Collection.* Right and left jars - $35 ea., Center jar - $30

Inkstamp mark of pink cat jar. The paper label "Relco/Japan" appears on two lines.

Another cat, 8 inches high, with a "Japan" inkstamp. *Courtesy of Jazz'e Junque Shop, Chicago, Illinois.* $45

A fruit fest, 6-3/4 inches high, with "Japan" inkstamp. *Courtesy of Jazz'e Junque Shop, Chicago, Illinois.* $20

Just like the pink cat above, it even has the same inkstamp mark. But the paper label is different—"Richard/Japan" on two lines. *Courtesy of Jazz'e Junque Shop, Chicago, Illinois.* $40

This canister jar, 8 inches high, is marked "Maple Ware/(likeness of a maple leaf)/Made in Japan" on three lines. *Courtesy of Jazz'e Junque Shop, Chicago, Illinois.* $20

The 6-1/4 inch high jar on the left is not marked, while the 6-3/4 inch high jar on the right is identified by the paper label "Betson's/Japan" on two lines. *Oravitz Collection.* Left - $35, Right - $60

This jar, 8 inches high, is marked "Dresden/Ware/Japan" on three lines. *Oravitz Collection.* $20

239

This canister jar is only 6-1/2 inches high, with a "Made in Japan" inkstamp. *Courtesy of Jazz'e Junque Shop, Chicago, Illinois.* $20

This unique jar is 9-1/2 inches high. The impressed mark reads "Shafford/Original©1979" on two lines, while the paper label is "Shafford/Japan" on two lines. *Oravitz Collection.* $55

An owl canister, 10-1/4 inches high, marked "OMC/Japan" on two lines. *Courtesy of Jazz'e Junque Shop, Chicago, Illinois.* $25

The height is 7 inches, and the inkstamp mark is "Japan." *Oravitz Collection.* $20

A rather plain cookie jar, 10 inches high, with "Made in Taiwan" impressed. *Courtesy of Jazz'e Junque Shop, Chicago, Illinois.* $20

# Chapter 31
## *Jars From Other Countries*

Mention foreign cookie jars and thoughts automatically turn to Japan. But several other countries have made cookie jars, too, some of the jars being of very high quality. Italy appears to be the most prolific. The Italians apparently were not immune to the carbon copy syndrome, as you will see if you compare the Italian clown head below to the Morton Pottery clown in Chapter 21, upon which it was obviously based.

Duck, 9-1/4 inches high. The inkstamp reads "Hand/Painted/Made in Brazil" on three lines. Paper label is shown. *Oravitz Collection*. $20

The jar on the left is 8-3/4 inches high, with "Japan" impressed. The jar on the right is 8-1/4 inches high and marked "Hand/Painted/Made in Brazil" on three lines. *Oravitz Collection*. $25 ea.

Weiss paper label of the duck cookie jar.

These two jars have the same inkstamp—"Hand-painted/Made in Brazil" on two lines. The left jar is 8 inches high; the right one is 8-1/4 inches. *Oravitz Collection*. $20 ea.

This biscuit jar, 6-3/4 inches high without the handle, was made in Czechoslovakia. Mark is shown. *Oravitz Collection.* $85

Paneled biscuit jar, 7-1/2 inches high without handle. The mark is "Made in England" with crown above. *Courtesy of Jazz'e Junque Shop, Chicago, Illinois.* $30

English pig, 11-1/4 inches high. The mark is shown. *Bosson Collection.* $100

Reverse of Czechoslovakian biscuit jar.

This glass jar is 10-3/4 inches high. On the lid is "Triomphe/France" on two lines. On the bottom, "France/3L" on two lines. *Zera Collection.* $15

Mark of the English pig cookie jar.

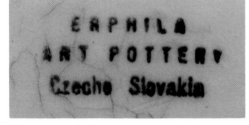

Inkstamp mark of Czechoslovakian biscuit jar. Erphila is an acronym for Ebeling & Reuss, a Philadelphia importer that started in business in 1886 and is still going today.

Stoneware bean pot, 7 inches high, made in England. Mark is shown. *Courtesy of Jazz'e Junque Shop, Chicago, Illinois.* $20

Mark of the bean pot.

Robin Hood's friend Friar Tuck, made by Goebel, the manufacturer of world famous Hummel figurines. In addition to a Goebel "V" mark on the bottom, it has "K29" and "©1957." There is also a Friar Tuck sticker on the back. Goebel is not believed to have made very many cookie jars. A Goebel cat head jar appeared in the October 1990 issue of *Crazed Over Cookie Jars. Bosson Collection.* $225

West German chalet cookie jar, 6-3/4 inches high. The original price sticker inside says $1.25 with a date code that appears to indicate February of 1959. Mark is pictured. *Zera Collection*. $40

This 10-inch high terra cotta pig is fairly common, and more desirable than many other foreign jars as it is hand thrown with the legs and ears attached. This one is unmarked, but "Made in Italy" is clearly indicated on the yellow one. *Oravitz Collection*. $50

Conestoga wagon, 10 inches high, with a mark that shows it was made in Italy. *Bosson Collection*. $45

Mark of the West German chalet jar.

Italian look-alike of the Morton clown head jar, 10-1/4 inches high. The mark is an unreadable number with "Italy" impressed. *Oravitz Collection*. $65

Inside of the red pig showing the ridges indicative of hand throwing.

This jar is 10-3/4 inches high, and marked "Italy." *Courtesy of Jazz'e Junque Shop, Chicago, Illinois.* $25

Hand thrown pig, signed "Italy." *Bosson Collection*. $50

The cookie house is 8-1/2 inches high, marked "Le/324/Italy" on three lines. *Oravitz Collection*. $25

243

The M & M's jar is 7-1/2 inches high. Impressed around the base of the bottom is "M & M's TM Cookie Jar/ ©Mars, Inc. 1982." Because this jar's bottom was covered with felt, it hasn't been determined if there were any additional marks or paper labels. *Courtesy of Betty and Floyd Carson.* $60

This jar, 11 inches high, was a 1990 mail-in premium offer from Frookie Cookies. On the bottom is a "Made in Taiwan" paper label. On the back is a "RWFrookie" decal. *Courtesy of Betty and Floyd Carson.* $25

Keebler elf, 11-3/4 inches high. Paper label reads "Made in Taiwan." *Oravitz Collection.* $40

Unmarked Nestlé Toll House cookie jar, 9-3/4 inches high. Reverse is shown below. *Courtesy of Betty and Floyd Carson.* $65

An Almost Home mail in premium cookie jar, 10 inches high. According to the Roerigs, this was made by Holiday Designs. The inkstamp mark and original advertising are shown below. *Zera Collection.* $75

Say hello to Dan the Dog, lover of Alpo dog biscuits. The jar is 8 inches high, and its mark is shown. *Zera Collection.* $50

Mark of Alpo dog biscuit jar.

Reverse of Nestlé Toll House cookie jar.

This mark appears inside the Almost Home jar.

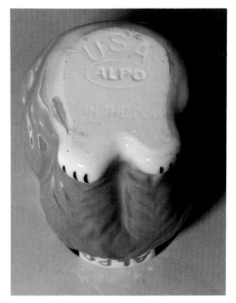

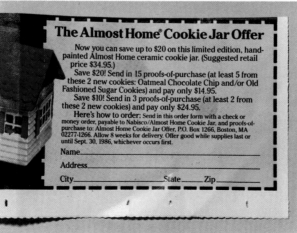

Original newspaper advertisement for Almost Home cookie jar.

This Milk-Bone jar is 7 inches high and marked "Roman/Made in Taiwan" on two lines. *Courtesy of Heidi and Nicci, the DiRenzo's Dobermans.* $100

Daisy
unkn

Sleepi
"Rulor
name
indicat
Cough

The Pillsbury jar is 11-3/4 inches high, with a "Made in Taiwan" paper label. Also marked "©1988 The Pillsbury Company" in the shape of a horseshoe. *Courtesy of Jazz'e Junque Shop, Chicago, Illinois.* $25

An earlier Pillsbury jar, 10-1/2 inches high. The mark is "©The Pillsbury Co. 1973" on one line. *Courtesy of Jazz'e Junque Shop, Chicago, Illinois.* $50

247

This 13-inch high unmarked jar, from an Alberta's mold, sings hobby ceramics loud and clear in several different voices. The entire jar was painted by hand, which again would have been too expensive a procedure for a professional pottery; it has that paint-by-number look that home ceramists were known for a few decades back. No one but a beginning hobbyist would have picked such an appalling color scheme. *Courtesy of Jazz'e Junque Shop, Chicago, Illinois.* $20

Same rocking horse but marked "Alberta/©1956" on two lines. Probably a hobby ceramist. *Oravitz Collection.* $20

No doubt everyone has had the experience of seeing another person who is super attractive from the back, only to have them turn around and display a face even a mother couldn't love. That's the way it is with this 12-1/2 inch high cookie jar. From the rear it is absolutely stunning. But the face is so awful it looks like it couldn't have been decorated by the same person. The signature on this jar is shown below, as is, sadly, the front. *Zera Collection.* $300

This jar is 11 inches high. It has no mold mark but the initials "V.K" are scratched in bottom. *Courtesy of Jazz'e Junque Shop, Chicago, Illinois.* $25

Front of the cookie jar which has the beautiful back. Decoration on the front is nice, face is poorly done, hands were modeled like boxing gloves. Carl & Gari McCallum, of California, have this jar painted as a black woman, and carrying an incised mark on the bottom, "Brayton-Laguna-California-K-27." They also have a matching salt and pepper shaker of the woman and a male companion.

Different story here. Same jar, but finished by either a pottery or a decorating firm. Main clues are its professional look, the use of airbrushing where possible, and the dependence upon clear glaze to keep the cost low. Jars decorated in this same manner show up in collections throughout the nation. *Courtesy of Betty and Floyd Carson.* $50

*Right*: This cookie jar exemplifies one of the pluses and one of the minuses of homemade jars. The hobby ceramist was able to take the time to neatly paint the tiny packages in Santa's sleigh and the houses, but the jar is beginning to craze, which often happens with home ceramics. *Zera Collections.* $25

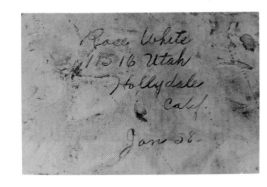

*Left*: Bottom of the lady with the pretty back. The fact that the bottom is not glazed is puzzling. The quality of the decoration on the dress would seem to indicate a studio artist. However, the face would seem to indicate a beginner.

The pear is 11-1/2 inches high, with "Marianne 77" scratched in the bottom. *Oravitz Collection.* $20

Little Red Riding Hood, 11-3/4 inches high. "M.D. 1969" is scratched in the bottom. *Oravitz Collection.* $25

Although the Porky Pig cookie jar comes from a Duncan mold, at least three of the four jars shown—the ones with single color hats—were probably executed by a professional pottery or decorating company. This jar is 11 inches high with "Duncan/©1975 Warner Bros. Inc." impressed in the back. *Coughenour Collection.* $60

The same height as the pear, 11-1/2 inches, this jar has "©1973" impressed at the base and "E.H." scratched in the bottom. *Zera Collection.* $40

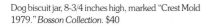

Dog biscuit jar, 8-3/4 inches high, marked "Crest Mold 1979." *Bosson Collection.* $40

Here's another guess. Both jars are made of the lightweight whiteware normally associated with hobby ceramics, both are entirely hand decorated instead of airbrushed, and the jar on the right has what appears to be an unreadable mold company mark. The jars are 11 inches high. *Courtesy of Country Heirs Antique Shop.* $20 ea.

This Porky may be a hobby ceramic product. Brush strokes seem unsteady where the yellow-orange and brown glazes meet, the cap was made unnecessarily complicated by using two colors, and the letters in Porky Pig were not executed with the same authority as the others. *Courtesy of Jazz'e Junque Shop, Chicago, Illinois.* $55

251

Nice work. Note the flower decals on the yellow chair. *Bosson Collection.* $60 ea.

Here's why hobby ceramics make it tough on cookie jar collectors. The cow shown in this picture and the pumpkins in the next picture were taken from a 1988 Gare catalog. The catalog showed eight different cookie jars plus a milk can canister set. Each jar has the potential to have been decorated by several hundred hobby ceramists, each free to chose his own unique design. And that is just one of the many companies. When these jars are finished by skillful hands, there is no reason to suspect they weren't done by a professional pottery. There is also no reason to exclude them from a collection.

Three ghostly pumpkins from Gare. In the future you will no doubt see them at flea markets and antique shows.

# Chapter 34
## *Other Unknown Jars*

The cookie jars shown below lack identifiable marks, paper labels, or attributable characteristics to indicate beyond any doubt what companies made them, and in many cases, what countries they originated from.

Obviously, many of these jars are Japanese. They would have been included in Chapter 30 Pacific-Asian Cookie Jars, except that readers deserve more than a guess when an author declares positive identification. And no matter how much a cookie jar may look or feel Japanese, calling it such would still amount to nothing but an educated guess if there wasn't a paper label or a mark to back it up. Also, as you move on through the 1970s, 1980s, and into the 1990s, the once clear differences between American and Pacific-Asian cookie jars become fuzzier and fuzzier.

Hopefully, in time, all of the jars in this chapter will be identified.

Mark of the lady in the pink dress.

This graceful lady is 10-1/2 inches high. The jar's mark is shown but gives no clue to its identity. *Oravitz Collection*. $90

Dutch woman, 11-1/2 inches high, unmarked. Quite possibly hobby ceramics. *Zera Collection*. $45

For years collectors assumed this unmarked jar was American Bisque, but when the Roerigs interviewed the late A.N. Allen, former owner of American Bisque, he claimed the company didn't make it. The height is 13 inches. *Courtesy of Mercedes DiRenzo.* Value not determined.

Unmarked peasant girl, 11 inches high. *Oravitz Collection.* $70

Some call her a "kitchen witch," others call her "Thelma." She is unmarked, 11-1/2 inches high. *Coughenour Collection.* $70

If the paint on this jar hadn't peeled, wouldn't it have made a great enlargement for the back cover? The height is 10 inches. Mark is "Circus/by/David Surell" on three lines. *Bosson Collection.* $35

Same mold as the example above, but 11-1/2 inches high, unmarked. *Zera Collection.* $70

Similar to the example above, but 1/4 of an inch taller. Note that the *eyes* of both jars are holes in the bisque. *Courtesy of Jazz'e Junque Shop, Chicago, Illinois.* $70

This unmarked mammy is 11-1/4 inches high. Possibly put together from two jars as the top is noticeably whiter than the bottom. *Oravitz Collection.* $100

On the left is a 9-inch high granny cookie jar, on the right an 8-1/2 inch high granny bank. Neither is marked. *Bosson Collection.* Left - $50, Right - $30

This jar is 12-1/4 inches high. It is not marked. *Bosson Collection.* $50

Chinese man, 10-3/4 inches high and not marked. *Zera Collection.* $40

Pirate, 10 inches high, with an unreadable remnant of paper label. *Bosson Collection.* $50

This Starnes jar is 11-3/4 inches high, unmarked. A matching boy, not shown, is dressed in bib overalls. *Oravitz Collection.* $400

This jar is 9-1/4 inches high. Mark is shown. *Bosson Collection.* $125

This fellow is made of stoneware and stands 12-3/4 inches high. Its paper label is shown. *Zera Collection.* $55

Mark of the above jar.

Unmarked Amish boy, 9-1/2 inches high. *Courtesy of Betty and Floyd Carson.* $90

255

Stoneware Designs West lady, 12 inches high. The paper label is below the collar and is basically the same as the example on the previous page; except the word at the top is "Porcelone" instead of "Stoneware." *Saxby Collection.* $50

This jar might be a mate for the Dutch girl on page 253 as the heights are the same (11-1/2 inches) and so is the blue glaze. *Courtesy of Jazz'e Junque Shop, Chicago, Illinois.* $50

A donut chef, 11 inches high and unmarked. *Coughenour Collection.* Value not determined.

Sounds like good advice to me. The unmarked jar is 9-1/2 inches high. *Courtesy of Betty and Floyd Carson.* $25

This jar is 10-1/4 inches high. It is unmarked with the exception of an extremely provocative phrase "Old Shawnee Test" written on the bottom. It was photographed near Zanesville, Ohio, the home of Shawnee, so anything is possible. *Bosson Collection.* Value not determined.

Clown head, 11 inches high and unmarked. The jar is heavily poured, suggesting an American origin. In the picture of the aluminum shelves in Chapter 6, it is featured next to a duplicate that has red hair, a yellow hat with a green brim, and a yellow and green bow tie. *Blumenfeld Collection.* $350

This unmarked jar is 12 inches high. It also appears in a glaze two or three shades darker than Pottery Guild's blue. *Oravitz Collection.* $110

The clown biscuit jar is 9-1/2 inches high excluding the handle. It is unmarked. *Blumenfeld Collection.* $50

Unmarked standing clown, 12-1/2 inches high. *Bosson Collection.* $35

Unmarked clown, 12 inches high. *Bosson Collection.* $95

Uncle Sam minus his top hat? Charles Dickens character? Or just a head jar that is 9-1/2 inches high and unmarked? *Zera Collection.* $75

No mark here, either. The height is 7-1/4 inches excluding the handle. *Oravitz Collection.* $35

Metlox chef head is 11-1/4 inches high and unmarked. *Oravitz Collection.* $200

Very similar to the William Hirsch monk shown in Chapter 21, but with a flat bottom. If you look closely, you'll see small differences in the mold, too. The unmarked jar is 11-1/2 inches high. *Oravitz Collection.* $45

This monk is only 10 inches high. It is not marked. *Oravitz Collection.* $40

This jar at least has an inkstamp, "E-4499," which unfortunately doesn't tell much. The monk is 9-3/4 inches high. *Oravitz Collection.* $40

The height here is 10-1/4 inches. The jar has an unreadable paper label. *Oravitz Collection.* $50

According to owner Mercedes DiRenzo, this jar was made in Mexico by a monk who makes cookie jars when the spirit strikes him. It is 11 inches high, unmarked. *Courtesy of Jazz'e Junque Shop, Chicago, Illinois.* $100

Like the Metlox Cookie Boy in the bottom right, but with much of the original paint intact. Its height is 9-1/4 inches, and it has the remnant of a paper label. *Oravitz Collection.* $125

A young buccaneer, 8 inches high. The inkstamp mark is "SJ-501." *Courtesy of Betty and Floyd Carson.* $50

Monk head jar, with "Thou Shalt Not Steal Cookies" barely visible on the base. The jar is 8-1/2 inches high and has an "A3438" inkstamp and the remnant of a paper label. *Oravitz Collection.* $85

This jar is 8 inches. Possibly the work of a hobby ceramist from the "M.E." that is scratched in the bottom. *Zera Collection.* $50

This jar is 11-1/4 inches high and unmarked. The hymnal is decorated with gold. The bottom, shown on the following page, has the unglazed dot in the center that's characteristic of Abingdon. *Oravitz Collection.* $300

The jar on the left is 8-1/2 inches high, and the jar on the right is 9-1/4 inches high. They are the Cookie Boy and Cookie Girl, made by Metlox. Neither is marked. *Blumenfeld Collection.* $125 ea.

Bottom of "Sweet Notes" jar.

Obviously a pair, but a pair of what? The scarecrow is 10-1/2 inches high, his companion 10-1/4 inches. *Bosson Collection.* $75 ea.

Candle boy, 11 inches high with no mark. *Oravitz Collection.* $35

Both were made by California Originals and are 11 inches high. Neither one is marked. *Blumenfeld Collection.* $90 ea.

Commonly called a Beatle boy after the English rock group of the 1960s, this unmarked jar is 13-1/2 inches high. *Courtesy of Jazz'e Junque Shop, Chicago, Illinois.* $150

The left pixie, by California Originals, is 11 inches high, and the right pixie is 10 inches high. Both are unmarked. *Blumenfeld Collection.* Left - $90, Right - $40

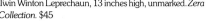

The difference in size is more noticeable in this photo than in the one above, even though it is actually less. The two outside jars are 10-3/4 inches high, the center jar 10-1/4 inches. None of the pixies are marked; the two outside jars were made by California Originals. Note that the eye treatment on the center jar is quite different than that of the other two jars. *Oravitz Collection.* Left and right jars - $90 ea., Center jar - $40

Twin Winton Leprechaun, 13 inches high, unmarked. *Zera Collection.* $45

A pixie couple, she is 12 inches high, and he is 12-1/2 inches high. No marks. The eyes look similar to those above; perhaps there is a connection. *Blumenfeld Collection.* Left - $100, Right - $100

The same unmarked jar as above, but with red trim around the neck instead of blue. *Oravitz Collection.* $100

The jar on the left is 6-1/4 inches high, and the jar on the right is 7-1/4 inches. Neither is marked. *Oravitz Collection.* Left - $45, Right - $45

This Doranne of California is 13 inches high and lacks a mark. *Oravitz Collection*. $70

A bear with a belly button, 12-1/2 inches high and unmarked. *Bosson Collection*. $35

They talk about pink elephants, so why not pink bears? The jar is 10-1/2 inches high. It has a remnant of a paper label but it is unreadable. *Courtesy of Jazz'e Junque Shop, Chicago, Illinois*. $35

Both of these jars are 10 inches high. Neither is marked. The jar on the left is a little bigger around at the top, so the lids aren't interchangeable. *Bosson Collection*. $85 ea.

The big question about this cookie jar is why someone would model one of the baby's ears to look like a bear's, the other a rabbit's. The jar is 13 inches high, unmarked. *Saxby Collection*. $35

This nicely finished unmarked teddy bear is 12 inches high. *Oravitz Collection*. $40

This jar appears to be identical to one made by Maurice of California, but it is not on par with that company's work. It is 10-1/8 inches high and unmarked. *Courtesy of Jazz'e Junque Shop, Chicago, Illinois*. $30

Unmarked bear, 13-1/2 inches high. *Oravitz Collection.* $45

Except for the baby, this is very similar to a panda made by Metlox. The unmarked jar is 11-1/4 inches high. *Oravitz Collection.* $40

Another panda, this one is 10-1/4 inches high, unmarked. *Oravitz Collection.* $30

Candycane bear, 11 inches high and unmarked. *Oravitz Collection.* $45

"Cookie Panda," 12-1/4 inches high. This jar is heavily poured but unmarked. *Oravitz Collection.* $35

If you don't look closely at this jar you might miss the kitten. The height is 10-1/4 inches, no mark. *Oravitz Collection.* $50

*Left*: This unmarked jar is 9-1/4 inches high. The chain is metal. Look closely and you will see that the bear cub is beginning to push the lid off of the can. *Courtesy of Country Heirs Antique Shop.* $50

*Right*: What a dude! The jar is 11 inches high and is unmarked. *Oravitz Collection.* $40

262

Unmarked, 11-1/2 inches high. *Lilly Collection.* $25

Sailor cat, 10 inches high with no mark. *Oravitz Collection.* $20

Another unmarked cow, this one is 10 inches high. *Courtesy of Jazz'e Junque Shop, Chicago, Illinois.* $35

Mother and kitten, 11-1/2 inches high and unmarked. *Saxby Collection.* $35

Kitty biscuit jars, both 5-1/4 inches high, both unmarked. *Oravitz Collection.* $35 ea.

This unmarked cat is 12 inches high. *Oravitz Collection.* $25

Moving from the house to the farm for a moment, this cow is 9-1/4 inches high. It is not marked. *Courtesy of Jazz'e Junque Shop, Chicago, Illinois.* $40

An unmarked dog, 11 inches high. *Oravitz Collection.* $30

This canine, 6-1/2 inches high, is also unmarked. *Oravitz Collection.* $20

This elephant was made by Los Angeles Potteries. It is unmarked, 10-3/4 inches high. *Courtesy of Grinder's Switch Antique Shop.* $25

The Scottie biscuit jar is 6-1/2 inches high, unmarked. *Zera Collection.* $75

This jar is 6-3/4 inches high. It is not marked. A companion pig was made in a blue basket. *Oravitz Collection.* $30

Small monkey jar, 7 inches high, unmarked. *Oravitz Collection.* $25

The unmarked elephant with a straw hat is 12-1/2 inches high. *Oravitz Collection.* $30

Froggy went a courtin', as they say. The unmarked jar is 10-3/4 inches high. Possibly Sierra Vista. *Zera Collection.* $250

Hippo on a scooter, 10-3/4 inches high, unmarked. *Oravitz Collection.* $45

This mouse looks like a strong candidate for hobby ceramic status. It is 9 inches high, and not marked. *Oravitz Collection*. $35

It seems no other name but "Sneaky Pig" would be suitable here. The jar, 11-1/2 inches high, is unmarked. *Oravitz Collection*. $35

This rabbit is 12-1/4 inches high and unmarked. *Oravitz Collection*. $35

A pig chef, 11 inches high and unmarked. *Oravitz Collection*. $30

This rather simple oinker is 9-1/4 inches high. It is not marked. *Oravitz Collection*. $25

Possibly kinfolk to the standing elephant on the previous page, this jar is 6-1/2 inches high and unmarked. *Oravitz Collection*. $25

A pig head, 9 inches high, with no mark. *Oravitz Collection*. $40

Rabbit jar, 12-3/4 inches high. It is marked "Patented/USA" on two lines. A unique feature is that the opening is diamond shaped instead of rounded. *Oravitz Collection*. $45

The same jar as above, although is looks a bit different because it was photographed at a different angle. The mark is different, too: "Pat.Pen." *Zera Collection*. $45

A rabbit mailing what apparently is a love letter. The jar is 11-1/2 inches high, unmarked. *Oravitz Collection*. $45

This turtle is 10-1/2 inches tall and unmarked. *Oravitz Collection*. $35

An unmarked chicken, 9-3/4 inches high, believed to be McCoy. *Lilly Collection*. $45

Unmarked, 12-1/2 inches high. *Bosson Collection*. $35

Rooster, 9-1/2 inches high and unmarked. *Oravitz Collection*. $40

Mother-of-pearl glaze, 11-1/2 inches high and unmarked. Possibly a hobby ceramics jar. *Courtesy of Jazz'e Junque Shop, Chicago, Illinois*. $25

Snail, 9-3/4 inches high and unmarked. *Oravitz Collection*. $35

This 9-3/4 inch high jar, made by Red Wing, is not marked in any way. The bottom is heavily crazed. *Courtesy of Dorothy Coates*. $70

This canister-type chicken cookie jar is 12-1/4 inches high. It is marked with an impressed "Made in California 1408/USA" on two lines. *Oravitz Collection*. $35

This jar is always referred to as a baby duck, but the pointed beak seems to indicate a chick. There is a very similar jar with a longer, rounded bill that looks more like a duckling than this one; the two more than likely are made by the same company. Both jars exhibit characteristics common to those born of the American Bisque—American Pottery—Ludowici Celadon triad. *Zera Collection.* $85

Same duck with lighter red and a different impressed mark—"USA-10." *Oravitz Collection.* $40

A 9-1/2 inch high unmarked duck. *Lilly Collection.* $35

This unmarked duck is 12 inches high. *Courtesy of Virginia Sell.* $35

This duck is 12-1/2 inches high with "USA" impressed. It was made by Hull. *Zera Collection.* $40

The "Mother and Her Babies" is 10-1/2 inches high. It is not marked. *Courtesy of Jazz'e Junque Shop, Chicago, Illinois.* $30

The scarf on this duck is cloth. The jar is 7-1/2 inches high and unmarked. *Lilly Collection.* $30

Exquisitely styled Art Deco duck, 12 inches high. It is not marked. *Zera Collection.* $125

The lovebirds jar is 10-3/4 inches high and ahs a "H7525" inkstamp. *Oravitz Collection.* $95

The penguin is 12-1/2 inches high. It is unmarked. *Courtesy of Jazz'e Junque Shop, Chicago, Illinois.* $30

The same apple as the one attributed to Hull, but marked with an "E" inside the lid. This jar was also made in yellow and possibly other colors. *Oravitz Collection.* $40

This owl is 10-1/4 inches high and unmarked. It is often seen without paint or repainted. *Courtesy of Jazz'e Junque Shop, Chicago, Illinois.* $45

This apple is 8-1/2 inches high and unmarked. Westfall credits this apple to Hull, but an exhaustive search yielded nothing to substantiate the jar's origin. *Zera Collection.* $50

Apple, 9 inches high. At first glance one might be inclined to think it was made by Metlox because of the blossoms. But the quality is lacking, and the jar is decorated entirely with paint that is inconsistent with Metlox's penchant for glaze. *Zera Collection.* $25

There was felt on the bottom of this owl cookie jar so whether or not it is marked is hard to determine. It is 11-3/4 inches high. *Oravitz Collection.* $30

These unmarked apples are 8-1/2 inches high. *Zera Collection.* $30 ea.

As you can see, this unmarked apple was made in several colors. It is 9-1/4 inches high. *Zera Collection.* $30

This apple is 11 inches high and has "©USA" impressed. Doranne of California. *Courtesy of Jazz'e Junque Shop, Chicago, Illinois.* $50

Standing 11-1/2 inches high, this jar has "8218" impressed inside the lid, "©USA 8218" impressed in the bottom, and was made by California Originals. *Taylor Collection.* $60

This apple is also unmarked and is 9-1/4 inches high. *Courtesy of Jazz'e Junque Shop, Chicago, Illinois.* $30

Barrel of apples, 7-1/2 inches high, with no mark. *Taylor Collection.* $45

Unmarked pear, 11-1/2 inches high. *Courtesy of Jazz'e Junque Shop, Chicago, Illinois.* $45

This one solves part of the mystery. Around the bottom is the impressed mark "USA." *Courtesy of Jazz'e Junque Shop, Chicago, Illinois.* $30

Orange, 7-1/2 inches high, with a "9316" inkstamp. *Taylor Collection.* $30

Pear or lemon? The shape suggests a lemon, and the stem suggests a pear. The jar is 11-1/4 inches high and marked "3732." *Courtesy of Jazz'e Junque Shop, Chicago, Illinois.* $40

This pear is 10-3/4 inches high and inkstamped "C-8262." Compare it to the Los Angeles Potteries' wedding pineapple shown in Chapter 21, and draw your own conclusion. *Zera Collection.* $25

Unmarked strawberry, 9-1/2 inches high. *Lilly Collection.* $35

An unmarked cookie stack, 8-1/2 inches high. *Courtesy of Jazz'e Junque Shop, Chicago, Illinois.* $25

Heavily poured pineapple, 13-1/2 inches high, with a "1386" inkstamp. *Taylor Collection.* $75

This strawberry is 11-1/2 inches high with "8215" impressed in lid. It was made by California Originals. *Courtesy of Jazz'e Junque Shop, Chicago, Illinois.* $45

Strawberry pie, 8 inches high and unmarked. Doranne of California. *Bosson Collection.* $60

This 8-1/2 inch high pumpkin is marked "SFA 1966." *Saxby Collection.* $30

The mark here is "GK3/USA" on two lines. The strawberry is 9-1/2 inches high. *Zera Collection.* $30

Gingerbread house, 11-3/4 inches high. There is no mark. Made by CaliforniaOriginals. *Zera Collection.* $65

Gingerbread house on a smaller scale than the one above, only 8-1/2 inches high, unmarked. *Oravitz Collection.* $40

Unmarked log cabin, 11-1/2 inches high. *Zera Collection.* $35

Unknown, unmarked castle, 11-1/4 inches high. *Courtesy of Jazz'e Junque Shop, Chicago, Illinois.* $75

Unmarked house, 10 inches high. *Bosson Collection.* $35

Metlox Lighthouse, 12-3/4 inches high, unmarked. *Oravitz Collection.* $300

This windmill is 14-1/4 inches high. It is not marked. *Bosson Collection.* $30

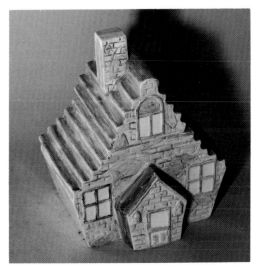

This jar is 10-1/4 inches high and unmarked. Possibly hobby ceramics. *Bosson Collection.* $35

This unmarked jar is 13-1/2 inches high. *Courtesy of Jazz'e Junque Shop, Chicago, Illinois.* $30

Same windmill in blue. The height is 14-1/4 inches and it has no mark. *Courtesy of Jazz'e Junque Shop, Chicago, Illinois.* $30

Noah's Ark, 10-1/2 inches high and unmarked. *Courtesy of Jazz'e Junque Shop, Chicago, Illinois.* $45

This locomotive is 9 inches high. It is not marked. *Courtesy of Jazz'e Junque Shop, Chicago, Illinois.* $30

Cookie car, 6-1/2 inches high and unmarked. *Bosson Collection.* $30

Another ark, 10 inches high, also unmarked. *Oravitz Collection.* $40

At the rear of this engine are the words "Cookie Cargo." The unmarked jar, 6 inches high, is made of redware. *Zera Collection.* $45

This clock is stamped "H4219." It is 11-1/2 inches high. *Courtesy of Jazz'e Junque Shop, Chicago, Illinois.* $25

A Conestoga wagon, 6-1/2 inches high and unmarked. *Oravitz Collection.* $50

This San Francisco cable car is 6-1/2 inches high. It is not marked. *Zera Collection.* $35

This unmarked car is 6-3/4 inches high. *Courtesy of Jazz'e Junque Shop, Chicago, Illinois.* $45

More clocks. The jar is 8 inches high. It is unmarked. *Oravitz Collection.* $30

272

Being separate from the rest of the jar, the propellers on this airplane actually turn. The unmarked jar is 6-1/2 inches high, 15-1/2 inches long. According to the Roerigs, it was made by North American Ceramics. *Coughenour Collection.* $500

Shawnee Carousel, 9-1/2 inches high. The mark is "S4 USA." *Bosson Collection.* $150

This unmarked jar is 10-1/2 inches high. *Courtesy of Jazz'e Junque Shop, Chicago, Illinois.* $35

This jar is 9-3/4 inches high, has "USA" in raised letters on the bottom. *Zera Collection.* $50

The same jar in the same size as above, the only difference is that the "USA" is impressed instead of raised. This jar appears to be a hobby ceramic piece as it is hard to imagine a professional pottery turning out something so poorly painted. The other jar could be the product of a hobby ceramist or a professional pottery. *Oravitz Collection.* $30

The jar on the left is 6 inches high and unmarked. It has a different scene on each side. The jar on the right is 7-1/4 inches high and has a "T25" inkstamp. *Oravitz Collection.* $35 ea.

This cookstove is 7 inches high and unmarked. *Zera Collection.* $35

Unmarked potbelly stove. *Bosson Collection.* $25

Unmarked coffee grinder, 10-1/2 inches high. *Bosson Collection.* $30

Potbelly stove, 11-1/2 inches high, with no mark. *Courtesy of Jazz'e Junque Shop, Chicago, Illinois.* $25

This milk can is 12 inches high. Though unmarked, on the front it says "Cookies/Revere Milk Co." on two lines, which might make it an advertising jar. *Oravitz Collection.* $35

A 12-inch high coffee pot, unmarked. This jar is very much like the Japanese coffee pot shown in Chapter 30, and it also may have been made by the same company. *Saxby Collection.* $25

This potbelly stove is also unmarked. It is 11-3/4 inches high. *Coughenour Collection.* $30

Cookie barrel with wicker handle, 6-1/2 inches high. Unmarked, it is made of redware. *Courtesy of Jazz'e Junque Shop, Chicago, Illinois.* $20

Shoe, 10-1/2 inches high and unmarked. *Bosson Collection.* $40

Chef head jars, 8 inches high and unmarked. *Blumenfeld Collection*. $45 ea.

The unmarked rag doll is 12 inches high. *Oravitz Collection*. $40

Same unmarked jar as above, but 7-3/4 inches high. This side is displayed when it has cookies in it. The reverse, shown below, is displayed when empty. *Oravitz Collection*. $40

Snowman, 9-1/4 inches high. Impressed in bottom is "©B.C." The Roerigs show it with "Made in USA" also impressed. *Zera Collection*. $50

Doll, 10-1/4 inches high, with no mark. *Oravitz Collection*. $50

Reverse of chef head jar.

The top half of this snowman is a teapot with the handle on the right and the spout on the left. The jar is 13-1/2 inches high, marked "Riddell/©" on two lines. *Bosson Collection*. $90

This unmarked jar is 8-1/4 inches high. It is thought to be by Holiday Designs, Inc. *Oravitz Collection*. $30

The flower pot is 8-1/2 inches high and unmarked. It's a California Originals jar. *Courtesy of Jazz'e Junque Shop, Chicago, Illinois.* $30

The drum is 8-3/4 inches high. It is not marked. The drumsticks look remarkably real. *Courtesy of Jazz'e Junque Shop, Chicago, Illinois.* $50

Old jar, 7-1/2 inches high, with "USA" in raised letters. *Zera Collection.* $30

This 10-inch high jar is marked "4261/USA/J.G." impressed on three lines. The remaining bits of a nearly destroyed paper label read "...Hutchin...S, of NE...NA." The bottom appears to be from the same mold as the Abingdon money sack. *Courtesy of Betty and Floyd Carson.* $50

Liberty Bell, 9-1/2 inches high, no mark. *Bosson Collection.* $35

This simulated bamboo jar is assumed originally to have had a bamboo or rattan handle. It is 7 inches high, unmarked, and made of redware. *Oravitz Collection.* $20

Also missing a handle, this jar is 8 inches high and unmarked. *Zera Collection.* $25

This jar has a metal finial. It is 9-3/4 inches high with "516/USA" impressed on two lines. *Courtesy of Grinder's Switch Antique Shop.* $45

An American made jack-in-the box, the mark on the bottom is "USA." The jar is 12-1/2 inches high. *Courtesy of Jazz'e Junque Shop, Chicago, Illinois.* $200

You can get cookies from both ends of this cookie jar. It is 8 inches high. The handle is missing. The mark is shown below. *Courtesy of Jazz'e Junque Shop, Chicago, Illinois.* $20

This isn't a cookie jar but a sucker jar, which like grease jars and canisters, often finds its way into cookie jar collections. This particular jar has a reversible lid. It is 7 inches high, unmarked. *Oravitz Collection.* $65

This jar is 8 inches high. It is not marked. *Oravitz Collection.* $45

Mark of double-entry jar.

Good old Kilroy. The mark of this jar is shown, but attempts to trace it were unsuccessful. *Zera Collection.* $40

Mark of the Kilroy cookie jar.

This unmarked jar is 10 inches high. Though it appears to be lacking a handle, there would be no way to securely attach one. *Courtesy of Jazz'e Junque Shop, Chicago, Illinois.* $25

Locomotive with a glaze identical to that of the rag doll on page 275. The jar is 6-3/4 inches, unmarked. *Oravitz Collection.* $25

Sucker jar showing lid reversed.

Unmarked jar, 9 inches high. This is similar, but not identical, to a jar shown by Westfall that was made by Los Angeles Potteries. *Courtesy of Grinder's Switch Antique Shop.* $30

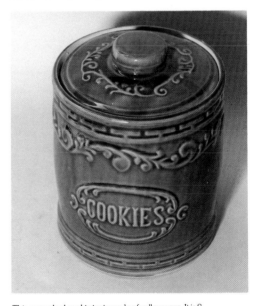

This unmarked cookie jar is made of yellowware. It is 8-1/2 inches high. *Courtesy of Jazz'e Junque Shop, Chicago, Illinois.* $25

The height here is 8-3/4 inches. The jar is unmarked. *Zera Collection.* $25

A 12-1/4 inch high bull, unmarked, made by California Originals. *Oravitz Collection.* $50

This raccoon is 12-3/4 inches high. The jar is not marked. *Oravitz Collection.* $45

This jar is 11-1/2 inches high. The only mark is "©Mopsy" at the base of the bottom. *Courtesy of Betty and Floyd Carson.* $80

This appears to be the same bull as above. Though a different color, it is the same size and has no mark. California Originals, *Courtesy of Jazz'e Junque Shop, Chicago, Illinois.* $50

The turtle jar is marked "KJ20/USA" on two lines between the feet. The height is 9 inches. *Oravitz Collection.* $40

The elephant is 12 inches high and unmarked. DeForest of California. *Oravitz Collection.* $45

This bull is from a different mold than the other two. It is 11-1/2 inches high, unmarked but Twin Winton. *Oravitz Collection.* $50

A bear with his hand in the cookie jar. The height is 8-1/2 inches. There is no mark. *Bosson Collection.* $30

Game warden bear, 12 inches high with no mark but by DeForest of California. *Oravitz Collection*. $50

The little kitty is 11 inches high and has no pedigree. *Oravitz Collection*. $30

This companion puppy for the cat is 10-1/2 inches high, Made by Twin Winton. *Oravitz Collection*. $60

Pig, 11 inches high with no mark. *Oravitz Collection*. $30

Unmarked cat, 9-1/2 inches high. *Bosson Collection*. $45

Unmarked monkey, 11-1/2 inches high. *Oravitz Collection*. $45

The cat in the basket is 9-1/2 inches high and not marked. It was made by Twin Winton. *Courtesy of Betty and Floyd Carson*. $60

Lion and lamb, 14-1/4 inches high. The mark on the bottom is "928" in raised numerals. *Oravitz Collection*. $45

This walrus is 10 inches high and has "Calif." incised on the bottom. Some are unmarked. *Bosson Collection*. $50

This van is 8 inches high. *Bosson Collection.* $65

This guy must have gotten into a cookie poker game. The jar is 12-1/2 inches high and marked "R77 USA." *Bosson Collection.* $50

Unmarked shoe, 12 inches high. *Courtesy of Jazz'e Junque Shop, Chicago, Illinois.* $50

This jar is 9-3/4 inches high. It was made by California Originals. *Bosson Collection.* $50

Space cadet, 12-1/2 inches high, no mark. *Zera Collection.* $95

Nearly the same size as the other shoe, 12-1/4 inches, this jar is also unmarked. The Roerigs show it as California Originals. *Oravitz Collection.* $50

Milk can, 12 inches high, unmarked. *Oravitz Collection.* $45

This crock is 8 inches high. It appears very much like the Coors crock in Chapter 21, but is two inches shorter, with a slightly different shape, and not marked. *Courtesy of Dory and Don Jones.* $25

The lid is the same as the white crock, and the double ring at the shoulder is the same, but handles have been added. The height of this one is 9-1/2 inches. It is not marked. *Zera Collection.* $25

It looks like McCoy, but the handles are too big. It looks like Ransburg, but lacks the concave curve on the outside of the neck. It is 9-1/2 inches high, marked with a "CBK89" inkstamp. *Lilly Collection.* $25

Whoever modeled this jar did a nice job of making it appear to be hand thrown with attached handles; however, inside you can see by the hollow handles that the jar was poured. Its 8-1/2 inches high and unmarked. *Courtesy of Jazz'e Junque Shop, Chicago, Illinois.* $30

Very plain, this crock possibly had painted decoration at one time. Its height is 9-1/2 inches, and it has no mark. *Zera Collection.* $20

Southwestern scene, 8 inches high and unmarked. *Courtesy of Jazz'e Junque Shop, Chicago, Illinois.* $35

What kind of cookie jar leads to a collection of more than 600? This 8-inch high unmarked yellowware jar is one. It is the first cookie jar purchased by Richard and Susan Oravitz, who haven't stopped buying since. $25

This unmarked jar is 9-3/4 inches high. *Oravitz Collection.* $35

Silhouette jar, 10-1/2 inches high, marked "Made in USA." *Zera Collection.* $35

Mary and her lamb, 8-1/4 inches high. The mark is "697" impressed. *Oravitz Collection.* $35

Like gingerbread boy jar above, but in tan. *Courtesy of Jazz'e Junque Shop, Chicago, Illinois.* $35 each

This appears to be the same basic jar as the three blind mice above, and was probably made by the same company. The height is 8-1/4 inches, no mark. *Oravitz Collection.* $35

The bear is the same size as the rabbit and carrot, 9-3/4 inches, no mark. *Oravitz Collection.* $30

This canister-type jar is 8-3/4 inches high, and marked "4253/USA" on two lines. It seems very likely that it is a recent McCoy. *Lilly Collection.* $30

Like the gingerbread boy, this unmarked jar is 9-3/4 inches high. The condition of the paint decoration seems too good to be original. Maybe it received excellent care, perhaps a wedding present that was left in the box and never used, a fate undoubtedly common to a great many cookie jars. *Oravitz Collection.* $35

The jar on the left is 9-3/4 inches high, the jar on the right is 8-1/2 inches high. Neither is marked. *Oravitz Collection.* $30

This unmarked jar is 9-1/4 inches high. *Lilly Collection.* $30

Because it is a slightly different color, it is possible the lid on this cookie jar is not the original. The jar is 10 inches high with "USA" in raised letters on bottom. *Courtesy of Jazz'e Junque Shop, Chicago, Illinois.* $30

Nice detail in this general store mold. The jar is 9 inches high with no mark. The reverse is shown. *Courtesy of Jazz'e Junque Shop, Chicago, Illinois.* $20

Unmarked, 8-1/2 inches high. The same jar is seen in white. *Zera Collection.* $20

The height of this jar is 11 inches, and it has "USA" impressed. *Oravitz Collection.* $25

Not much to say about this plain Jane except that it is 7-1/2 inches high, marked "1528/USA" on two lines, and has a rubber gasket in the lid. Based on the mark, it is believed to be recent McCoy. *Lilly Collection.* $25

Reverse of the general store canister jar.

This obviously older jar is 7-1/2 inches high and unmarked. *Zera Collection.* $65

Nicely detailed, 9 inches high, and unmarked. The reverse is shown. If you have this jar or the green jar above and want to research them, a good place to begin might be old Hull Pottery catalogs. *Zera Collection.* $90

This canister is 13 inches high and unmarked. *Courtesy of Jazz'e Junque Shop, Chicago, Illinois.* $20

Reverse of canister jar on previous page.

Bean pot, 6-1/2 inches high, with its mark shown. *Courtesy of Homer and Bev Simpson.* $25

Mark of brown bean pot, possibly that of the West Bend Company, of West Bend, Wisconsin.

Bean pot, 7-1/2 inches high, marked "Made in USA." *Courtesy of Jazz'e Junque Shop, Chicago, Illinois.* $30

Cookies bean pot, 7-3/4 inches high, marked "USA." *Courtesy of Jazz'e Junque Shop, Chicago, Illinois.* $25

There are hand-painted flowers on this jar, while its mate below has a transfer decoration. The height is 7-1/4 inches, and there is no mark. *Courtesy of Jazz'e Junque Shop, Chicago, Illinois.* $30

Bean pot, 8 inches high, with no mark. *Oravitz Collection.* $25

This one is 7 inches high and marked "USA." *Zera Collection.* $25

Marked "USA," this bean pot is 6-1/4 inches high. *Courtesy of Jazz'e Junque Shop, Chicago, Illinois.* $20

Like the jar above, this is 7-1/4 inches high, but it is marked "USA." *Zera Collection.* $30

Look closely and you'll see some raised fruit around the bottom of this bean pot. It is 7-1/4 inches high and marked "USA" in raised letters on the bottom. *Zera Collection.* $20

Bean pot, 6-1/4 inches high. The mark is an impressed "USA." *Courtesy of Grinder's Switch Antique Shop.* $30

Pot O' Cookies, 7 inches high, with no mark. *Courtesy of Jazz'e Junque Shop, Chicago, Illinois.* $25

The height is 6-1/4 inches, and it has "USA" impressed. This appears to be the same as the tan jar above, but with a less prominent ridge below the knob on the lid. *Courtesy of Jazz'e Junque Shop, Chicago, Illinois.* $25

These two jars, 9 inches high, were made by the Jeanette Glass Company, of Jeanette, Pennsylvania, during the 1940s. The milk glass version was also made in Jeanette's shell pink color. *Zera Collection.* $40 ea.

Pear shape with applied finial, 11-1/2 inches high, no mark. *Zera Collection.* $75

Hobnail milk glass jar, 8-1/2 inches high, maker unknown. *Zera Collection.* $20

Paper label on wood base of hexagon glass cookie jar. $75

This 10-3/4 inch high jar is marked. On the front it says "©Carlton 1982," and on the bottom "Carlton Glass/3L/USA" on three lines. *Courtesy of Grinder's Switch Antique Shop.* $10

As the pictures show, this jar has been made in several different colors. It is 9-3/4 inches high. *Courtesy of Jazz'e Junque Shop, Chicago, Illinois.* $10

This glass jar is 8-1/2 inches high and is often seen without its wood base. The paper label on base is shown. *Courtesy of Sharon Isaacson.* $15

Slag glass cookie jar, 10-1/2 inches high, unmarked. *Zera Collection.*

Orange and yellow version of above jar. None of these jars are marked. *Zera Collection.* $10

Another glass jar that has been made with several different decorations. The jars are 8-1/4 inches high. They are not marked. *Oravitz Collection.* $15 ea.

Red with petals and leaves, or pears and plums if you prefer. *Zera Collection.* $10

B.C. comic characters, 8-1/4 inches high. *Zera Collection.* $15

Glass Liberty Bell, 7-3/4 inches high. The mark is "Barlett-Collins/Sapulpa, Oklahoma" on two lines. *Zera Collection.* $25

Yellow with flowers. *Courtesy of Jazz'e Junque Shop, Chicago, Illinois.* $15

Aluminum apple and orange, each 8-1/2 inches high. The same jar was made in green. They were part of a canister set of four different sizes. Their maker is unknown. *Zera Collection.* $15 ea.

## Metal Cookie Jars

The majority of metal cookie jars are made of steel. A few are made of aluminum. The current trend in metal cookie jars is for companies to pack their products (often cookies) in them to attract consumers.

METAL COOKIE JARS

Aluminum pear, 11-1/2 inches high, possibly by the same unknown company as the apple and orange, unmarked. *Zera Collection.* $15

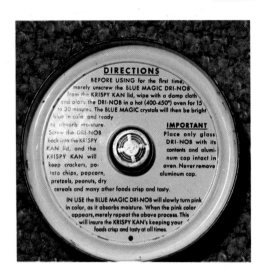

Inside of Krispy Kan lid, which gives instructions on how to use its "dri-nob." Note that it mentions potato chips, popcorn, and several other foods but not cookies.

The metal clown jar is 7-1/2 inches high, unmarked. The knob on top is made of wood. *Zera Collection.* $10

Cookie can marked "Weibro Div./J.L.Clark/Chicago/ USA" on four lines. It is 8-1/2 inches high. *Courtesy of Jazz'e Junque Shop, Chicago, Illinois.* $15

Embossed mark of Krispy Kan, patent no. 2543168, indicates a patent date of 1951.

Chein Industries, of Burlington, New Jersey, made this 9-inch high cookie tin. Its mark is shown. *Courtesy of Jazz'e Junque Shop, Chicago, Illinois.* $10

Embossed mark of Chein Industries.

Blue Magic Krispy Kans, made by the Luce Manufacturing Company, of Croton, Vermont. Cans are 8-1/2 inches high, and their mark is shown. Other designs were used, including Howdy Doody. *Courtesy of Jazz'e Junque Shop, Chicago, Illinois.* $15 ea.

Chein Holly Hobbie tin, same size and mark as above. *Courtesy of Jazz'e Junque Shop, Chicago, Illinois.* $10

Barnum's Animals tin, 7 inches high. It says on the tin that it's a replica of a 1914 design and shows a copyright date of 1979. *Courtesy of Jazz'e Junque Shop, Chicago, Illinois.* $10

Part of advertisement for above tin from 1988.

Yellow and green Paddy
*Oravitz Collection.* $35 e

This Chein tin is 7-1/2 inches high. Its mark reads "Sun Giant Raisins/Cheinco/Housewares/J.Chein & Co./Burlington NJ/09010" on six lines. *Zera Collection.* $10

Nestlé chocolate chip tin from 1988. *Zera Collection.* $10

Maurice Lentil plastic coo
visible at upper right. The
is Airlite logo ("Airlite" wr
very large "A"), plus "Om
*Collection.* $3

This is the 1989 Nestlé Toll House chocolate chip tin. It is 6-1/4 inches high. *Zera Collection.* $10

Burroughs jars are colore
upper half is always white
Flowers are another popu
mark is shown. *Zera Colle*

## Plastic Cookie Jars

Without a doubt the most popular non-pottery cookie jars are made of plastic. Plastic jars include both soft and hard. It's the hard plastic, and the older the better, that captures the most attention.

### Fiedler and Fielder Mold and Die Works

One of the early pioneers in hard plastic cookie jars was Fiedler and Fiedler Mold and Die Works of Dayton, Ohio, commonly called F & F because the initials appear on its logo.

## PLASTIC COOKIE JARS

Aunt Jemima, made by F & F for Quaker Oats during the 1950s. It is 11-1/2 inches high, marked with standard F & F log. *Zera Collection.* $250

F & F made this dog as a premium for Ken-L-Ration dog food. It's 6-3/4 inches high, standard F & F mark. *Courtesy of Jazz'e Junque Shop, Chicago, Illinois.* $125

In th
F & F to
ums for
shown a
creamer
jar spice

Aun
Rutt, co-
the vaud
and Farn
to a song
wearing
associati
song, ar
Baker ar

The Pearl China Watermelon Mammy stands 11 inches high. Unmarked, its distinctive bottom is shown. *Courtesy of Gary and Mimi Rhinehimer*. $4000

This is a Tat-L-Tale jar by Helen Hutula,. It is 11-1/4 inches high, and its mark is shown. *Courtesy of Gary and Mimi Rhinehimer*. $950

Mark of the Helen Hutula Tat-L-Tale jar.

Bottom of Pearl China Watermelon Mammy.

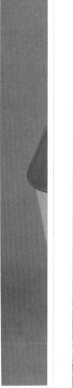

The Keebler

OTHER

Smokey Bear. 10 inches high, unmarked, and maker unknown. *Courtesy of Gary and Mimi Rhinehimer*. Undetermined value.

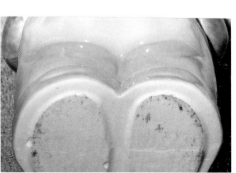

Paddy Pig w
high. *Zera C*

Bottom of Smokey Bear.

Another Tat-L-Tale. Note that this one has suffered the fate of many in that the left forefinger has been broken off. A restoration specialist could fix this problem. *Courtesy of Denise Teeters*. $600, as shown; $950, undamaged.

298

Raggedy Ann, 10-1/4 inches high, with "Pat Applied For" impressed. This jar was made by Dwight Morris, of East Palestine, Ohio. Salt and pepper shakers were made in the same design. So were banks and figurines. Some animals, too. *Courtesy of Denise Teeters.* $250

This is Olive Oyl, a reproduction of the original American Bisque jar by J.D. James of Buckeye Lake, Ohio. It is 10-1/2 inches high. Its mark is shown. While the jar itself looks about the same, the lid is somewhat different than the original. *Courtesy of J.D. James.* $150

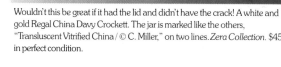

Bottom of the J.D. James Olive Oyl jar. It shows the jar was made in 1993, and was number 43 in an issue of 250. This information is under the glaze.

Wouldn't this be great if it had the lid and didn't have the crack! A white and gold Regal China Davy Crockett. The jar is marked like the others, "Transluscent Vitrified China / © C. Miller," on two lines. *Zera Collection.* $450, in perfect condition.

The J.D. James much more recent, and much less expensive, Rubbles House. It measures 9-1/8 inches high, is signed, "J.D. 1993," in ink under the glaze. *Courtesy of J.D. James.* $150

This is the Regal China Alice in Wonderland described in Chapter 16. Unmarked, it stands 13-1/4 inches high. *Bosson Collection.* $2500

# Appendix 1: Sources

Chapter 5
Married Mammy cookie jar (Brayton Laguna mammy
  reproduction)
Mary Jane Giacomini
MJ's Collectibles
782 Verano Avenue
Sonoma, California 95476

Chapter 6
*An Illustrated Value Guide to Cookie Jars,* by Ermagene
  Westfall.
Collector Books
P.O. Box 3009
Paducah, Kentucky 42002-3009

*Collector's Encyclopedia of Cookie Jars, Volumes I, II and
  III,* by Fred and Joyce Herndon Roerig
Collector Books
P.O. Box 3009
Paducah, Kentucky 42002-3009

*Cookie Jarrin'—The Cookie Jar Newsletter* Joyce Roerig,
  Editor
Cookie Jarrin'—The Cookie Jar Newsletter
R.R. #2, Box 504
Waterboro, South Carolina 29488

*Lehner's Encylopedia of U.S. Marks on Pottery, Porcelain
  & Clay,* by Lois Lehner.
Collector Books
P.O. Box 3009
Paducah, Kentucky 42002-3009

Chapter 21
*Pennsbury Pottery,* by Lucille Henzke.
Schiffer Publishing, Ltd.
4880 Lower Valley Road
Atglen, Pennsylvania 19310

Indian head cookie jar.
Southeast Minnesota Pottery
P.O. Box 93
304 Belvedere
Kellogg, Minnesota 55945

Chapter 28
Rick Wisecarver
42 Maple St.
Roseville, Ohio

Chapter 29
Keith Herklotz
Down to Earth Ceramics Studio
RR1 118-C
Franklin, Maine 04634

# Appendix 2: Ceramic Mold Companies

Listed below are the names of ceramic mold companies you might encounter on cookie jars. In most cases these are only the catch words, often followed by "Molds," "Company," "Co., Inc.," etc.

Alberta's Molds, Inc.
Arnel's, Inc.
Arrow
Atlantic Mold Corp.
B & D
Bama Molds
Bay State Mold Co., Inc.
Bell
Boothe
Byron
C-ramics
Castle
Central Penn
Ceramichrome
Class A
Clay Magic
Cramer
Crest
Delta Molds
Doc Holiday Molds, Inc.
Dom's
Dona's Molds, Inc.
Duncan
E.S.
Fantasy
Fash-en
Frank Gleason Ceramic Molds, Inc.
Gare, Inc.
Georgie's Bulldog

Glenview
Gold Rush
Hershey
Holland Mold, Inc.
Hallmark
Indiana Hobby
Jamar-Mallory
Jay-Kay Molds
Jones Mold Co.
Kentucky
Kelly
Kimple Mold Corp.
Lonestar
Longview
Macky
McCloud
Mike's
Nowell's Molds
O.C.S.
PCM
Provincial
R Molds
Riverview Molds, Inc.
Robin Hood
Santmire
Scioto Ceramic Products, Inc.
Tampa Bay Mold Co.
Trenton Mold Co.
Tri Star
Vern Elliott
Weaver
White Horse
Yozie

# Appendix 3: McCoy Cookie Jar Designs by Year

The Number of New Cookie Jar Designs Offered Each Year by McCoy, 1939-1987

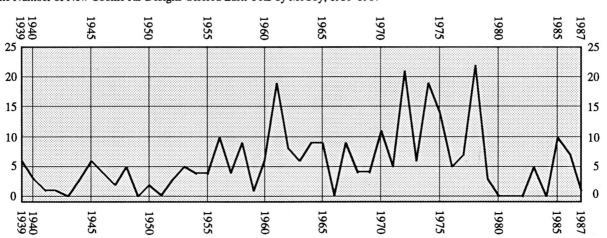

The Number of Different McCoy Cookie Jars Offered Each Year, 1939-1987

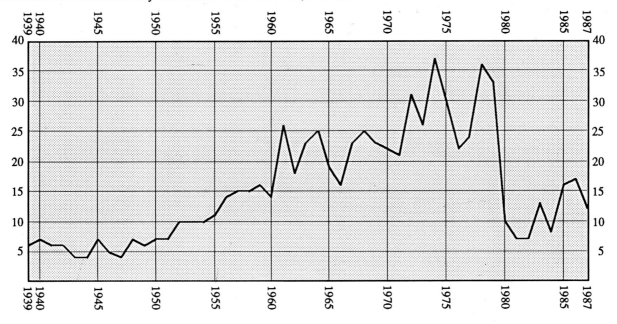

# Bibliography

*American Export Register: 1990*, Thomas International Publishing Inc., New York, 1990.

*Brands and Their Companies—9th Edition,* Donna Wood, Editor, Gale Research Inc., New York, 1991.

Bruce, Scott, *Fifties and Sixties Lunch Box, The,* Chronicle Books, San Francisco, 1988.

Chappel, James, *The Potter's Complete Book of Clay and Glazes,* Watson-Guptill Publications, New York, 1977.

*Companies and Their Brands—9th Edition,* Donna Wood, Editor, Gale Research Inc., New York, 1991.

Cunningham, Jo, *The Collector's Encyclopedia of American Dinnerware,* Collector Books, Paducah, Kentucky, 1982.

DePasquale, Dan and Gail, and Petersen, Larry, *Red Wing Collectibles,* Collector Books, Paducah, Kentucky, 1983.

Derwich, Jenny B., and Latos, Dr. Mary, *Dictionary Guide to United States Pottery and Porcelain (19th and 20th Century),* Jenstan, Franklin, Michigan, 1984.

*Directory of Corporate Affiliations-1991,* National Register Publishing Company, Wilmette, Illinois, 1990.

Drury, Elizabeth, editor, *Antiques,* Doubleday, Garden City, New York, 1986.

Florence, Gene, *Collector's Encyclopedia of Depression Glass, The,* Collector Books, Paducah, Kentucky, 1982.

———, *Kitchen Glassware of the Depression Years,* Collector Books, Paducah, Kentucky, 1981.

Hamer, Frank and Janet, *The Potter's Dictionary of Materials and Techniques,* Watson-Guptill Publications, New York, 1986.

Hasten, Bud, *Bud Hasten's Avon Bottle Collector Encyclopedia, 11th Edition,* Bud Hasten, Las Vegas, Nevada, 1988.

Heide, Robert, and Gilman, John, *Cartoon Collectibles,* Doubleday, Garden City, New York, 1983.

Heiss, Willard and Virginia, "Pottery Cookie Jar Put Ransburg on Road to Success," *Antique Week,* March 21, 1988.

Henzke, Lucille, *Pennsbury Pottery,* Schiffer Publishing Ltd., Atglen, Pennsylvania, 1990.

Huxford, Sharon and Bob, *Collector's Encyclopedia of McCoy Pottery, The,* Collector Books, Paducah, Kentucky, 1982.

———, *Collectors Encyclopedia of Roseville Pottery, The* Collector Books, Paducah, Kentucky, 1976.

———, *Collectors Encyclopedia of Roseville Pottery,* Collector Books, Paducah, Kentucky, 1980.

———, *The Collector's Encyclopedia of Weller Pottery,* Collector Books, Paducah, Kentucky, 1979.

Jensen, Elsa, "How Elsa Became Cat Cookie Jar Crazy," *Crazed Over Cookie Jars,* October, 1990.

Ketchum, William C. Jr., *Pottery & Porcelain,* Knopf, New York, 1983.

Kovel, Ralph and Terry, *Kovel's Advertising Collectibles Price List,* Crown, New York, 1986.

Lehner, Lois, *Lehner's Encyclopedia of U.S. Marks on Pottery, Porcelain & Clay,* Collector Books, Paducah, Kentucky, 1988.

Marquette, Arthur F., *Brands, Trademarks and Goodwill—The Story of The Quaker Oats Company,* McGraw-Hill, New York, 1967.

McDonald, Ann Gilbert, *All About Weller,* Antique Publications, Marietta, Ohio, 1989.

Meugniot, Elinor, *Old Sleepy Eye,* The Printing Press, Tulsa, Oklahoma, 1973.

Nichols, Harold, *McCoy Cookie Jars from the First to the Latest,* Nichols Publishing, Ames, Iowa, 1987.

Oravitz, Richard and Susan, handwritten notes from Mike Clum cookie jar auction, Zanesville, Ohio, July 18, 1990.

Purviance, Louise and Evan, and Schneider, Norris F., *Zanesville Art Pottery in Color,* Mid-American Book Company, Leon, Iowa, 1968.

Rinker, Harry, "How an Ohio Rubber Factory Became a Major Toy Maker," *Antique Week,* April 4, 1990.

Roberts, Brenda, *Collector's Encyclopedia of Hull Pottery, The* Collector Books, Paducah, Kentucky, 1989.

Roerig, Fred and Joyce Herndon, *The Collector's Encyclopedia of Cookie Jars,* Collector Books, Paducah, Kentucky, 1991.

Roerig, Joyce, "Jarrin' with Joyce," *Cookie Jarrin'—The Cookie Jar Newsletter,* January-February, 1991.

Saxby, Clifford and Maureen, "January Mystery Jars," *Crazed over Cookie Jars,* January, 1991.

———, "December Mystery Jars," *Crazed over Cookie Jars,* December, 1990.

Schneider, Mike, "Hobby Ceramic Mold Companies," *Crazed over Cookie Jars,* November, 1990.

Simon, Delores, *Red Wing Pottery with Rumrill,* Collector Books, Paducah, Kentucky, 1980.

Supnick, Mark E., *Collecting Shawnee Pottery,* L-W Book Sales, Gas City, Indiana, 1989.

Weatherman, Hazel Marie, *Colored Glassware of the Depression Era 2,* Weatherman Glassbooks, Ozark, Missouri, 1982.

Westfall, Ermagene, *An Illustrated Value Guide to Cookie Jars,* Collector Books, Paducah, Kentucky, 1989.

Williams, George III, "The Original McCoy Pontiac Indian," *Crazed Over Cookie Jars,* November, 1990.

Young, Jackie, *Black Collectibles—Mammy and Her Friends,* Schiffer Publishing Ltd., Atglen, Pennsylvania, 1988.

Zera, Stan and Karen, "Cookie Jar Market is Still Influenced by Warhol Sale," *Antique Week,* April 3, 1989.

———, "Cookie Jars Don't Have to Be Pottery to Be Collectible," *Antique Week,* January, 21, 1991.

# Index